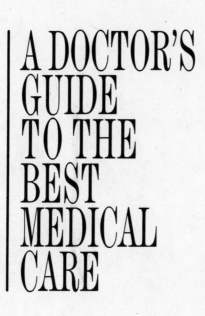

A DOCTOR'S GUIDE TO THE BEST MEDICAL CARE

A DOCTOR'S GUIDE TO THE BEST MEDICAL CARE

A Practical No-Nonsense

Evaluation of Your Treatment Options for

Over 100 Conditions and Diseases

MICHAEL OPPENHEIM, M.D.

Medical Reviewer: John H. Renner, M.D.
President of Consumer Health Research Institute and
Associate Chairman for Research,
Department of Family Medicine,
University of Missouri-Kansas City

WINGS BOOKS
New York • Avenel, New Jersey

Copyright © 1992 by Michael Oppenheim

All rights reserved. No part of this book may be reproduced or transmitted in any form or by any means, electronic or mechanical, including photocopy, recording, or any other information storage and retrieval system, without the written permission from the publisher.

Editor: Alice Feinstein
Book Designer: Jeanne Stock
Copy Editor: Patricia E. Boyd

This 1994 edition is published by Wings Books, distributed by Outlet Book Company, Inc., a Random House Company, 40 Engelhard Avenue, Avenel, New Jersey 07001, by arrangement with Rodale Press, Inc.

Random House
New York • Toronto • London • Sydney • Auckland

Printed and bound in the United States of America

A CIP catalog record for this book is available from the Library of Congress.

ISBN 0-517-10161-0

8 7 6 5 4 3 2 1

Contents

Introduction

This book will describe for you the best treatment for each of a host of disorders. Not all are miracles, but they are the best medical science can offer, so you should ask for an explanation if your doctor decides on something else.

These treatments will remain the best for a long time, perhaps well into the twenty-first century. Good treatments don't change as rapidly as the media want you to believe (for strep throat and arthritis they haven't changed in 50 years).

The treatments featured in this book are the best from your point of view as well as the doctor's. A drug that gives you normal blood pressure but also causes dizziness, drowsiness, and an upset stomach can't be the best because we can control blood pressure with no side effects. It may, however, take some trial and error to find the right drug for you. Don't settle for less.

Expect plenty of surprises in this book. Doctors can treat impotence and acne better than you think. Our treatments for coughs and sore throats are much worse than you probably expect. Doctors are so unhappy with the best treatment for viral upper respiratory infections (URI) that they hate using it (one reason is that patients also don't like it). So they've invented a disease ("bronchitis") that's much easier to treat. When "bronchitis" doesn't respond to treatment, they decide it's not a viral URI but something else that they *can* cure. Thus, a viral sore throat becomes "strep."

Sometimes even our best treatment is not so good. People who have chronic bronchitis and emphysema are miserable most of the time. When given the best possible treatment, they are still miserable *some* of the time—a definite improvement but hardly dramatic. I give medical science a "C." Obesity scores lower still. Almost everyone loses weight when he or she begins receiving the best medical treatment. After a year almost everyone has gained it back. I give us a "D."

To understand my grading system, you need to pay attention to my ground rules. The grade is awarded to *medical science.* How much can we shorten the course of the disease? How often do we actually cure it? How well can we relieve your discomfort in ways that you can't manage by yourself? This is a very concrete grading system.

It ignores other reasons for seeing a doctor. It ignores the information we can give: what you have, how you got it, what's in store for you, when (if ever) it will go away. The grade ignores our advice on home treatment, advice available in plenty of popular health books. It ignores our sympathy and reassuring words, if any. Just because your ailment scores a "D" or even an "F" is no reason to stay away from the doctor's office. But if you want your disease or at least your discomfort to disappear, the grade shows how well we do.

Here's the explanation for the grade I provide at the beginning of each chapter:

F: Total failure.   We never cure it. Nothing we can provide in the office or by prescription is superior to what you can do for yourself. Examples—the common cold, sudden infant death syndrome.

D: Nothing to be proud of.   Cures are rare. We sometimes help in lesser ways by improving symptoms, avoiding complications, and prolonging life. Examples—lung cancer, osteoporosis, obesity.

C: Fair.   When a cure is possible, we succeed sometimes. We often make you feel better and improve your quality of life. Examples—herpes, arthritis, low back pain.

B: Good.   Cures are common, and we almost always improve things in some way. Examples—acne, menstrual cramps, cancer of the uterus, impotence.

A: A medical triumph.   You should expect a complete cure almost every time. Examples—most bacterial infections (strep throat, tuberculosis, impetigo, many pneumonias), many surgical conditions (appendicitis, gallstones), gland failures such as hypothyroidism.

PART ONE

Best
Treatments

Acne

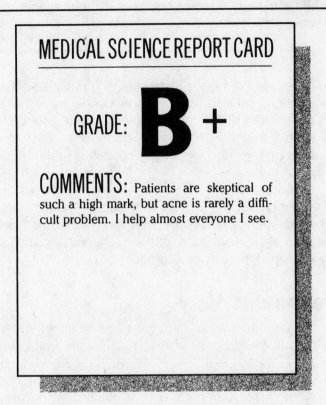

MEDICAL SCIENCE REPORT CARD

GRADE: **B**+

COMMENTS: Patients are skeptical of such a high mark, but acne is rarely a difficult problem. I help almost everyone I see.

Although not fatal, acne can make life seem not worth living. Even if you're middle-aged, you can't assume that you're home free. While acne mostly affects teenagers, I care for a few grown men and women who never got rid of it or who experience it for the first time late in life. Some rare diseases and many medications produce acne, but most people who have it, including those who are older, can blame it on their sex hormones.

We know what causes acne: male hormones (andro-

PEARL

Boys *without testicles and girls without ovaries never have acne.*

gens). Female hormones (estrogens) don't cause acne; they suppress it. Upon learning this, some people may wonder why girls suffer from this disorder, too. The answer, of course, is that women have plenty of male hormones—and men have female hormones, too. Puberty generates a surge of both sex hormones in both sexes.

Androgens stimulate the skin's sebaceous glands, which secrete an oily substance (sebum) through the pores (follicular openings). People who have acne don't produce more androgens than normal; their sebaceous glands simply respond too vigorously to androgens.

Treatments Vary

There are several different types of acne. You should know about these types because your doctor might not—and treatment for each is different. Material pouring from an over-active sebaceous gland often plugs the follicle, producing a tiny, skin-colored bump called a whitehead. Exposure to air causes chemical changes that turn the bump into a more visible blackhead. Whiteheads and blackheads (the medical word: *comedones*) are one class of acne.

Beneath this plug, more sebum piles up. Normally, harmless bacteria feed on this sebum plug, producing waste products that add even more to the trapped material. Nothing happens as long as everything remains inside the follicle, but if the follicle wall finally ruptures, this irritating material oozes into the surrounding layer of skin to produce a small infection. The smallest infection produces a red bump (papule), but the traditional badge of acne is the red bump with a white dot in the middle—the pimple. Papules and pimples make up what most people think of as acne. This is the second type. The medical term is *papulopustular.*

Left alone, a pimple heals without scarring. Some unfortunate victims have ferociously overactive glands or very sensitive skin, so that a ruptured follicle leads to an ugly cyst or boil. The third type of acne, known as cystic acne, is the worst type; cysts produce scars.

The Worst Treatment

If you believe two myths about acne, you'll make it worse.

Myth 1: Acne is caused by poor hygiene. The black of a blackhead isn't dirt in your pores; it's a chemical change in the follicle plug. Scrubbing and washing won't help eliminate blackheads, but if you're vigorous enough you'll rupture the follicles and cause *more* pimples. Remember: In ordinary acne, pores plug from below. Keeping the surface clean is all right, but you must do more than that to keep acne at bay.

Myth 2: Oily skin provokes acne. Sebum is oily, and people with acne produce an excess, but as long as it flows freely the complexion won't suffer. On the contrary, sebum is a natural moisturizer. There's no point in washing it off and replacing it with a commercial skin cream. Attacking

PEARL

Acne is a disease of Western industrialized nations. While enthusiasts claim that lack of acne in poor countries results from a diet high in fiber and low in sugar and other bad things, it's actually due to malnutrition. Starvation suppresses sex hormones. That's why victims of anorexia nervosa stop having menstrual periods. They also have a smooth complexion. When humans are well nourished, some develop acne.

your face with chemicals also misses the point. Some acne treatments dry your skin by suppressing sebum production, but ordinary drying agents like alcohol don't do this.

The Best Treatment

The best acne treatment is tailored to the specific type of acne.

Whiteheads and Blackheads

Retinoic acid (Retin-A) stands .head and shoulders above the rest as a treatment for whiteheads and blackheads. An alternate name, vitamin A acid, gives the impression that this substance is a *natural* medicine, but it's a completely synthetic derivative of the vitamin.

Retin-A works by thinning your skin and making sebaceous material more watery, so that pores are less likely to plug. It also loosens the plugs themselves. Most treatment failures occur because patients just aren't patient enough. *Treatment takes three months.* You probably won't notice improvement before two months, and during the first month you'll look worse because your plugs will become inflamed. Be persistent.

Like many powerful drugs, Retin-A has an unpleasant side. The cream is irritating and may sting when you put it on. A few patients can't tolerate this. Don't assume you must wash your face before applying Retin-A; that only makes it more irritating. My instructions are to apply it every other evening to unwashed skin. After a week you can begin applying every evening.

Skin treated with retinoic acid becomes delicate and sensitive to the sun, so you must apply an SPF (Sun Protection Factor) 15 sunscreen every morning. A pleasant side effect for people with thin, delicate skin is the disappearance of fine wrinkles. I'll discuss this in the chapter on wrinkles.

Papules and Pimples

The best treatment for papules and pimples is an antibiotic, but don't nag your doctor for pills. Creams alone work fine except for the worst cases.

Try benzoyl peroxide first. Among creams sold over the counter are Vanoxide, Oxy-5, Clearasil, and Loroxide, but many more exist. Ignore other ingredients listed on the label; ignore the concentration of benzoyl peroxide. There's no evidence that 10 percent benzoyl peroxide works better than 5 percent or 2½ percent.

Benzoyl peroxide is irritating, so use it carefully once a day for a few weeks, then work up to twice a day. Wash your face beforehand, but dry thoroughly before applying the cream. If it still stings, don't wash. On the other hand, the cream *should* be a *little* irritating. If it isn't, put it on immediately after washing your face. *Use it religiously for three months* before giving up and seeing a doctor.

The best prescription treatment for typical acne combines Retin-A (to keep pores unplugged) with an antibiotic. Besides prescription benzoyl peroxides (not necessarily better than the over-the-counter creams listed above), other topical medications contain more familiar antibiotics such as erythromycin, tetracycline, or clindamycin. Not one is superior. Apply Retin-A at night and antibiotic (plus sunscreen) in the morning. I schedule a return appointment in two months.

When a patient has a large number of pimples, antibiotic pills work best. Tetracycline is the first choice, and the initial dose is as high as for an ordinary infection—perhaps 500 milligrams two or three times a day. Within a month there should be enough improvement to taper to 250 milligrams once or twice a day, a safe dose for long-term treatment.

Minocycline, a relative of tetracycline, is slightly more effective but ten times as expensive, so you probably won't get it as the first choice. Other antibiotics such as erythromycin and trimethoprim-sulfamethoxazole (Septra, Bactrim) are not superior, but we use them when tetracycline fails or patients don't seem to respond.

Continue using the creams while you take the pills. Patients often believe that pills are so strong that everything else is unnecessary—a common cause of treatment failure. That's not the only reason for treatment failure—the most common is not taking the medicine long enough or regularly enough. Acne therapy never works quickly; it must continue for a long, long time.

Cystic Acne

Cystic acne, a devastating problem, used to be fairly painful for the doctor, too (grade: C−). The introduction of isotretinoin (Accutane) changed the outlook dramatically; it's a major medical advance.

Accutane, another distant relative of vitamin A, probably works by destroying sebaceous glands, reducing sebum production to nearly zero. A four-month course melts away most ugly cysts and nodules, and improvement often continues even after treatment is finished. About 30 percent of people with cystic acne require a second course. Because Accutane works so well, patients with less severe but still tiresome acne often beg for it. When they do, I tell them—Accutane is poison!

Accutane may be the most unpleasant drug prescribed for a nonfatal illness. Besides drying your sebaceous glands, it dries you from head to foot: your skin and lips will itch, crack, and peel; your nose will bleed; occasionally your eyes will water and your hair will fall out. It causes birth defects. And it's brutally expensive: $500 to $1,000 for one course. Despite the drawbacks, most victims of cystic acne are happy to endure.

The Food and Drug Administration has approved Accutane only for cystic acne. This means the drug is effective for that single condition. However, no law forbids doctors to prescribe it for something else, and I know several doctors who prescribe Accutane freely.

Almost every patient with ordinary acne who asks for Accutane insists that the usual therapy hasn't worked. Quizzing them I invariably find that they're bored with using creams and taking pills day after day, so they've stopped. Long and sad experience has taught me to be wary of patients who don't like the usual treatment and are eager to try something new and risky. In my youth, I'd allow patients to talk me into something against my better judgment. That's when I found one bit of evidence for the existence of God. With horrifying regularity those patients came back to haunt me—for example, by suffering a catastrophic side effect. Today, if you come to me, you get the treatment proved to be the best. If you have your own ideas, plenty of other doctors will accommodate you.

Age Spots

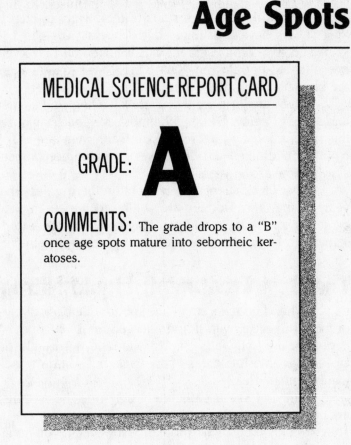

MEDICAL SCIENCE REPORT CARD

GRADE: **A**

COMMENTS: The grade drops to a "B" once age spots mature into seborrheic keratoses.

Among signs of aging that worry my patients, baldness and wrinkles head the list. This is a waste of worry, because these are hard to prevent and not very satisfactory to treat. If you want to worry constructively, pay attention to the age spots that appear around age 40 as small flesh-colored or tan freckles.

Since people are familiar with their faces and the backs of their hands, that's where they tend to notice the first telltale spots. But these spots also grow on the arms, chest, abdomen, and (out of sight and profusely) the back.

Slowly these pale age spots enlarge, thicken, and become darker. They finally turn brown, occasionally even black. As they grow, their surface starts to look warty or greasy, and they always have a distinct edge. They appear glued to the skin, and a vigorous scrape with a fingernail may even tear one off—but not always; don't try it. These mature age spots are known as seborrheic keratoses.

They are also called warts of aging and sometimes barnacles of aging. By age 60 almost everyone has dozens of them, occasionally hundreds. Like warts, they are absolutely benign, but unlike warts they never go away; more appear and slowly grow as the years pass.

My older patients rarely mention them unless they appear on the face. Doctors are willing to remove almost any keratosis on the face, and you may convince them to do the same with large ones elsewhere, but plenty will remain.

The Best Treatment: Liquid Nitrogen

When I notice a small age spot on the back of my hand or face, I freeze it with liquid nitrogen for 10 seconds. A few days later it quietly falls off. My wife reports several ripe keratoses over invisible areas of my back, but so far my face and hands remain clear.

Unless I see a particularly ugly one, I never mention my patients' age spots, and they rarely mention them to me. They are only a cosmetic problem. However, if you don't look forward to being speckled by brown, warty bumps, pay atten-

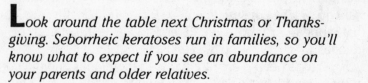

PEARL

Look around the table next Christmas or Thanksgiving. Seborrheic keratoses run in families, so you'll know what to expect if you see an abundance on your parents and older relatives.

tion to these little freckles, and have your doctor get rid of them as soon as they appear. Forget over-the-counter bleaches; only destruction works.

Be prepared to hear your family doctor explain that age spots are nothing to worry about. He or she is right, and a campaign to prevent seborrheic keratoses means a lifetime commitment to at least one visit per year. You may decide that the effort is worthwhile, but convincing your doctor will take persistence. Dermatologists are happy to freeze age spots, but they charge more. Work on your family doctor first.

Liquid nitrogen is also the best treatment for a small keratosis, but patients tend to wait till it grows so large— perhaps over ¼ inch—that liquid nitrogen becomes impractical.

Why You Don't Want to Wait

The best treatment for a large seborrheic keratosis is surgically scraping it away—with or without local anesthesia.

Unless you're a stoic, choose anesthesia. Some keratoses rip away after a few scrapes, but others are stubborn.

Allergies

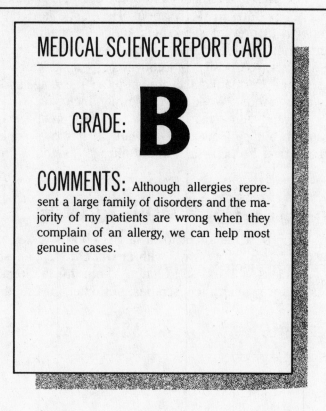

MEDICAL SCIENCE REPORT CARD

GRADE: **B**

COMMENTS: Although allergies represent a large family of disorders and the majority of my patients are wrong when they complain of an allergy, we can help most genuine cases.

If erythromycin, aspirin, codeine, or cafergot upset your stomach, it's probably not because you're allergic to it. If Retin-A or other acne creams burn your skin, don't blame an allergy. I hate cigarette smoke as much as the next person, but people who complain that they're allergic are wrong.

My patients love medical terms, and "allergic" comes often to their lips, usually incorrectly. Mostly these claims are harmless, because I know what they mean (but do you want your doctor to believe that he "knows what you mean" when you talk to him?).

Allergy versus Annoyance

Just because something irritates you, don't assume you're allergic to it. An allergy is an inappropriate reaction to something that is normally harmless.

Smog, smoke, chemicals, and many drugs are genuinely irritating. Burning eyes or an upset stomach is a sensible response, not an allergy. You may prefer to endure an erythromycin bellyache rather than pay five times as much for a substitute. But if you're genuinely allergic to a drug such as penicillin, you must never take it unless your life is threatened—and then only in a hospital under close watch.

When it does its job properly, your immune system attacks harmful invaders—mostly germs and bacteria—with specialized defense cells, chemicals, and sticky proteins known as antibodies. When your immune system attacks a harmless intruder—a pollen, food, or drug—you experience allergy symptoms. This inappropriate defense is a genuine mistake, not much different from the behavior of the average car alarm. It's more evidence that nature doesn't design perfect animals.

Allergy Symptoms

Allergy can produce a great many symptoms, depending on the target organ of the body's misguided attack. Let me mention a few that *aren't* typical of an allergy: drowsiness, mood swings, depression, fatigue, difficulty concentrating. If you disagree, you'll find plenty of enthusiasts to assure you that everything that bothers you about life is an allergy.

Most stomach upsets in adults are a direct action of something (a virus, food toxin, an irritating drug), not an allergy. Finally, patients with upper respiratory tract symptoms worry about an allergy, but allergies don't cause fever, severe sore throat, swollen glands, or a bad cough. If you think you have hay fever, pay attention to the following: Allergies itch.

Most allergies affect the respiratory tract and skin. In the respiratory tract they cause a runny, itchy nose and red, itchy eyes. A persistent runny nose without itching is probably a cold or a reaction to something irritating in the environment.

13

The usual allergic rash is hives: itchy red welts from the size of a pinhead to a silver dollar that appear, last a few hours, then fade, to be replaced by others. When hives affect the delicate tissues of the face, your eyes and lips swell. Hives can also cause itchy, swollen palms. An extensive rash that *doesn't* itch is probably not an allergy. Hives are generalized, so a local itchy patch is not typical.

Allergies attack other target organs less often but sometimes more severely. Although it seems reasonable for foods to affect the digestive tract, they don't except in infants. Mostly they cause hives or hay fever symptoms. Drug allergies produce hives as well as a host of other rashes. Less often they mimic almost any serious disease, from pneumonia to kidney failure to anemia to some types of cancer.

Life-Threatening Allergies

Most of us know of someone who suffered a violent reaction to a bee sting or penicillin shot or erupted into intense itching in the middle of a lobster dinner. This extreme reaction is called anaphylaxis. If ordinary allergy is a misguided defensive response, anaphylaxis is sheer insanity. The same chemicals that cause the swelling in your nose and face gush in such huge quantities that the entire respiratory tract swells— including the larynx and bronchial tubes, cutting off breathing. These chemicals can also make blood pressure collapse and stop the heart or kidneys. Anything can cause anaphylaxis, but the most common causes are insect venoms, penicillin, aspirin, many vaccines, shellfish, nuts, and eggs.

Best Treatment: Adrenalin

Adrenalin is a lifesaver in anaphylaxis. Patients who have survived one attack carry a kit to inject themselves at the first sign of another. Adrenalin works for less severe attacks, too, and I often give a shot to a patient miserable with hives.

Histamine is the body's defensive chemical responsible for most itching and hives, so antihistamines are a reasonable treatment (grade: B−). They work best when taken regularly because they prevent histamine release from cells that store it. Any histamine already in action will continue to act. Cheap antihistamines such as Chlor-Trimeton are sold over the counter; they are as good as anything a doctor can prescribe. If antihistamines make you drowsy, ask the doctor for one of the newer—and more expensive—brands that don't do this.

Shots May Help

Despite a universal yearning for shots to make allergies disappear, allergy hyposensitization is only a fair treatment, earning a "C –." Seventy percent of patients have a "good" response, meaning a 60 percent reduction in symptoms after a year of injections. Shots work best against insect stings and for typical hay fever and other pollen allergies that flare up during certain seasons. People who have dust allergy or multiple allergies and those whose symptoms persist most of the year don't respond well. Shots work even more poorly for food and drug allergies.

Avoiding Allergy

One method of handling allergy earns an "A": avoidance. Since this strategy is prevention, not treatment, it doesn't qualify for inclusion in this book on medical care. But if you don't want allergy symptoms, avoidance works best. I see patients' eyes glaze over when I bring up the subject. This method of dealing with allergy isn't real medicine, my patients are convinced. Surely some scientific treatment can enable them to tolerate their house plants, pets, or favorite foods. But avoidance is superbly scientific—it's based on the truth, and studies prove that it works.

Alzheimer's Disease

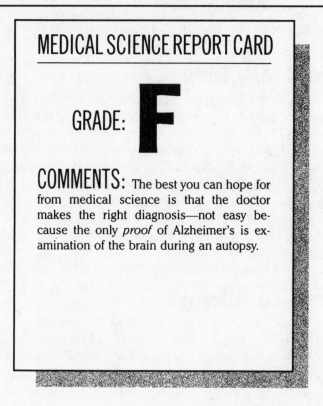

MEDICAL SCIENCE REPORT CARD

GRADE: **F**

COMMENTS: The best you can hope for from medical science is that the doctor makes the right diagnosis—not easy because the only *proof* of Alzheimer's is examination of the brain during an autopsy.

Every older person who becomes forgetful and careless should have a complete mental and physical exam and tests, including computerized tomography (CT) or magnetic resonance scans of the brain, in the hope that he or she *doesn't* have Alzheimer's disease. A good family doctor or internist can arrange for these tests.

Fifteen percent of the luckiest have something we can cure: anemia, depression, thyroid disease, drug reactions, some types of brain tumors. Another 25 percent have conditions we can help, such as kidney failure, severe emphysema, strokes, and other brain diseases. The rest suffer this most common and devastating chronic disease of the elderly.

An Unknown Cause

Theories abound about what causes Alzheimer's, but I feel comfortable blaming a virus. Some experts agree; others search for causes in environmental toxins, hereditary defects, or derangement in nerve function. Each one of these theories has some evidence in its favor.

As far as the viral theory goes, history is on my side. Although first discussed in 1907, Alzheimer's was considered rare until I was out of medical school, when we gradually realized that it was extremely common and grows more so with age. Twenty percent of those past 80 have it.

Both experts and the media always reach for exotic explanations when they encounter a new, frightening disease. Three diseases that made headlines when the first cases appeared were Legionnaires' disease, toxic shock syndrome, and acquired immune deficiency syndrome (AIDS). All gave rise to wild theories, but all turned out to be the result of an infection. Nature seems to abhor a vacuum; as we free our bodies from older infections, it invents new ones.

Not only that, several obscure diseases with strange names have a pattern ominously similar to that of Alzheimer's. In medical school we listened to lectures on kuru, a disease confined to cannibals in central New Guinea. It affected mostly women and children because they tasted half-cooked brains (men had more patience). After a very long incubation period—sometimes over 20 years—signs of brain degeneration appeared and the victim died in a year or two.

Although rare, Creutzfeldt-Jakob disease occurs around the world, mostly affects the elderly, and begins exactly like Alzheimer's, with confusion and memory loss. Progression is faster, with death occurring in a year or two. Like kuru, it spreads through contact with human nerve tissue; several unfortunate people were infected after a corneal transplant or injections of hormone prepared from human pituitary glands.

Because both these diseases (and half a dozen other rarities) have a very long incubation period, their agents are called slow viruses, but it's not certain that they're viruses at all. They are smaller and simpler than the usual virus and far more resistant to poisons and boiling. They may represent an entirely new form of infectious particle. Although I find them fascinating to read about, the implications are a bit frightening. I predict a viral cause for Alzheimer's will be found by the end of the century.

Symptoms of Alzheimer's

People who have Alzheimer's initially experience forgetfulness and loss of memory for recent events.

These symptoms mark the first signs, but they are common in everyone, so don't panic if they happen now and then. Once they begin to make life difficult—if someone persistently leaves home and gets lost or forgets to turn off the tea kettle—it's time to let the doctor know. He or she may do a short exam and assure you that the problem's caused by normal aging. Accept this explanation, but only at the first visit. If the problem persists for another month, return and ask for an investigation for Alzheimer's or referral to someone who will do it. It's a major undertaking that some family doctors are reluctant to launch.

Remember that Alzheimer's begins as dementia—deterioration of higher intellectual functions. Suspect a different disease if there are signs of local brain damage such as weakness of one side, abnormal movements, seizures, slurred speech, or difficulty with vision. These symptoms may appear late in Alzheimer's, but not at inception.

Best Treatment: Support

Plenty of drugs are supposed to help restore memory temporarily, but since early symptoms of Alzheimer's often improve for a time on their own, I suspect drugs don't work. Research on oxygen, hormones, and nutrition is unimpressive, although you'll find enthusiasts for them all.

Caring for someone with Alzheimer's may prove to be overwhelming. Never try this alone; Alzheimer's is so common that support groups exist everywhere. Join one.

Angina

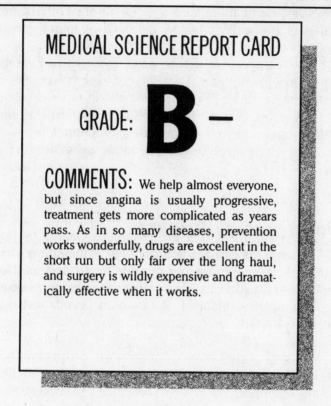

MEDICAL SCIENCE REPORT CARD

GRADE: **B –**

COMMENTS: We help almost everyone, but since angina is usually progressive, treatment gets more complicated as years pass. As in so many diseases, prevention works wonderfully, drugs are excellent in the short run but only fair over the long haul, and surgery is wildly expensive and dramatically effective when it works.

Angina is chest pain and the first sign of heart disease. Everyone should know about it.

Angina begins quietly enough. Long before you feel the first twinge of pain, cholesterol from your diet starts attaching itself to the walls of your arteries. In larger arteries, this buildup doesn't often cause problems; the vessels simply grow stiffer. This is known as hardening of the arteries or atherosclerosis. In smaller arteries, cholesterol buildup can narrow a vessel enough to cut off the blood supply. If this blockage happens in the brain, a stroke follows; if it's in the heart, a heart attack occurs.

Cholesterol piles up faster if you smoke, have a high level of cholesterol in your blood, or have high blood pressure or diabetes. Being male is also a disadvantage. Being fat and inactive is probably a factor, although evidence is not as strong.

You can prevent hardening of the arteries by eating a diet very low in cholesterol and fat, but experts who cheerfully give advice on this subject make it sound too easy. Only an extremely rigorous diet—on the order of the Pritikin program or pure vegetarianism—will provide protection. Modestly lowering your cholesterol intake will modestly slow atherosclerosis.

Symptoms of Angina

Vessels supplying the heart muscle (coronary arteries) are a weak spot in human design. Being so narrow, they are at risk of obstruction as cholesterol piles up. If a vessel becomes completely blocked, it causes a heart attack, which usually begins with chest pain identical to angina—but it's not angina.

Angina occurs when a coronary artery is narrow but not quite plugged. Enough blood squeezes through to nourish the heart muscle under normal circumstances, but when the heart works harder to supply a body that's mowing a lawn, walking up stairs, or even eating a heavy meal, the extra blood needed to do the job can't get through. Deprived of oxygen, the heart behaves no differently from a back, calf, or biceps muscle forced to work too hard. It hurts. Feeling pain, the person usually stops what he or she is doing. After a few minutes, the heart isn't working as hard, its blood supply is once again sufficient, and the pain goes away. This is angina, and if you experience it, you should let your doctor know.

Warning: If pain doesn't go away in 15 minutes, it's not angina; it may be a heart attack. Call the paramedics or hurry to an emergency room.

Pain Profile

Angina pain is focused in the chest, almost always in the center. It occasionally radiates to the jaw, arm, or back, but more rarely than medical textbooks claim. My patients often worry about left shoulder and arm pain in the absence of chest pain, but I've never encountered this pain pattern as a sign of heart disease.

Don't take "pain" too literally. Angina is not sharp or stabbing, and many patients deny that they're suffering pain. They describe what they feel as a pressure or squeezing sensation. Also, don't assume that angina is brought on only by exercise. Once you have coronary artery disease, a vessel may decide to go into spasm and reduce blood flow temporarily. This spasm can occur at any time and produces the same discomfort even if it happens while you're at rest.

The Best Treatment: Diet, Exercise, Drugs, and Surgery

You may remember an old Oppenheim rule: When doctors have many treatments for a disease, none is very good. Strep throat or appendicitis has a single treatment, and it works every time.

Angina is one of the few conditions for which prevention often begins *after* the disease appears.

That's because angina is not only a disease in itself, it's the forerunner of a more serious disease: heart attacks.

Of course, if you'd practiced prevention all your life, you wouldn't have angina, but that's water under the bridge. You can still prevent further disease. Here are the goals of the best treatment.

Relieve the heart of unnecessary work. This means stopping smoking and losing weight. Other experts advise reducing stress, but they're vague about how this is accomplished.

Make the heart work more efficiently. Everyone with a new diagnosis of angina should enter a supervised exercise program. Conditioning allows the heart to accomplish more with the same blood supply, thus reducing angina episodes.

Dissolve the cholesterol buildup. As I mentioned earlier, a *very* low fat diet prevents atherosclerosis. Evidence that the same diet reverses the process is tantalizing but not convincing. It seems to work in monkeys and *may* work in humans. I discuss the possibility with patients, but too few have the will power required to change their diets so radically. Despite the lack of proof, it's worth a try.

A few doctors claim excellent effects from chelation therapy—using drugs to clean out the cholesterol buildup. Their claims are irritatingly enthusiastic and backed by no evidence except testimonials from equally enthusiastic patients.

Medications That Work

Although exercise, a rigorous diet, and a clean lifestyle are helpful, most angina victims also require drugs (by contrast, self-help makes drugs unnecessary in a large number of people with hypertension). Here are the best drugs and their actions.

A class of drugs known as nitrates works by increasing blood flow to the heart.

Dissolved under the tongue (sublingual), ordinary nitroglycerin (Nitrostat, Nitrolingual) relieves pain within minutes and works for up to half an hour. Isosorbide dinitrate (Isordil, Sorbitrate) is a similar sublingual nitrate that takes a few minutes longer but lasts an hour or two. I tell patients to use it just before an activity likely to provoke chest pain, such as yard work or sex. Sublingual nitrate relaxes blood vessels throughout the body, and one consequence is a throbbing vascular headache. This reaction is so common that I tell patients to expect it—and to suspect that their pills are out-of-date if they stop getting it.

Sublingual nitrates work fast because veins in your mouth empty directly into the heart. Stomach veins first pass through the liver, which inactivates almost all the nitrate it receives. However, a small amount gets through, so doctors prescribe oral nitrates (Isordil, Peritrate, Nitro-Bid) in an effort to increase blood flow to the heart 24 hours a day. Patches applied to the skin have the same action, although they are much more expensive.

Long-acting nitrates definitely work, but many experts suspect that tolerance develops after several weeks or months. Since doctors tend to keep patients on drugs until they discover a reason to stop, it's up to you to let yours know if the drug no longer prevents pain.

Another class of drugs, known as beta-blockers, prevents the heart from overworking.

Also used to treat high blood pressure and prevent migraine, dozens of brands are on the market, among them Inderal, Lopressor, Tenormin, Corgard, and Blocadren. When you exercise, nerve impulses speed up the heart. So does adrenaline, a hormone released when you're frightened or nervous. Beta-blockers block both these actions and reduce angina attacks.

I know a patient is taking a beta-blocker when I measure a slow pulse of between 50 and 60 beats per minute. Under 45 is too slow; let your doctor know if your pulse gets this slow. A pulse over 70 means the beta-blocker isn't working. You may need a larger dose.

A third class of drugs, known as calcium blockers, decreases the heart rate and increases blood flow through the coronary arteries.

The calcium blocked has nothing to do with calcium in your diet but refers to tiny amounts that regulate the contraction of muscle cells. Under the influence of these drugs (Isoptin, Calan, Cardizem), coronary blood vessels relax, but so does the heart, which beats more weakly. Used carefully, these drugs help a great deal.

Bypass and Angioplasty: The Surgery Option

If angina remains intolerable despite medical therapy, a surgeon can detour a blood vessel around the narrowed section of coronary artery and plug it into a coronary artery further on. Even if angina is well controlled, you should have a bypass if certain vessels are blocked—for example, the left main coronary artery.

Although a major surgery, a bypass is surprisingly safe, with a mortality of 1 percent in skilled hands. It abolishes angina 90 percent of the time. Unfortunately, angina tends to return as years pass, because atherosclerosis progresses and some grafts become plugged. Bring up the subject of a bypass with your doctor if you can't stand your chest pain. If the doctor suggests it, listen carefully to the reasons; he or she may be right, but get more opinions. In my opinion, too many bypasses are done.

Angioplasty is another type of surgery sometimes used to treat angina. It involves stretching the narrowed artery.

This procedure is easy to describe but tricky in practice. The doctor threads a wire dragging a deflated balloon through the narrowed segment of the artery, then blows up the balloon. This eliminates the blockage more than 90 percent of the time. Three percent of the time it makes things worse, necessitating an emergency bypass. More tiresome is the speed with which blockage reappears: over one-quarter of patients are back within six months.

Bypass grafting has been around since the 1960s, so I don't expect dramatic improvements in results from that operation. I'm more optimistic about the future of angioplasty because it's only been popular since the early 1980s. As with most new procedures, doctors put it in practice before we understood how to use it. That means patients during this first decade contributed greatly to our knowledge. They were also participating in an experiment without being asked. I expect that doctors will become more skilled as they practice and the instruments they use will improve rapidly, so angioplasty should work much better in the 1990s and replace a great deal of bypass grafting.

Arthritis

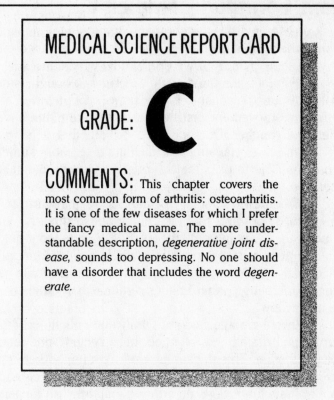

MEDICAL SCIENCE REPORT CARD

GRADE: **C**

COMMENTS: This chapter covers the most common form of arthritis: osteoarthritis. It is one of the few diseases for which I prefer the fancy medical name. The more understandable description, *degenerative joint disease*, sounds too depressing. No one should have a disorder that includes the word *degenerate*.

Mr. Jones, my exam and the lab tests show that you have a rash. For treatment, I'm prescribing . . ."

Would you let your doctor get away with that? Wouldn't you want to know what sort of rash it is, especially what caused it? Of course you would, yet patients rarely complain when told they have *arthritis*, a vague term that means joint inflammation. Fat textbooks cover the subject; hundreds of arthritides exist (yes, the plural of arthritis is arthritides; you never see it because writers think the word looks strange, so they rearrange their sentences to avoid it). Always ask which type of arthritis you have.

Most Common Complaint

Just as wrinkles accompany aging skin, osteoarthritis occurs when joints get old. By age 75 everyone has it, but not everyone feels pain. And we don't know what causes it.

All joints are lined with cartilage—a tough, smooth, flexible tissue that cushions the bone and provides almost friction-free movement. As the years pass, cartilage becomes stiffer and rougher. Doctors often explain that it is wearing out—a simple explanation as inaccurate as most simple explanations. The truth is that no one knows why cartilage deteriorates.

Osteoarthritis tends to attack weight-bearing joints (knees, hips) or joints that take much abuse (fingers), so this supports the "wearing out" theory. But if joints wore out, runners and people in strenuous jobs would suffer more arthritis, and they don't. Perhaps osteoarthritis is an inevitable part of aging; some people inherit better cartilage than others, so they age more slowly.

When cartilage becomes thin and rough, moving the joint hurts. Irritated and inflamed, unprotected bone reacts by growing thicker. This thickening doesn't help, and after a few years an arthritic joint becomes permanently swollen and less mobile. In its final stage, an arthritic joint may no longer hurt, but it also doesn't bend.

The Best Treatment: Reducing Inflammation and Improving Function

Unlike skin, injured cartilage doesn't heal, so you can never reverse the damage. However, you should suppress the pain and inflammation produced by excessive friction. Pain serves no useful purpose except to warn you that something is wrong, and you know that already.

Try aspirin first. It costs far less than newer anti-inflammatories and works as well. If your stomach can tolerate it, take up to three every 4 hours. If you aren't satisfied with the results, try the nonsteroidal anti-inflammatory drugs (Motrin, Naprosyn, Feldene, Clinoril, Indocin, Tolectin). Although all are chemically related, most patients find one that works best. Give each a month's trial and *keep a list,* because your doctor will soon forget, and other doctors you may consult in the future will need to know.

I engage in this sort of dialogue time and again.

DOCTOR: Have you tried Naprosyn?

PATIENT: Is that the same as Indocin?

DOCTOR: No.

PATIENT: Well . . . I think I tried it, and it didn't work.

DOCTOR: Voltaren is fairly new. Did your doctor prescribe that?

PATIENT: Hm-m-m . . . Is it a little blue pill?

DOCTOR: I don't know. What about Clinoril?

And so on. It's frustrating for your doctor to work in the dark, and it makes helping you all the more difficult. Make sure you never inflict this scenario on your doctor.

A Warning about Bleeding

All the drugs mentioned above cause stomach bleeding, usually without pain. Serious bleeding is not common, but when it happens, it can be catastrophic. The elderly run a higher risk. Although massive bleeding isn't common, it's also not rare, and experts are beginning to fret. Worried editorials are appearing in medical journals. Doctors still prescribe pain-relief drugs freely, but I have a gut feeling that a big shift in medical opinion may take place in the 1990s, and we'll become less generous with these drugs. My gut feeling is not always right, but keep your eyes open.

Cortisone Injections

Don't be shy about asking for a cortisone injection, especially if one joint is making life miserable. It can dramatically reduce pain and swelling for months. Some family doctors don't inject joints, so they have no personal experience with the power of cortisone, but we all know the dangers, so you can expect to hear about them. Your doctor will tell you that cortisone slows the healing process and temporarily reduces resistance to infection. For these reasons, cortisone is risky. But in the hands of an expert, an occasional (not more than twice a year) joint injection is fairly safe, and the benefits are impressive. Be persistent.

Finally, if you're crippled by hip arthritis, ask your doctor about surgery. Hip replacement verges on a medical miracle (grade: A− to B+). It eliminates pain and gives you almost complete movement. Other artificial joints don't work so well, but this is an area of steady progress, so ask your doctor to discuss this option with you.

Balding

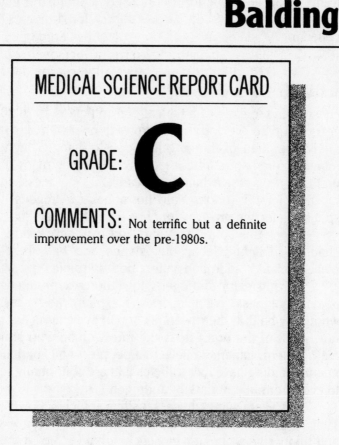

MEDICAL SCIENCE REPORT CARD

GRADE: C

COMMENTS: Not terrific but a definite improvement over the pre-1980s.

Hair is the fastest growing tissue in the body, averaging half an inch per month. One hair grows for about three years, then enters a resting phase for several months before a new hair growing from below pushes it out. Then the cycle repeats. We begin life with about 100,000 hair follicles. Three years equals about 1,000 days, so a simple calculation reveals that everyone loses 100 hairs per day.

When a healthy young person complains of hair loss, I look for visible scalp disease (which I rarely find). Then I instruct him or her to collect all hair for 24 hours and bring it to me in an envelope for a count. Try it yourself if you think you are going bald; do not shampoo for 48 hours before collecting.

Cause of Balding

The life span of a typical hair follicle is 15 to 20 three-year cycles, so everyone's hair grows thinner with age. Patients rarely complain of thinning hair due to aging. They worry a lot about premature baldness, however. While many diseases produce progressive hair loss leading to baldness, they are too rare for this book. Male hormones (androgens) are responsible for the great majority of premature balding cases.

Does this sound familiar? You may have read it in the chapter on acne. Sebaceous glands and hair follicles are closely related; androgens affect both in unpleasant ways.

Giving extra androgens to either sex produces male-pattern baldness, but this doesn't explain most cases. Men who grow bald in their twenties don't have excess androgens, nor (most of the time) does the rare woman who shows the male pattern. Experts believe that people who experience premature balding have hair follicles that are abnormally sensitive to even normal amounts of androgen.

As years pass, these sensitive follicles slowly wither. They never disappear entirely but continue to produce smaller and thinner hair. Looking closely at a bald scalp, you can see a fine fuzz.

The Best Treatment: Minoxidil

Minoxidil has long been available to treat high blood pressure. Although effective, it is also powerful and has many side effects, so the average doctor has stayed away. I never used it, but specialists such as cardiologists grew familiar with it because they dealt with more difficult cases. Hairiness was a common side effect, so women didn't like minoxidil.

PEARL

Boys *without testicles and girls without ovaries never grow bald.*

During the 1970s doctors began to notice that many balding cardiologists weren't bald any more. Not only had their scalp filled in, but hair flourished everywhere, so that their morning shave included forehead, nose, neck, and ears as well as the usual areas. Sly jokes from colleagues were a small price to pay; these cardiologists were happy to have hair again. They were, we knew, consuming large amounts of minoxidil.

This side effect was not lost on its maker, the Upjohn Company, which began financing research on the effect of minoxidil rubbed into the scalp—a much safer method. In the meantime a thriving gray market sprang up; pharmacists made a tidy income grinding up minoxidil tablets and dissolving them in whatever they had on hand, and dermatologists prescribed the resulting lotions liberally. This wasn't illegal. Remember, once the Food and Drug Administration approves a drug for one thing, a doctor can prescribe it for anything. I tried it myself for six months but lost interest. My baldness doesn't bother me that much.

Limitations of Treatment

Before the advent of topical minoxidil (Rogaine) a young man anxious to ensure that he would never grow bald could have himself castrated. Although a grade A treatment, it never caught on, but now the man can do almost as well by rubbing Rogaine into his scalp twice daily for the rest of his life.

Experts don't know how it works. Minoxidil won't grow hair where no follicles exist and doesn't affect hormone levels.

Apparently it reverses the shrinkage of follicles so that hairs become thicker and more visible. However, it only works for the early stages of shrinkage. It's useless once an area is bald. Ideally, a young man or woman should begin using it before any thin spots are visible, but it's also fairly effective when thinning first appears over the top or front of the scalp. Once you start using it you should see improvement for about a year. After that you won't get better, but if you continue treatment, you shouldn't get worse. Once you stop, baldness proceeds.

Barrier Contraceptives

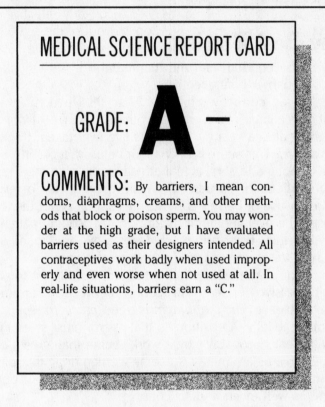

MEDICAL SCIENCE REPORT CARD

GRADE: **A** −

COMMENTS: By barriers, I mean condoms, diaphragms, creams, and other methods that block or poison sperm. You may wonder at the high grade, but I have evaluated barriers used as their designers intended. All contraceptives work badly when used improperly and even worse when not used at all. In real-life situations, barriers earn a "C."

Thousands of years ago, our ancestors began to suspect that a direct connection existed between pregnancy and the act of sex. Barrier contraceptives appeared almost at once.

Records from 3,500 years ago mention that women inserted half a lemon into their vagina to block the cervix. Modern spermicides have the advantage of working, but ancient creams—honey, beeswax, or opium—were more natural. Men once fashioned condoms from animal intestines. (Although still available, they are not as reliable—modern latex is less porous.) Casanova's lady friends received a gold ball to insert in their vagina and were assured that it would prevent pregnancy. History does not record whether they believed him, but few refused the gold.

The Best Barriers

The condom and the diaphragm tie for first place as the best barrier contraceptive.

Used correctly, both are 97 to 98.5 percent effective. That percentage represents a woman's chance of *not* being pregnant after a year. In any class I've ever taken, 97 percent gets an "A." This score is only a hair below that of birth control pills. Among all users, actual effectiveness plummets into the neighborhood of 70 percent. While pregnancies occur from improper use of barrier contraceptives, this is not the leading cause. The overwhelming majority of my women patients admit that they have unprotected sex now and then. *Barrier contraceptives don't work if you don't use them.*

The diaphragm is not a barrier. Although it looks like an impressive rubber obstruction, sperm swim around the edge with ease. *The diaphragm is a receptacle for spermicide.* It holds the jelly in position so that sperm must swim directly into it. That's probably why it works better than cream or jelly alone. Creams are messy, so some women hope that popping in an empty diaphragm provides some protection, but they might as well insert a lucky charm.

An Added Benefit

Barrier contraceptives protect against sexually transmitted diseases.

Men have long worn condoms as protection against sexually transmitted disease, but women using any kind of barrier also suffer fewer serious venereal diseases such as gonorrhea. They also experience less yeast infection and fewer annoying vaginal infections in general. Besides this, good evidence exists that barriers prevent viral infections such as herpes and acquired immune deficiency syndrome (AIDS).

Birth Control Pills

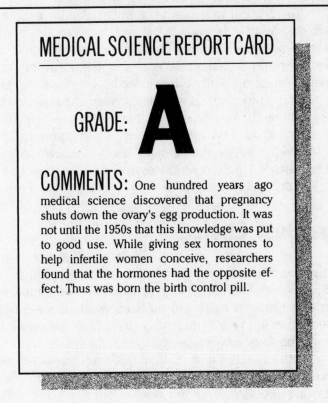

MEDICAL SCIENCE REPORT CARD

GRADE: **A**

COMMENTS: One hundred years ago medical science discovered that pregnancy shuts down the ovary's egg production. It was not until the 1950s that this knowledge was put to good use. While giving sex hormones to help infertile women conceive, researchers found that the hormones had the opposite effect. Thus was born the birth control pill.

To say that birth control pills work by mimicking pregnancy is too simple. Pregnancy feels too unpleasant to tolerate in exchange for convenient contraception, as women who took the Pill 30 years ago can attest. Hormone doses in those early pills were almost as high as during pregnancy.

Nowadays, the Pill provides one-quarter of the hormones in the old dose. Most users don't experience the same nausea, weight gain, breast tenderness, and emotional swings as the average pregnant woman—but some do. Equally important, low-dose pills are just as effective as the old ones: virtually 100 percent in those who take them religiously, 96 percent for the average woman who skips a pill now and then.

Today's Pill makes a woman "a little bit pregnant" to upset the delicate hormonal balance between the brain, the pituitary, and the ovaries. These three areas secrete half a dozen hormones that must rise and fall in strict order to provoke ovulation. Only a hint of extra estrogen and progesterone in the blood confuses these cycles and shuts down the ovary. Although as effective as early pills, today's minimal doses give much less margin for error. Forgetting to take the Pill for even a single day is more likely to allow the cycle to resume long enough to produce an egg.

The Best Choice

The best birth control pill is any that contains 0.35 milligrams of estrogen. Examples are Ortho Novum or Norinyl 1/35, Brevicon, Modicon, Ortho Novum 777, and Triphasil. Pills with less estrogen exist and probably work as well, but they have less margin for error and a fairly high incidence of annoying spotting between periods.

Pills containing more than 0.35 milligrams of estrogen provide equally good contraception but more side effects. If you don't like estrogen, your doctor can prescribe pills containing only progestins (Micronor, Ovrette). Only about 98 percent effective, they are not quite as good as combination pills and produce a great deal of irregular bleeding.

My patients worry that spotting between periods means that their pill is weak, that is, not protecting them. This is absolutely not so. Besides interfering with ovarian function, oral contraceptives also suppress the menstrual cycle, sometimes in unpredictable ways. Spotting is one result. I can usually eliminate this annoying problem by increasing the estrogen dose, but I do so only when a woman insists that she can't stand the inconvenience. Increasing estrogen is never necessary to assure protection against pregnancy.

The Bad Side Effects

During the 1950s and early 1960s, everyone called the Pill a miracle drug. Taking it was the mark of an independent woman, free as never before to live life with no worries about getting pregnant at the wrong time. We forget how revolutionary that was. Oral contraceptives (along with votes for women and *The Feminine Mystique*) make up the roots of feminism today.

In the mid-1960s an ominous note was sounded—reports of women on the Pill who had suffered blood clots in the brain or lung. Only a few reports appeared in medical journals, and many doctors did not believe that oral contraceptives were to blame, but several small studies hinted at the contrary.

Researchers launched a massive effort to find a definite answer. It had to be massive, because fatalities were so rare. Thousands of hospital records were reviewed. Tens of thousands of women on the Pill were observed for years to compare their medical problems with those of nonusers.

The answer finally appeared, and further studies confirmed it. Users have a higher risk of blood clots. They also have more heart attacks, but this risk is almost entirely limited to smokers, whose risk of clots is also far greater than that of nonsmokers. Many doctors, including me, don't prescribe the Pill to smokers. Other side effects are predictable because pregnant women also have them: more gallstones, higher blood pressure, and elevated blood sugar.

This isn't the first time doctors embraced a new drug before they knew the side effects, and it won't be the last. Serious side effects from taking the Pill aren't common, but every potential user must decide for herself whether the risk is worth the convenience.

The Good Side Effects

Seventy-five percent of American women believe oral contraceptives are a major health hazard, 50 percent believe taking the Pill is riskier than childbirth, and 33 percent believe that it causes cancer. They're wrong on all counts. The Pill is not a major health hazard—pregnancy and childbirth are more dangerous, and oral contraceptives don't seem to cause cancer. In fact, the best studies show that it prevents certain types of cancer. Users have about half the ovarian and uterine cancer risk of nonusers. Ovarian cancer is common, difficult to detect early, and usually fatal. Reducing your risk by half is a major benefit.

Because the Pill suppresses the activity of a woman's reproductive tract, users have less menstrual bleeding (and, as a result, less anemia). They also experience fewer ovarian cysts, uterine fibroids, and benign breast lumps. The Pill protects against serious pelvic infections, although not as well as barrier contraceptives. Finally, you should know that most studies of the bad side effects took place when women were taking higher-dose pills. Today's low-dose Pill is almost certainly safer.

Bladder Infections

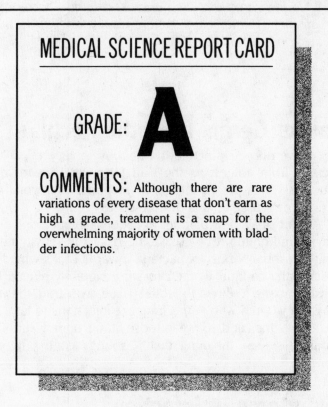

MEDICAL SCIENCE REPORT CARD

GRADE: **A**

COMMENTS: Although there are rare variations of every disease that don't earn as high a grade, treatment is a snap for the overwhelming majority of women with bladder infections.

Bladder infections (cystitis) are almost always a female problem. They are 50 times as common among young and middle-aged women as among men. Because of its length, the penis provides an excellent barrier to germs. By contrast, the short female urethra allows easy access to the bladder.

Since most bladder infections are bacterial, you can have confidence in the doctor's antibiotic prescription for your bladder infection. It's probably a cure, not a placebo.

PEARL

Bladder infections are the most common bacterial infection. Humans suffer more respiratory illness, but these are usually viral.

Cause: Germs from the Rectum

Even if you practice the best hygiene, you can't keep bacteria from colonizing the skin for several inches around your anus. This places the germs responsible for bladder infections near the genitals of both sexes.

Nuns have few bladder infections, so apparently sexual activity and childbirth increase the risk. Any activity near the genitals probably pushes bacteria inward. That's why doctors traditionally caution women to wipe carefully after a bowel movement and to direct the toilet tissue away from the vagina. We warn women who suffer frequent infections to take showers, not baths, and to wear loose-fitting underwear. This is common sense—meaning that it sounds good but no one knows if it helps.

Symptoms of Infection

Germs and their waste products irritate the sensitive bladder lining, so you can guess what symptoms follow. The irritated bladder contracts, giving the feeling that you absolutely must urinate (urgency); it does this too often (frequency), but after you rush to the bathroom the urine often refuses to appear (hesitancy) or barely comes out (dribbling). An infected bladder may bleed, causing bloody urine (hematuria). Although a frightening sight, blood in the urine is not an ominous sign and doesn't mean that your infection is worse than usual. Don't worry about it, but do see your doctor.

Painful urination (dysuria) is trickier to interpret. It's

not a bladder symptom but a sign of inflammation of the urethra, the tube that carries urine from the bladder to the outside. Bladder infections can hurt, but so can a vaginal infection that irritates the urethral opening. Don't insist that you have a bladder infection if it hurts to urinate. Patients often argue with me, probably because they don't want a pelvic examination.

If you don't jump out of bed to urinate throughout the night, it doesn't matter how much urgency and frequency you suffer during the day. The diagnosis is probably stress, not cystitis.

I see this stress-related behavior regularly. Remember that the bladder is a muscle. Neck muscle contraction gives you a tension headache, bowel muscle contraction an irritable bowel, and bladder muscle tension the urge to urinate.

Nonsigns and Nonsymptoms

Question: What is the likely diagnosis in a woman with urgency, frequency, dysuria, bloody urine—and excruciating low back pain?

Answer: Bladder infection plus low back pain. Bladder infection can produce a nagging ache in the pubic area or low back, but the ache is never severe. Fever, chronic fatigue, an upset stomach, and constant vaginal burning are worth bringing to the doctor's attention, but these symptoms are not typical of bladder infection.

Women with bladder infection plus low back pain worry that they might have a kidney infection, but *low back pain is not the sign of kidney disease!* The kidneys don't lie in the low back but much higher: in the midback behind the lower ribs. If you have a kidney infection you're likely to know that something is really wrong.

A kidney infection (pyelonephritis) makes you sick!

You shouldn't feel ill with a simple bladder infection, but germs in the kidneys cause fever, chills, and general misery, often with nausea and vomiting. Pain in the kidney area occurs, but it's not necessarily severe. A kidney infection may or may not give symptoms like those of bladder irritation.

The Best Treatment: Antibiotics

Twenty years ago when doctors believed that patients followed instructions, we treated cystitis for two weeks. The first researchers into patient compliance discovered that practically no one completed the course. Fortunately, it wasn't necessary, and we reduced it to one week. Energetic researchers reduced this still more, and ten years ago enthusiasts encouraged us to give a single large dose. Some doctors still do so, although good studies show that it doesn't work as well as longer courses; the cure rate is perhaps 85 percent. This is fine if you're among the 85. Taking the medication for five to seven days is better.

If you suffer half a dozen bladder infections every year, don't rush off to a urologist for plumbing repairs. If you did not have urinary problems as a child, your urinary tract is probably normal. I see many women who have undergone brutal urethral dilatations because a urologist suggested that the opening was too narrow; even urologists agree that this procedure is vastly overdone.

When a healthy woman is plagued by recurrent bladder infections, many doctors prescribe an antibiotic for prophylaxis—to prevent an infection. The most common is nitrofurantoin (Macrodantin). This drug is excellent for the bladder because it's excreted so fast that it doesn't enter other tissues, so it's useless for infections elsewhere. If a woman knows that sex provokes an infection, I tell her to take one pill afterward. If she doesn't know what brings on the infection, she should take one pill every night.

Breast Lumps

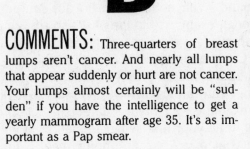

MEDICAL SCIENCE REPORT CARD

GRADE: **B**

COMMENTS: Three-quarters of breast lumps aren't cancer. And nearly all lumps that appear suddenly or hurt are not cancer. Your lumps almost certainly will be "sudden" if you have the intelligence to get a yearly mammogram after age 35. It's as important as a Pap smear.

Breast tissues respond energetically to sex hormones, swelling as much as 50 percent before a period and shrinking afterward. Some women are uncomfortably aware of these changes, but all women have them.

Examine Your Breasts

During childbearing years, milk ducts are so numerous and active that *breasts are normally nodular.* You should become familiar with your own knots, cords, thick areas, cysts, and bumps. It will save you terrible worry and doctor visits.

Here is a scenario that typifies the experience of 90 percent of younger women who discover a lump. Like most women, this patient doesn't examine her breasts regularly or does so only superficially. Then at some point, time hangs heavy on her hands—perhaps during a touch of insomnia or a dull TV show. Her fingers wander to a breast and she begins to feel around. With nothing else to do, she performs a far more thorough exam than in the past—so she's guaranteed to find something. And she does. Panic mounts. Is it normal? Is it a lump? Could it be cancer? Is this the beginning of the end?

Depending on her degree of panic, hours to weeks may pass before I can (almost always) reassure her. Do yourself a favor and examine your breasts carefully every month. If you haven't yet done your first self-examination, *don't do it now!* You'll ruin your day. Make an appointment with your family doctor, then give yourself a thorough examination a few hours before the visit. This will keep terror to a minimum.

Then make sure you *tell the doctor what you found!* Many patients keep quiet during the exam and feel reassured when the doctor announces that the breast is normal. That lump I found must be nothing, they think. Otherwise, the doctor would have mentioned it. The sad truth is that he or she probably didn't feel it. You're more familiar with your breasts than your doctor is. He or she needs your help.

What Causes Lumps?

A firm, rubbery, mobile, painless mass is almost certainly a benign fibroadenoma in a woman in her twenties and probably in an older woman as well.

A cancer tends to be harder than a benign lump, but don't depend on it.

A woman worried about cancer should feel reassured by the appearance of several lumps, because that's rarely an ominous sign.

Doctors once told women with multiple lumps that they had fibrocystic breast disease, but recently we decided that it was unfair to use *disease* for a condition affecting 20 percent of women all the time and almost every woman at some point in her life.

Hormones affect some breasts so intensely that swollen ducts are always palpable around the period or even the entire month. Fluid secreted at the end of the month pours out in such quantities that some of the liquid becomes permanently isolated in cysts. Women with fibrocystic breasts *don't* have a higher risk of cancer, but they don't have a lower risk, either. They and their doctors must grow intimately familiar with such breasts, because they will see a great deal of each other. All new lumps *must* be checked by a doctor and monitored.

Best Treatment: Aspiration or Surgery

Today a doctor (a surgeon if your family doctor doesn't have this skill) will probably stick a needle into your lump. Although this sounds gruesome, it solves your problem instantly when it succeeds. Many frightened women see their lump vanish as the needle fills with fluid. Once aspirated, a cyst rarely returns—and many firm lumps also turn out to be filled with fluid. Women with severe fibrocystic breasts may get tired of doctor visits and needles; they should consider the drug I discuss in the chapter on breast pain.

In the past, if a lump was solid you went to a surgeon, who admitted you to the hospital and took it out in the operating room. This was expensive. Removing breast lumps is very minor surgery, so experts decided that it would be safe and much cheaper as an outpatient procedure. So hospitals built ambulatory surgery clinics, where patients arrived in the morning, had their operation, and left in the afternoon. Everyone agrees that this is terribly cost-effective.

My wife had an outpatient breast biopsy in 1989. She arrived at 9:00 A.M., and I picked her up at 3:00 P.M. For half a day's use of the facilities, the hospital charged $2,150. The surgeon's fee was $1,500. The anesthesiologist sent a bill for $480. Several hundred dollars each were due the radiologist and pathologist. Nothing converts one to a fervent advocate of socialized medicine better than such an experience.

Wrong Use of Mammograms

If your doctor orders a mammogram to investigate your lump, you haven't had the best treatment.

No matter what the mammogram reveals, a new or changing lump must be aspirated or removed unless the doctor is almost certain that it's benign. If your doctor has reason to believe it's benign, then it's all right to wait a few months to make sure it grows and shrinks with the menstrual cycle.

A mammogram (like a Pap smear) is actually a poor way to diagnose cancer; too many suspicious findings turn out to be normal. But both procedures are superb at arousing our suspicions. *That's why we use them.*

Mammograms and Pap smears work best when nothing is wrong.

That's why you should have them regularly when you feel fine. If a doctor has already found something abnormal, such as a lump, the next step is a more accurate test such as a biopsy.

Breast Pain

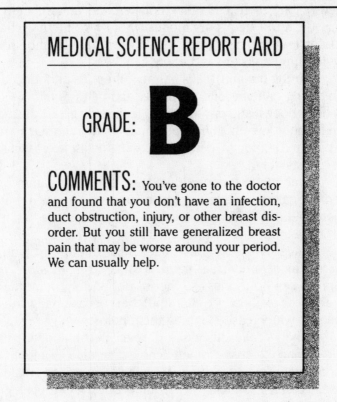

MEDICAL SCIENCE REPORT CARD

GRADE: **B**

COMMENTS: You've gone to the doctor and found that you don't have an infection, duct obstruction, injury, or other breast disorder. But you still have generalized breast pain that may be worse around your period. We can usually help.

Although both generalized breast pain and menstrual cramps are provoked by hormones, these two pains are only distantly related. Hormones cause the release of chemicals known as prostaglandins in the uterus. Prostaglandins produce muscle spasm and pain. These same hormones also make breast tissue swell. With no extra space available in the average breast, anything that expands rapidly squeezes against neighboring tissue and hurts.

Male Hormone Helps

Although the male hormone danazol (Danocrine) is the best treatment, it shouldn't be the first thing you try. Aspirin or even ibuprofen and other nonsteroidal anti-inflammatory drugs (NSAIDs) help only modestly, but give them a chance. And don't wait to hear from your doctor that you should wear a well-fitting brassiere and apply heat.

During the mid 1980s a flurry of reports announced that eliminating caffeine often provides dramatic relief. Although self-help books and my medical texts still give this recommendation a few lines, I suspect that it's a fading fashion. It's worth a try, although cutting out caffeine is not as easy as enthusiasts claim.

Feel free to try nutritional supplements. Vitamin E, 200 international units three times a day, has a few reputable experts behind it. Don't use supplements for more than three months without telling your doctor.

Since female sex hormones aggravate breast pain, the best treatment suppresses them. Birth control pills don't really suppress sex hormones, so they're not an important therapy, but they occasionally help. And they occasionally make it worse, in which case stopping them helps.

When you're miserable despite all the above, you deserve danazol. Most women feel better after a month and become pain free after three. A synthetic androgen (male hormone), danazol shuts down your ovaries nicely, but giving male hormones to a female has predictable side effects, such as hair growth, acne, irregular periods, and shrinking breasts, as well as hot flushes from diminished estrogen. On the other hand, male hormones increase sexual drive. Not all women suffer side effects, and others consider them a reasonable trade-off for pain relief. You must make the decision after talking to your doctor.

Bronchitis

Bronchitis is one of the most frustrating conditions I encounter. Time and again, I have a variation of the following dialogue.

"You have a nasty virus that's given you that cough and cold," I say. "I'll prescribe a good cough medicine that'll take the edge off, but here are other things you can do. First . . . "

"Excuse me, doctor," the patient interrupts. "It's not a cold. It's bronchitis."

I always agree, explaining that *bronchitis* is simply a

word meaning inflammation of the bronchi. Any inflammation of the bronchial tubes makes you cough, just as inflammation of the nose (rhinitis) makes it run, inflammation of the throat (pharyngitis) makes it hurt, and inflammation of the larynx (laryngitis) makes you hoarse. Anything that irritates the bronchi causes bronchitis—dust, chemical fumes, allergies, asthma, and viral infections.

"I have a tendency to bronchitis. I need an antibiotic to knock it out," the patient invariably declares.

Having given my mini-lecture on bronchitis, I must now deliver my why-antibiotics-don't-work-for-this-condition explanation. It's an excellent explanation, which you'll read several times in these chapters—antibiotics kill bacteria; they don't have any effect on viruses. Patients often look puzzled. They can't understand why I don't prescribe the good medicine that their previous doctors gave "for the same thing." It would be outrageous for me to explain that their previous doctors had diagnosed a fictitious disease in order to justify giving a powerful drug, so I don't. But I'm telling you here.

Not a Disease

Here's an amazing medical secret: Bronchitis doesn't exist—at least not as a medical diagnosis.

Everyone knows that there's no cure for the common cold and other viral upper respiratory infections, so when doctors want to prescribe an antibiotic they must call it something else. They often call it bronchitis.

In my more pugnacious youth, I would confront such doctors. This usually happened when one of their patients gave me a hard time for refusing to give antibiotics. Marching to his or her office, I would hand over the patient's chart.

"I see you've given this patient antibiotics for his respiratory infection," I would announce. "What were you treating?"

"Bronchitis," the doctor would answer after inspecting the chart.

"I'm a little unclear on bronchitis," I would continue innocently. "Could you enlighten me? What is it? What are the symptoms? How do you evaluate it?"

If the doctor tried to comply, I would point out that

everything he or she described could be explained by an ordinary viral upper respiratory infection. Eventually the doctor would realize that I was there to cause trouble and would wave me off with the advice: "Look it up if you don't know."

"Good advice!" I'd declare triumphantly. "Let's look it up in Harrison." *Harrison's Principles of Internal Medicine* is the doctor's bible, a huge tome of over 2,000 pages. A copy probably stood on the shelf in that very office. I would snatch it down, and we would search . . . and search.

Harrison doesn't mention it! A long chapter discusses chronic bronchitis, but this is a severe disease of old smokers with emphysema and badly damaged lungs—not what we were looking for. Although these doctors were always surprised at the absence of bronchitis, they did not thank me for this information, nor did they stop giving out antibiotics. You can read why in the chapter on throat infections.

Coughing as a Symptom

Coughing is the main symptom of inflamed bronchi. Don't be upset if you cough up mucus. Everyone makes a quart per day. When your respiratory tract is irritated, it makes more. Many coughers think this mucus is terrible stuff and spit it out as fast as it comes up. In fact, mucus is a natural product and full of protein. Swallowing it won't make you sick; you should recycle it.

Don't make too much of the sensation that mucus is stuck in your chest. Patients insist that they'd feel better if they could only "bring up the phlegm," but this is deceptive. Irritated bronchi make you feel like something is stuck down there (just as irritated eyes feel sandy), but nothing is there.

Viruses to Blame

Bronchitis exists when an infection makes you cough, because coughing is the only way the bronchi can complain. Pneumonia also makes you cough (see the chapter on pneumonia), because infection in the nearby lung tissue irritates the bronchial tubes.

The bronchial tubes of otherwise healthy people are

51

surprisingly resistant to bacterial infections but susceptible to viruses.

By *healthy* I mean not suffering emphysema, cystic fibrosis, or other serious pulmonary disease. Many patients are convinced that they have weak lungs because they suffer frequent colds. This is not true. And "tendency to bronchitis" is another condition invented by doctors.

Treat the Symptoms

Patients often ask for a strong cough medicine, and I comply with a prescription for one containing codeine or hydrocodone. Handing it over, I always add encouraging words like, "This will make you feel better." Once a patient takes the trouble to come in, I won't announce that over-the-counter cough suppressants are equally strong, but that's the truth. Look for dextromethorphan on the label.

If a tickle in your throat makes you cough, use cough drops, not cough medicine. Breathe in steam or take a decongestant if you don't like your mucus production, but don't worry about it.

I often see patients worried because a nagging cough has dragged on several weeks. I can't remember the last patient who had anything other than a simple virus, but you should let your doctor know if a cough persists.

If it's severe and accompanied by a fever, let us know within a few days. You might have pneumonia. We can cure pneumonia.

Cancer

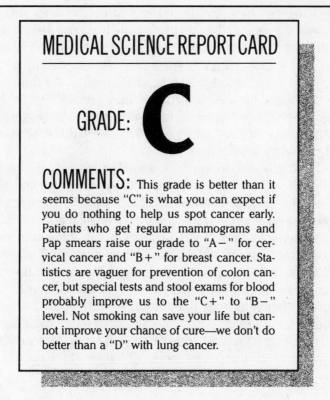

MEDICAL SCIENCE REPORT CARD

GRADE: C

COMMENTS: This grade is better than it seems because "C" is what you can expect if you do nothing to help us spot cancer early. Patients who get regular mammograms and Pap smears raise our grade to "A−" for cervical cancer and "B+" for breast cancer. Statistics are vaguer for prevention of colon cancer, but special tests and stool exams for blood probably improve us to the "C+" to "B−" level. Not smoking can save your life but cannot improve your chance of cure—we don't do better than a "D" with lung cancer.

People think of cancer as a wild growth of cells, and this isn't a bad explanation. But it doesn't explain the few cancers in which cells don't multiply—they do the opposite.

You and I started life as a single cell created when sperm joined egg. During the first hours of our existence in the womb, that solitary cell divides and divides again, making exact duplicates of itself. At first those cells are very primitive—meaning they don't do anything interesting. They just multiply. But being primitive also means that there are few restrictions on what they can do. If, when you were only a ball of 2, 4, 8, or 16 cells, those cells fell apart, each could develop into a normal, identical copy of you.

Soon these early cells begin to specialize: Some of their genes are permanently turned off; others go into action. At first, while you are still a tiny ball, cells become merely inside, middle, and outside cells. Then they form simple organ systems. Some cells begin to specialize into, for example, blood cells. But these blood cells are still primitive. As time passes these blood cells develop further into primitive white blood cells. Then the white cells mature further into lymphocytes, plasma cells, leukocytes, and other specialized white cells that perform useful functions.

All this development is governed by signals—probably chemical—under the control of the genes. Some messenger chemicals are growth factors, which stimulate cell division; others are inhibitory factors, which do the opposite. Mostly, these chemical controls help the fetus mature—the tissues become more complicated. But occasionally these chemicals switch the cells into reverse. After an injury, for example, cells revert to a primitive stage, multiply vigorously, fill in the wound, then return to their mature form and settle down. Under the microscope, cells repairing an injury look like cancer cells; sometimes an expert can't tell the difference. During an injury, of course, the process is under strict control—the body turns the cells on, then turns them off again.

Current Cancer Theory

Cancer happens when the body loses control. Normal cell tissue stops growing when its cells start bumping up against neighboring cells. Cancer cells just keep on growing, squeezing their neighbors or spreading around them. Normal cells literally stick together. But cancer cells lack the ability to stay where they belong, so many float off and grow elsewhere. They also don't do their normal job—a gland cell stops making hormone or makes far too much, for example.

Why do cells escape control or regress? Plenty of theories have come and gone, but those favored today are supported by more and more evidence.

Unwanted Inheritance

Many cancers tend to run in families. You may have double or triple the risk if more than one relative has the same form of cancer. But what exactly is it that you inherit that can lead to cancer? It must be something in your chromosomes— structures in the nucleus of each cell that contain genes that regulate every aspect of a cell's behavior. You inherit your chromosomes from your parents, but things happen to those chromosomes as you age.

Over the past decades, researchers looking hard at human genes have made discoveries that will bear fruit in the next century. They have spotted visible abnormalities in the chromosomes of cancer cells, indicating that pieces are missing or have moved from one place to another. Not only that, each type of cancer has a specific chromosomal abnormality. The next step the researchers must take is to learn why and how these defects produce cancer. I don't think the answer is far off.

Cells out of Control

What exactly causes a normal cell to turn into a cancer cell?

A normal gene making a substance that stimulates cell division functions with its regulatory gene nearby, keeping an eye on things. That's how cells operate—a gene that works is controlled by a regulatory gene that turns it on and off. Sometimes the chromosome breaks, and the piece carrying the regulatory gene moves somewhere else. Chromosomes break all the time; they're usually repaired quickly, but sometimes the cell makes a mistake and sticks a piece of chromosome where it doesn't belong. This mistake may have no consequence or it may be so crippling that the cell dies. But if it simply deprives a growth factor gene of control, that gene begins churning out growth factor without restraint, and the cell multiplies wildly. A chilling thought: This need only happen in a single cell to make a cancer.

You can probably think of other ways a cell can turn cancerous. A poison (a drug, cigarette smoke, radiation) can damage the regulatory gene. Viruses can disrupt a chromosome and even insert genes that force the cell to multiply. Advancing age may make the chromosome repair process less efficient. Defects in the immune system—including advancing age—may make the body incapable of getting rid of cancerous cells.

Although I keep hammering home how defective we are, this is one instance where we're almost perfect. Two out of three Americans never get cancer.

Cancer Symptoms

You're probably familiar with the mass effect that cancers produce when expanding into an area where other tissues belong. Expanding cancers cause pain when they compress tissue or block passages. Normal function diminishes when tumors replace healthy tissue. For example, large lung cancers make it difficult to breathe; a pancreas full of tumor produces less digestive enzyme.

But remember that cancer cells are deranged—meaning their genes don't exert the proper control. So they can behave in very odd ways.

In a crazy way, cancer cells occasionally behave as if they were other parts of the body. It's not rare for a lung cancer to produce hormones normally made by the pituitary gland. One tumor, called a dermoid, is filled with hair, teeth, skin, and other clumsy attempts of cells to switch roles.

The Best Treatment: Destruction

The best treatment currently available for cancer involves destroying the tumor—whether by surgery, chemicals, or radiation.

Medical science should do better. Destruction works fine for a localized disease in an unnecessary tissue (e.g., appendicitis, hemorrhoids). But destruction is a crude way of treating cancer. We should develop something as benign as antibiotics. Eventually we will, but I can't predict when.

PEARL

All your cells contain exactly the same genes. That's what makes you an individual.

A kidney cell works differently from one in your eyeball, fingertip, or thyroid because most of its genes are permanently turned off and a few are working under strict control. As I explained earlier, this turning on and turning off of genes (i.e., speciali- zation) occurs rapidly in the womb but continues as you grow up. By the time you're an adult, your cells are mostly fixed and don't normally change function except in a few situations such as wound repair.

But each cell contains all your genes. Think of the possibilities! One could take a cell from your skin, turn off certain genes, turn on others, and con- vert it into a nerve or blood cell. In theory one could grow a kidney or a complete arm from that cell. In fact, by turning off everything, one could revert that cell to a state identical with the fertilized cell from which you began. Then, by turning on the develop- ment process, one could grow a human identical to you. Although theoretically possible, it will require more knowledge of gene control than we have now. I don't foresee it in our lifetime.

Many observers find our lack of treatment options in- furiating. Cancer research soaks up billions of dollars every year and produces fascinating discoveries about cancer genes and viruses and amazing machines to take pictures of cancers deep inside the body. Yet no treatment breakthrough has oc- curred, and despite my familiarity with research, I can't see any in the works. Are we on the right track? Probably. Here's why I think so.

During the 1860s researchers discovered that germs

cause disease. That was incredible because it was completely unpredictable. If you had told the wisest physicians in any civilization over the entire history of the human race that the most important cause of disease was tiny bugs, they would have agreed that you were stupid. Everyone knew that disease was caused by unhealthy habits, an improper diet, bad attitude, evil spirits, imbalance of bodily forces, overwork, or sin (doctors in other times *always* knew what caused disease; only today's doctors admit that sometimes they don't know). But no culture ever has blamed tiny bugs.

Until well into the twentieth century, germs remained the leading cause of disease—and dying of tuberculosis, typhoid, blood poisoning, or meningitis was *not* less painful and prolonged than dying of cancer can be today.

During the decades following the first discoveries of germs, scientists refined their knowledge, pinpointed the germs responsible for the major diseases, studied them in the lab, and explained how they behaved when they infected and killed people.

By the 1890s doctors were getting irritated. "Who cares about germs," they wrote impatiently. "For 30 years our journals have churned out articles about the amazing things scientists are discovering. But what about our patients? All this expensive research hasn't produced a single cure."

They were right. Eventually diphtheria antitoxin appeared—not a cure but an impressive advance. Half a dozen other important vaccines followed, but until well into the 1930s, a person sick with a bacterial disease got little help from our knowledge of bacteriology. Then came antibiotics, and within a few decades germs were literally conquered.

Other experts write that cancer is a complex disease requiring many approaches, so we can expect only slow, steady progress, which is what we have now. I think science will soon do better and that something like antibiotics will appear; like antibiotics it will seem to come out of nowhere. Unfortunately, although the *National Enquirer,* the evening news, and even reputable health magazines announce such a discovery regularly, they are unreliable. Your doctor will let you know when a reliable cancer cure becomes available.

Chronic Bronchitis and Emphysema

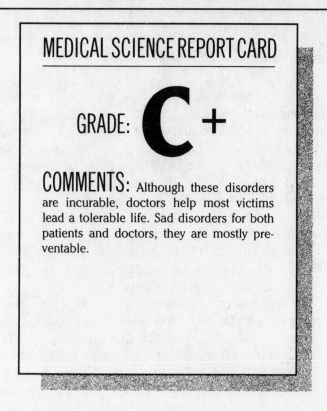

MEDICAL SCIENCE REPORT CARD

GRADE: **C**+

COMMENTS: Although these disorders are incurable, doctors help most victims lead a tolerable life. Sad disorders for both patients and doctors, they are mostly preventable.

Both chronic bronchitis and emphysema are caused by smoking.

Smoke damages bronchial tubes so that the lining swells and produces more protective mucus—which doesn't protect as well as it should, because the injured lining can't move mucus up and out smoothly. The mucus piles up, obstructs the tubes, and becomes infected, leading to more damage. This condition is called chronic bronchitis.

Smoke also destroys the delicate lung tissue through

which air passes into your blood. As years pass, lung tissue simply fades away, so that the chest x-ray of an old smoker shows a heart surrounded by emptiness. Absence of lung tissue makes breathing difficult. This is emphysema.

What about Smog?

I'm obliged to mention other causes; smokers want to know, and the tobacco industry is anxious to inform you.

Perhaps 1 percent of people with emphysema inherit an absence of alpha-antitrypsin, an enzyme that protects the lungs from damage. They develop terrible disease in their thirties. An additional 5 to 14 percent of the population inherit a partial deficiency. Experts suspect that this deficiency makes their lungs more vulnerable. Doctors don't routinely test for alpha-antitrypsin, but we may eventually do so in an effort to scare young people off smoking.

Air pollution fascinates smokers. They invariably bring up the subject when I'm on the attack outside the office, but even patients find it a useful defense.

"Why pick on cigarettes?" they complain. "I've been breathing dirty air 24 hours a day since I was born. That must cause terrible lung damage. Why quit smoking if I still have to breathe smog? I'll wait till you eliminate pollution."

Air pollution is not healthy, but evidence that it causes chronic bronchitis and emphysema is surprisingly thin. We know that heavy smog days harm people who already have chronic bronchitis and emphysema, but studies comparing people who grow up in the country with those in the city don't find much difference in lung disease. Smog is not good for you, but smoking is very bad for you.

Symptoms: Breathing Problems

The symptoms of chronic bronchitis and emphysema are wheezing, difficulty breathing, persistent cough with sputum production, and frequent respiratory infections.

In medical school I learned that chronic bronchitis and emphysema were distinct disorders at opposite poles of some-

PEARL

A *researcher studied chronic bronchitis and emphysema to determine the influence of smoking. Afterward he announced a revolutionary discovery.*

"The patients I interviewed who had mild and moderate disease were almost all smokers, as we suspected. But only a minority of the most severe cases smoked. This means that smoking can't be the whole story. Something else must cause the worst lung damage."

When good scientists do an experiment and announce their results, they're not necessarily right. Popular writers and the media are quick to trumpet new findings, but you should wait until other scientists have checked it out.

In this case, others discovered a fatal flaw. Almost everyone in the study had smoked, but the sickest had quit when breathing became almost impossible. The less sick hadn't reached that point. The interviewers had asked the wrong question ("Do you smoke?"); although the patients answered truthfully, their information was worthless.

This story illustrates the perils of research, but it also makes a point about chronic bronchitis and emphysema.

thing called chronic obstructive pulmonary disease. Each had unique signs and symptoms, which we memorized.

People with emphysema must labor to breathe because this condition has destroyed most of their lung. When a doctor listens with a stethoscope, breath sounds are soft, even inaudible. Tapping on the chest produces a hollow sound. These people are thin because breathing is such hard work that they lose weight. Their cough is mostly dry, and a respiratory infection can be catastrophic because they have so little reserve lung tissue.

People with chronic bronchitis are heavy, possibly because they're so inactive but also because the condition leads to heart failure, which causes water retention. They cough up a great deal of sputum and even more when they suffer one of their frequent respiratory infections. This extra sputum plus their inflamed bronchial tubes obstructs air flow, so oxygen doesn't reach the blood. The result is often a bluish hue to the skin. Obstruction also causes wheezing and difficulty breathing, which respond to bronchodilators. Bronchodilators are the same medications we give to young people with asthma. Patients with pure emphysema struggle for breath because they have too little lung, so bronchodilators don't work for them.

It's all right to remember these patterns, but almost every patient is a mixture of the two.

The Best Treatment

A family doctor can manage the initial stages of these conditions with a few pills and an occasional course of antibiotics, but this approach won't work once a patient's life begins to revolve around his or her lungs—a common fate. Chronic lung disease kills 75,000 people per year; it's our fifth leading cause of death and one of the few that's still rising. The century will end before the decline in smoking that began in the 1970s affects these statistics.

Once coughing, wheezing, puffing, and bloating become a daily concern, the best treatment includes:

Pills to dilate the bronchial tubes. These are almost always theophylline (Theo-Dur, Theobid, Slo-Phyllin, Theolair). A relative of caffeine (coffee was the leading bronchodilator in the nineteenth century), theophylline also helps the wheezing of allergies and asthma.

Sprays to dilate the bronchial tubes. These include relatives of adrenaline (Alupent, Ventolin, Proventil) and of belladonna (Atrovent).

Many patients ask me to persuade their medical insurance companies to pay for a home nebulizing machine, but despite its size and the impressive noise it makes, it's inferior to a properly used hand-held inhaler. If your doctor can't demonstrate how to use an inhaler, he or she doesn't see enough patients with your problem, and you should find another doctor.

Antibiotics. People with chronic bronchitis should suspect a lung infection when the cough gets worse and sputum pours out even more generously than usual. It means that bacteria have invaded the stagnant sputum clogging the lungs. A two-week course of antibiotics helps. Many patients require this treatment a dozen times per year.

Getting rid of mucus. Everyone agrees that people with chronic bronchitis should keep their mucus thin and get rid of it as quickly as possible. A hospital physiotherapist does a good job by pounding on patients' chests while they cough. You may think that science has developed more clever ways to deal with mucus, but you'd be wrong. I doubt that any drug or expectorant (although many are available) makes your mucus thin, and most experts agree. Self-help health writers claim that drinking extra fluids helps you cough up mucus, but this isn't true for any practical volume. Go ahead and drink fluids—it's unwise to allow yourself to get dehydrated. I urge patients not to become obsessed with mucus.

Cortisone. Cortisone suppresses inflammation, so it helps chronic bronchitis. Long-term cortisone therapy is risky, but specialists use it for the worst cases when simpler therapy fails.

Exercise. Everyone with chronic lung disease bad enough to limit normal activities should enter a pulmonary rehabilitation program. Hospitals provide them, and your doctor will recommend one. Training increases your energy and your body's ability to use oxygen, and you'll learn to breathe efficiently to get the most from your remaining lung tissue.

Oxygen. If you consider oxygen a drug, it's the most expensive of all. Home oxygen rarely costs less than $500 a month, so insurance companies and Medicare look very closely at any request. Fortunately, studies show that it's a lifesaver, doubling life expectancy for patients with end-stage (depressing word!) chronic lung disease. Oxygen won't pep you up if you're tired, and it's no use if you're short of breath now and then, but if you stop to rest several times while walking to the corner mailbox, you're a candidate.

PEARL

Bronchodilators only work if your bronchi need dilating!

This is one of those simple-minded rules that everyone ignores. If you have chronic bronchitis, with heavy mucus production, coughing, and inflamed bronchi, you probably have bronchial obstruction. The doctor hears wheezing through the stethoscope as air struggles through constricted passages. If he or she wants to prove it, you will be sent for pulmonary function studies, where you blow into a machine before and after receiving a bronchodilator.

If breathing is difficult because most of your lung has vanished, dilating bronchi is irrelevant, but I see plenty of people with emphysema taking these drugs. I have an easy test to determine if they're helping. I ask, "Are they helping?"

"Yes." (A positive test result; drugs are helping.)

"I think so." (A negative result; they aren't.)

Too many patients are reluctant to tell a doctor that a treatment isn't working. It's easy to tell if a bronchodilator is working; you breathe easier. If you're not certain that they're working, they probably aren't. Don't hesitate to let your doctor know. If you are asked to try them a little longer, obey, but mention it again if there's no change. Doctors—even good doctors—prescribe too many bronchodilators for chronic lung disease because they're the only safe class of drugs, and it's often hard to predict who will benefit. You have the final say.

Colds and Flu

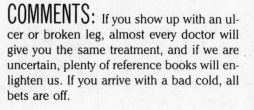

MEDICAL SCIENCE REPORT CARD

GRADE: **F**

COMMENTS: If you show up with an ulcer or broken leg, almost every doctor will give you the same treatment, and if we are uncertain, plenty of reference books will enlighten us. If you arrive with a bad cold, all bets are off.

Patients never lecture me on diabetes or brain tumors, but they're experts on their latest cold or viral upper respiratory infection (URI). They explain how they got it ("My husband left the window open last night"), why they're susceptible ("I've been working 12 hours a day; my resistance is low"), what I should prescribe ("Erythromycin knocks it out"), and what happens if I don't get the message ("It'll turn into bronchitis").

No one dies of a viral URI; medical students don't study it, and medical books dismiss it in a few pages. Nevertheless, these upper respiratory infections make up the *largest group of patients we see*—10 to 15 percent of everyone who walks in to be examined by a family doctor. We care for half a dozen every day, a few thousand every year, about 50,000 during a career. And we don't cure a single one. This is very unsatisfying, so we often pretend.

Antibiotics Don't Help

If you don't want useless drugs, stay away from the doctor for upper respiratory tract symptoms—sore throat, congestion, cough, runny nose.

Doctors throughout the world give antibiotics for these ailments because treating the symptoms gets us precious little gratitude. Patients are miserable, and they don't give thanks when told to gargle, take aspirin or cough medicine, and wait a few days.

Overprescribing antibiotics is a professional scandal. One expert called this torrent of unnecessary medications a "major environmental pollutant." I used to quarrel incessantly with colleagues for this lazy practice because it made my life difficult. No matter how carefully I would explain to patients that antibiotics had no effect on their infection (antibiotics kill bacteria but not viruses), they were puzzled and unhappy. That's what they'd always gotten, they insisted. Few were grateful for my sympathy and advice. Some were very resentful; a few were loudly abusive.

Today I am older and wiser. Patients come to us desperate for help, and doctors enjoy helping. If we can't, it's tempting to fake it, and giving antibiotics for common respiratory infections is this sort of faking. Most doctors can't resist.

Viruses Cause URIs

Perhaps a hundred strains affect the upper respiratory tract. As in most viral illnesses such as measles, mumps, and chicken pox, you're immune after you recover, but in the case

PEARL

You may believe that doctors earn their high in-comes and get their ulcers by caring for serious dis-eases like heart attacks. The truth is that heart at-tacks are easy. Experts tell us the best way to treat them—and doctors listen carefully and obey. Patients never argue with our judgment, and they appreciate our efforts.

This is definitely not the case for the coughs, sore throats, and congestion miseries of viral upper respiratory infections. Doctors invent their own treat-ments, and many patients have strong opinions on what they require. Treating an upper respiratory in-fection properly is often more stressful for the doctor than treating a heart attack. Improper treatment (i.e., antibiotics) pleases patients and makes the doctor's life easier. Giving antibiotics is so common that even good doctors do it; don't think of switching doctors when it happens.

of URIs, 99 other viruses remain to cause the same symptoms. Fortunately, your immunity grows. Children average half a dozen viruses per year, but the frequency steadily diminishes until middle age, when the average is less than one per year.

Again like measles, mumps, and the like, URIs are contagious. You catch them from another person, but despite the common belief, they are not easy to catch. If they were, doctors would be ill constantly. Good scientific studies prove that coughing and sneezing don't spread the virus easily. Most victims touch infectious secretions, then rub their eyes, pick their nose, or put fingers in their mouth, thus placing the virus where it can enter the body. If your spouse has a cold, don't touch one another, don't kiss, but do wash your hands. And don't pick your nose.

Treating Symptoms

Symptomatic is a medical term meaning, "Nothing shortens the illness; do what you can to make yourself feel better." Rest if you're tired (but rest does not make the illness go away quicker). Take aspirin or acetaminophen (Tylenol, Datril, Anacin-3) for pain or fever. Don't take them for any other URI symptom; they won't help. And don't give aspirin to children with fever. Over-the-counter cough medicines containing dextromethorphan (look for it on the label) are as strong as anything we can give by prescription. Look for the same ingredient in decongestants and throat remedies.

Drink lots of fluids if you're thirsty. Drink to replace the fluids lost by a fever. Otherwise, extra fluids serve no useful purpose.

By all means, take vitamin C if your friends urge you. It makes them feel helpful.

In deciding whether to see a doctor, follow the old Oppenheim rule: Sickness makes you sick. If you don't feel very sick, you're probably not very sick.

Go to the doctor if you feel sick: your cough is severe, your sore throat agonizing, you feel really bad. Be careful of reasons that disobey this rule. Here are some that I hear every day.

"It's gone on for five days."

"My mucus is green."

"My vacation begins Saturday, and I can't be sick."

"My wife had the same thing, and the doctor gave her tetracycline."

"I can't bring the fever down."

"It's my fourth cold of the year."

There's no harm in seeing a doctor for any of these reasons. We can explain why these are not ominous signs, answer your questions, and give the sort of advice you've just read. Furthermore, if you disagree with everything I've written and still want an antibiotic, you'll probably get one.

Constipation

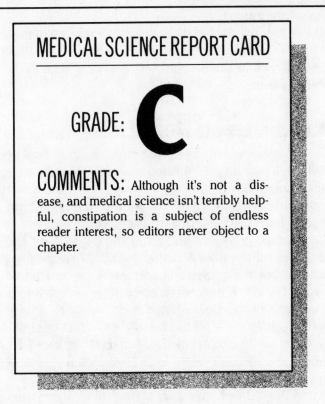

MEDICAL SCIENCE REPORT CARD

GRADE: **C**

COMMENTS: Although it's not a disease, and medical science isn't terribly helpful, constipation is a subject of endless reader interest, so editors never object to a chapter.

Constipation has lost status since I was young. Until the late 1960s most old people and plenty of young suffered without shame, and doctors lectured on the evils of laxatives and the merits of fruit. This was a tradition handed down for centuries.

Then good health became the rage, and everyone either exercised, ate lots of fiber, and felt virtuous, or they didn't and felt guilty. Popular writers taught that exercise and fiber cure constipation, so anyone who suffered must be slothful, poorly nourished, and otherwise negligent. Today patients tell me about stress, depression, gas, or bloating, but they avoid discussing the frequency of their bowel movements unless I bring it up. Constipation may be slightly less common than in the past but not much.

I no longer tell patients that a bowel movement every five days is normal for them. Although true, if a patient hates the way his or her body behaves, a doctor must agree that a problem exists.

Cause: Design Defects

Like the human back, the colon hasn't caught up with evolution. It was fine ten million years ago when our ancestors jumped energetically through the trees and ate huge amounts of vegetables. We live differently today, but the colon hasn't adjusted. It should be half its present size.

Storage is its job, and today the colon does its job too well. It has other minor functions, such as reabsorbing water and salts, but these aren't important. A colon isn't essential for your health. Nature developed it as a convenience for higher forms of life. Lower forms such as worms dribble waste as soon as it forms, and their neighbors don't complain.

The colon can easily hold ten days' residue—5 pounds of stool (average daily stool is ¼ to ½ pound). Although this is not unhealthy, people hate carrying it around. They hate the heavy feeling. They hate sitting on the toilet, trying unsuccessfully to get rid of it. Getting rid of waste isn't a high priority with the colon, but eventually the contents move out. If the wait makes you miserable, you don't have a disease, but you do have a problem.

Signs and Symptoms

Whatever you think represents constipation is your personal symptom—provided you feel it in your abdomen. Some people have a heavy sensation; some feel bloated. The urge to defecate without the ability to budge the stool is another. Other people complain of hard, painful, infrequent bowel movements.

Stool sitting quietly in the colon doesn't poison your body. Headaches, fatigue, and depression aren't signs, but I rarely say so anymore. As a doctor I can make only a limited number of statements that contradict my patients' deeply held beliefs before they suspect my competence.

Best Treatments: Fiber, Fluids, Exercise, and Drugs

If you eat enough roughage to give you gas and floating stool, you're doing your best. If you can't stand the calories or haven't time to chew a pile of vegetables, sprinkle unprocessed bran or psyllium seed (Metamucil, Konsyl, Effer-Syllium) over your food. Begin with 1 teaspoon per meal and increase until you're satisfied with the results.

Roughage by itself makes constipation worse. A lump of indigestible plant fiber moving through the small intestine (as the name hints, it's narrower than the colon) will occasionally wedge itself so tightly that only a surgeon can extract it. Fiber helps constipation only if it absorbs water, swells, and softens, so you must accompany it with fluids—two 8-ounce glasses per meal. Drinking without eating is useless. An empty stomach absorbs water, so it ends up as urine.

All your body functions, from creativity to excretion, proceed more briskly if you exercise regularly. *Exercise* means enough movement to make you tired, and *regularly* means almost every day. Like eating enough fiber, regular exercise requires a major change in the lifestyle of most Americans. Popular writers and doctors make it sound too easy. If you hold down a steady job in a big city or you're 60 with an arthritic hip, you must be particularly obsessive and persistent to stick to a good exercise program. In many cases it may be (here is why I'll never write a best-seller) *impossible*.

Outside Help

Patients who admit using laxatives are quick to assure me that they choose only "mild" ones. I find this as puzzling as those who take one aspirin for a headache instead of two, the recommended dose. These patients also assure me that

71

they only take laxatives when they "really need them" and they never, never abuse them.

My feeling is that if you want to use a laxative, you should make sure it works. So I advise something harsh and irritating such as magnesium citrate or castor oil. Suppositories and enemas are a good alternative because they bypass the digestive tract and go straight to where they're needed. If you don't use a laxative more than every few weeks, you won't get into trouble. If you're going to become an addict, you can do that as easily with milk of magnesia and other mild laxatives as with the powerful ones.

Depression

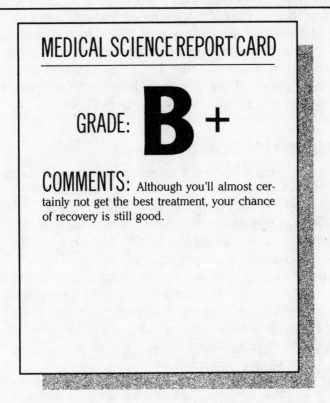

MEDICAL SCIENCE REPORT CARD

GRADE: **B**+

COMMENTS: Although you'll almost certainly not get the best treatment, your chance of recovery is still good.

Popular health writers explain that everyone feels sad sometimes and even worse after a personal tragedy. While we call this depression, perhaps we should call it sadness or grief, they advise, because real depression is severe, prolonged, and inappropriate—not triggered by an unhappy event.

Although not a bad explanation, it's not worth remembering. Nowadays we don't care if your depression came out of the blue or has a good explanation. If sadness is too painful, see a doctor. If someone you know is disabled by grief, treat it like any intolerable pain. Not every sad patient in my office is depressed, but plenty are. According to someone who counted, depression is the 12th most common diagnosis by a family doctor (4th in England, where you can't see a psychiatrist without a referral from a general practitioner).

Don't fool around trying to treat depression yourself— 15 percent of people who have it commit suicide, making depression more deadly than some cancers. And don't brush off people who talk about suicide. Despite the popular impression, people who talk about it *are* more likely to do it.

Cause Unknown

At the deepest level, no one really knows what causes depression—not like we know that T.B. germs cause T.B. But we can detect predictable abnormalities in the brains of people who are depressed—mostly in brain chemicals known as neurotransmitters. You should know about them.

You probably believe that the billions of nerves in your brain interact by sending electrical signals back and forth, then doing wonderful things with them—like a computer. But it's not so. Believe it or not, no electrical signal passes from one nerve to another, at least not normally; when it does happen it's called epilepsy.

Electricity does carry an impulse from one end of a nerve to the other end. Nerves fire slowly or rapidly, but that's about all. This is boring behavior—useful for simple actions like repetitive calculations (which is what a computer does!), but too inflexible for dancing, remembering, loving your child, appreciating a flower, and other interesting activities that make us human.

Nerves don't touch each other. When an electrical signal reaches an end (or 50 ends—one nerve may connect with dozens of others) it triggers a spurt of chemicals (neurotransmitters) that leap across the gap and influence the next nerve. Neurotransmitters don't simply carry an impulse between nerves; they change it. They may force the next nerve to discharge more rapidly or more slowly, or they may inhibit it— prevent it from discharging for a while.

Chemical Communication

Small changes in neurotransmitters produce complex interactions between nerves, a system far more flexible than a computer. Neurotransmitters that you may have heard of are acetylcholine, norepinephrine, serotonin, and dopamine. More are being discovered; it's a popular area of research.

Neurotransmitters regulate your mood, and drugs influence neurotransmitters. Many blood pressure medications work by reducing neurotransmitters in nerves that supply arteries. The same neurotransmitters are present in the brain, so these drugs make some patients sleepy or depressed. You feel bright and alert after a cup of coffee because caffeine produces a slight discharge of norepinephrine from nerve endings. Amphetamines (speed, diet pills) and cocaine produce an enormous gush of norepinephrine. This makes you exhilarated until the norepinephrine supply runs out. Then you feel very depressed.

Depressed patients suffer a deficiency of norepinephrine or serotonin. Antidepressants correct this much more slowly than amphetamines, so mood elevation doesn't occur, and no one takes antidepressants for fun.

I suspect that a temporary defect in certain brain nerve endings causes depression. An antidepressant stimulates those endings enough to relieve symptoms until they recover. After less than a year doctors taper the drug, and most patients don't relapse—at least not immediately—but depression may recur later.

Signs of Depression

You know what sadness feels like, but let me list other typical symptoms of depression. Most will not come as a surprise, but remember them.

Inability to feel pleasure.   People who are depressed enjoy nothing—food, hobbies, movies, sex. Men become impotent. Women lose interest in their appearance.

Hopelessness and helplessness.   You get nowhere criticizing depressed people; they agree wholeheartedly and add that they couldn't possibly improve. If you try to help, they

75

make sure you fail—either by rejecting help ("I'm sure I wouldn't like the play") or ruining your evening ("I told you I wouldn't like the play"). People who have other mental illnesses can be interesting despite their disability, but people suffering from depression cannot. The depressed are boring. Remember this if someone you know becomes very boring. Medical students are warned to think of depression when they find themselves growing irritated at a patient.

Fatigue.   When a healthy person below middle age becomes chronically tired with no other symptom (such as fever, pain, nausea, or diarrhea), depression is the leading possibility.

Derangements in the tempo of body functions. You might assume that depression slows body function, but it also does the opposite. Loss of appetite is typical, but so is an increase. (This cloud has no silver lining; in my experience fat patients get fatter and thin ones thinner.) Many patients become lethargic, mentally and physically. This can reach the absolute extreme of catatonia, where the patient remains motionless and must be fed and cared for. Agitated depression, with intense anxiety and restlessness, is at the opposite pole. Some patients have insomnia; others sleep too much.

Thoughts of death.   A bad sign even in the absence of sadness.

Best Treatment: Electroshock

Electroshock is a controversial but effective form of treatment that works 85 to 95 percent of the time in contrast to 70 percent for antidepressants. Drugs don't take effect for three weeks. Improvement with electroshock begins after the first treatment, so it can be a lifesaver in a suicidal patient. No one knows why this treatment works, but it must change the chemical behavior of nerve endings. The change is not instantaneous, because a series of shocks is necessary.

All medical treatment carries risks, and electroshock is no different. Broken bones were once a risk because the shock produces a convulsion. Nowadays patients are under anesthesia when the electrodes are applied to the skull so the convulsion won't spread beyond the brain. Everyone suffers some memory loss, but it's usually temporary. As treatments go, electroshock is safe—and it may be safer than drugs for sick or elderly patients. Antidepressants can have unpleasant effects on the heart, prostate, and blood pressure.

Your chance of getting the best treatment is almost nil. Only a scattering of hospitals and mental health centers have facilities for giving electroshock. Most private psychiatrists don't use it. And many of my medical references don't even mention it.

One reason for this rarity is that people think electroshock is barbaric. When doctors use an electric current to revive a diseased heart, everyone admires us. When we do the same to the brain, we become monsters. This has always puzzled me.

A second reason isn't puzzling. Electroshock was badly abused. When it was developed in the 1930s, everyone agreed that it was a wonderful treatment for depression and a few other psychiatric illnesses. During the 1940s and 1950s, medical insurance became popular. From the beginning to the present day, insurance companies have hated covering mental illness, and their benefits tend to be stingy and restricted. People who make up policies have simple minds. They feel comfortable with drugs, operations, and machines, but they are deeply suspicious of psychotherapy. (What goes on in those rooms? they think. Just talk? Why should we pay for that?) Today your insurance will pay for some psychotherapy, but older policies paid nothing. But electroshock required a machine no different from other medical machines. Underwriters had no objection, so insurance paid.

You can guess what happened. Since it was the only thing they could get paid for, psychiatrists found plenty of reasons to order it. Some set up "shock mills" and churned patients through on an assembly line. Electroshock acquired a sleazy reputation, and when antidepressants arrived in the 1960s, they quickly took over. A few more decades must pass before electroshock becomes respectable, and by that time we may have better drugs.

Diabetes

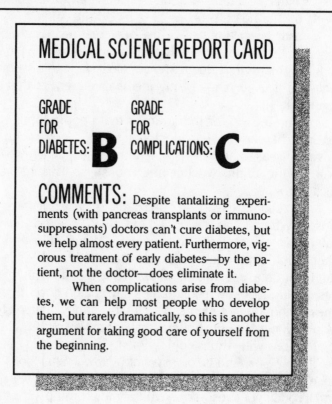

MEDICAL SCIENCE REPORT CARD

GRADE
FOR
DIABETES: **B**

GRADE
FOR
COMPLICATIONS: **C–**

COMMENTS: Despite tantalizing experiments (with pancreas transplants or immuno-suppressants) doctors can't cure diabetes, but we help almost every patient. Furthermore, vigorous treatment of early diabetes—by the patient, not the doctor—does eliminate it.

When complications arise from diabetes, we can help most people who develop them, but rarely dramatically, so this is another argument for taking good care of yourself from the beginning.

Like arthritis and pneumonia, diabetes is not a single disorder but a family of unrelated diseases. Their only common feature is a problem with insulin, a hormone with many interesting actions. You can think of it as a substance that allows your cells to obtain nourishment. Mostly, human cells nourish themselves from a simple sugar, glucose. Without it, they starve. The blood of a diabetic contains huge amounts of glucose, which can't get into the cells to nourish them, so it spills into the urine or accumulates in tissues and causes problems.

Type 1: Insulin Production Stops

You probably believe that lack of insulin causes diabetes, but the disease is more complex than that. Only about 10 percent of diabetics produce too little insulin. Most of these 10 percent receive their diagnosis before age 20. At one time they were called juvenile diabetics, a term now frowned upon because plenty of adults have this disease.

The proper term is now *Type 1 diabetes*. People who have this disease lack insulin because something destroys their beta cells—the cells in the pancreas that make insulin.

The trigger for Type 1 diabetes is probably a viral infection that provokes a deranged response from the immune system. Instead of attacking the virus, the immune response destroys the beta cells. This sounds crazy, but your body does crazy things more often than you think. Autoimmune diseases are fairly common. Many types of arthritis and hormone deficiencies occur when the body attacks itself.

Since the immune system causes this disease, you might think that immune suppressants would help, and you'd be right. Given soon after symptoms begin, these medications actually prevent the immune system from attacking the beta cells. Unfortunately, these drugs are poisonous, and diabetes returns as soon as they are stopped. Furthermore, by the time symptoms appear, most beta cells are already destroyed. They cannot regenerate. Still, this treatment is encouraging. Within a generation, doctors will use genetic analysis to detect those at high risk, then watch closely for the earliest sign of an autoimmune reaction, which will be easier to suppress.

Type 2: Too Much Insulin

Most adults with diabetes have what is known as Type 2 diabetes. They have normal numbers of beta cells that secrete abnormally high amounts of insulin. Adult diabetics have too much insulin, not too little.

Their blood sugars remain high despite this excess because their tissues are less sensitive to it. Adult diabetics are insulin resistant. Most are also overweight.

Overweight Adults Get Diabetes

Excess fat dulls the body's sensitivity to insulin, so beta cells must increase production. This extra insulin allows the fat person to assimilate excess food and continue to gain weight. As fat builds up, insulin resistance increases still more, so beta cells must work even harder. Eventually they can't keep up, so blood sugar rises.

Remember this explanation, because it explains why only one good treatment exists for overweight diabetics.

Symptoms of Diabetes

Once blood sugar rises to about double the normal level, the kidneys begin to get rid of it. Normally no sugar appears in the urine. Getting rid of excess sugar requires excess water, so people with diabetes discover that they are drinking a great deal. Excess thirst and urination are merely signs that your kidneys are struggling to excrete something. Plenty of disorders reveal themselves in this way, but only diabetes is common enough to mention here.

When insulin drops very low, a person's tissues will be

PEARL

Type 2 diabetes is more strongly hereditary than Type 1. If a parent or sibling has Type 2, your risk runs as high as 30 percent. If your identical twin falls victim, it's 100 percent. If Type 1 strikes your family, your risk is less than 10 percent. Even if your identical twin is affected, you'll escape half the time.

so starved that he or she will lose weight. Thirst, excess urination, and weight loss are almost always the first signs of
Type 1 diabetes. Occasionally, insulin drops so rapidly that
collapse and coma occur first. Coma rarely happens in Type
2 diabetes because the disease comes on much more slowly.
Most Type 2 reveals itself in an elevated blood sugar detected
during a routine exam.

Despite popular belief, diabetes is not heralded by a
craving for sweets and hardly ever by vague symptoms such
as fatigue, blurry vision, or simple hunger.

Treatment for Type 1: Insulin

In the past, drug companies bought pig or cow pancre-
ases from slaughterhouses and extracted insulin. Pig and cow
insulin is almost but not quite identical to ours, but it works
fine. Today you can buy pure human insulin made by bacteria
through genetic engineering. Using human insulin is not essential, except for a small minority who become allergic to
animal insulin, but it's probably advisable for first-time users.

In the past most diabetics gave themselves one injection before breakfast and followed their progress by checking
their urine with test-tape. Today if you do either, you're not
getting the best treatment.

Twenty years ago doctors argued over whether strict
control of blood sugar prevented long-term complications.
Strict control requires multiple injections, a careful diet, and
adjusting the insulin dose by checking *blood* (never urine)
sugars at home several times a day. This is work for the doctor
as well as the patient, and many doctors didn't insist on it
because they didn't believe it was necessary.

Today little argument remains. Experts agree that strict
control of blood glucose is better for your health than the
once-a-day injection of the past. Unfortunately, the nasty consequences of walking around with a high blood sugar won't
appear for years or even decades. So, many doctors haven't
learned to train patients in the self-care that's required, and
some patients aren't eager to take on the extra work. Don't be
among them.

Treatment for Type 2: Eat Less

The tissues of overweight diabetics resist insulin. As fat diminishes, so does resistance. An additional bonus: The less that people with diabetes eat, the less insulin they need to assimilate that food.

Eventually most diabetics who lose weight reach a point where they secrete enough insulin to handle their food intake and to normalize their blood sugar. This is ideal, because it means that beta cells are not straining. Many people with Type 2 diabetes who don't bring their condition under control eventually require insulin because their beta cells exhaust themselves and stop producing.

Pills to Boost Insulin

Oral antidiabetic pills (Diabinese, Orinase, Micronase, Glucotrol) stimulate beta cells to make more insulin. They are important for the rare person with Type 2 diabetes who is not fat and for those who lose enough weight but still have an elevated sugar.

The overweight diabetic on pills is not getting the best treatment. I see such patients all the time. If their blood sugars are normal, it's only because their poor beta cells are being driven to the maximum. This won't last.

Notice that I haven't mentioned a diabetic diet. Eating less is so important that I don't care how this is accomplished as long as the diet is balanced.

Complications of Diabetes

This section contains useful advice but no exciting news, so I'll begin on a pleasant note by dispelling one myth—that people with diabetes have poor resistance and suffer more infections.

This is probably not true. People with diabetes certainly don't suffer more colds or upper respiratory infections than normal, and they don't require special treatment when they do catch cold. On the other hand, severe bacterial or fungal infections can be stubborn and harder to treat. These conditions tend to strike people whose diabetes is poorly controlled; after all, sugar is food for other organisms besides humans.

Preventing Heart Disease

One serious complication of diabetes is atherosclerosis—otherwise known as hardening of the arteries or coronary artery disease.

The results of atherosclerosis, mostly heart attacks and strokes, are the leading cause of death in the United States. The leading cause of death in people with diabetes isn't diabetes; it's atherosclerosis. Diabetics have more heart attacks and strokes, and they have them earlier. Experts use the chilling adjectives *accelerated* or *premature* atherosclerosis for this complication.

All-Encompassing Treatment

There's no getting around it: The best treatment for atherosclerosis is a healthy diet and lifestyle. The four most dangerous risk factors for this condition are smoking, high cholesterol, high blood pressure—and diabetes. You can eliminate the first two, and with a doctor's help the third is no problem. Good control probably diminishes the risk of the fourth.

Despite all our exhortations, it's hard to persuade patients to quit smoking, eat right, exercise, and make other changes that everyone agrees are virtuous and healthy. In my experience, a heart attack does the trick. After a heart attack, most of my patients straighten out their lives. While it's never too late, doing something because "it's never too late" means that you should have done it sooner. Although not as catastrophic as a heart attack, a diagnosis of diabetes should be a loud signal to get your act together. Pay attention.

Protecting the Eyes

The most frightening complication, eye disease, eventually affects 85 percent of people with diabetes, although most never suffer serious visual loss.

In diabetes, small blood vessels in the eye become

leaky. Leakage into the retina, the light receptor at the back of the eye, causes minor visual problems. Major hemorrhages happen more rarely but cause more damage. More ominous is proliferation of the blood vessels—growth into areas where they don't belong, such as the clear fluid in front of the retina. These new vessels are fragile and prone to disastrous bleeding.

Luckily, a doctor can easily watch for these developments.

When a doctor peers into your eye with his ophthalmoscope, you may believe that he's checking your vision, but he isn't. He's looking at your retina, which is laced with arteries and veins. Your eye is the only part of the body where a doctor can look directly at your blood vessels, so we do it all the time. Peering into the eye, we can see the first evidence of atherosclerosis. Since the earliest eye damage of diabetes produces no symptoms, doctors occasionally diagnose the damage during a routine eye exam. Because detecting eye damage is so easy, everyone who has diabetes should see an ophthalmologist yearly.

Laser Treatment

Lasers are overrated in many areas of medicine, but they do important work in ophthalmology. Laser beams can cause burning and tissue damage, but so do cheaper instruments. A laser's advantage is that it can "damage" tissue that a doctor can't reach. The retina is one unreachable area. When an ophthalmologist sees leaky or proliferating blood vessels, he or she destroys them with a laser.

Protecting the Kidneys

A major complication, diabetic kidney failure, accounts for 25 percent of patients on dialysis. The appearance of protein in the urine marks the first sign that something is wrong with the kidneys. Protein in the urine produces no symptoms and is detected during routine tests. Proteins are large molecules—too large to pass through the filter of a healthy kidney. As time passes, more and more protein appears in the urine, and kidney function slowly declines. Decades may pass before kidney failure becomes severe, but most diabetics never reach this stage.

The Case for Blood Sugar Control

When protein excretion appears, strict control of blood sugar reduces it. Eliminating high blood pressure also slows the progress of kidney damage.

Having said this, I confess that as of 1991, no proof exists that rigid control of diabetes prevents kidney damage or stops its progress once it begins, although most experts believe this is the case. I tend to go along with experts, but they've been wrong before. Genuine scientific proof will require enormous work and millions of dollars. To obtain that proof, hundreds of people with diabetes must enroll in a study that follows them closely for at least ten years and that carefully compares kidney function in those with good and those with bad control of their blood sugar levels. Fortunately, the National Institutes of Health has sponsored such a study, so we should know before the end of the century.

Protecting the Nerves

Although rarely fatal, nerve damage is a common and troublesome complication of diabetes. The nerves of almost all diabetics conduct more sluggishly than normal, even in those who feel fine, and strict control of blood sugar improves nerve conduction. Once symptoms of nerve damage appear, however, good control doesn't have much effect.

Damage usually affects the feet first because these nerves are the longest and most vulnerable (a peripheral nerve must carry a signal directly to the spinal cord, so a single nerve supplying a toe may stretch 3 feet).

Doctors warn people with diabetes to care for their feet. Nerve damage (neuropathy) may dull pain sensation, enabling a minor cut to progress to a devastating infection with little discomfort. Foot care is crucial, but people with diabetes rarely complain when their feet are numb. They complain about tingling, burning, and sharp pains that usually affect both feet and are often worse at night. Sometimes pains are sharp and stabbing, at other times deep and aching. It's a miserable affliction and the most common symptom of diabetic neuropathy that I see.

Treatment: Antidepressants

Although pain medications provide temporary relief, narcotics are a bad idea for any long-term pain. Fortunately, good studies show that Elavil, Tofranil, and similar antidepressants provide modest relief when taken at bedtime every night. As in other chronic pain disorders, we don't really understand how antidepressants work, and the dose is usually (but not always) less than that required to treat depression. Frankly, these medications rarely give dramatic relief, but they usually help. This is an area receiving a good deal of attention from researchers, so better news may be on the way.

Earache

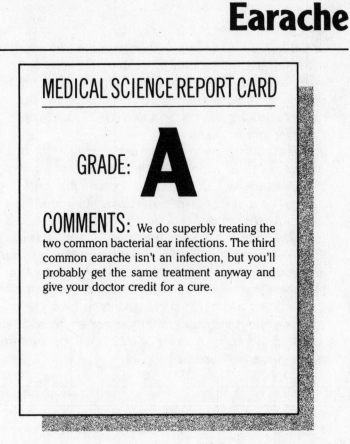

MEDICAL SCIENCE REPORT CARD

GRADE: **A**

COMMENTS: We do superbly treating the two common bacterial ear infections. The third common earache isn't an infection, but you'll probably get the same treatment anyway and give your doctor credit for a cure.

At a busy walk-in clinic, doctors enjoy seeing "earache" scribbled at the top of the next patient's chart. Ear pain is a "quickie." Along with "rash," it guarantees an easy diagnosis, easy treatment, and a grateful patient. Don't hesitate to see the doctor when your ear hurts; not only can we help, we enjoy ears more than most parts of the body.

However, when the nurse asks your problem, just say that your ear hurts.

PEARL

That lady in white who ushers you into the examining room and takes your blood pressure may be a
nurse. Then again, she may be a high school girl in
a uniform. Anyone can take a blood pressure, but
nurses earn big money. Sensible clinics don't use
them for simple tasks.

If the nurse seems warm and sympathetic, by all
means pour out your heart. But realize that none of
this information will reach the doctor! Time and
again, I've waited outside an examining room listening to the murmur of a patient giving a detailed history. Then the nurse appears, hands me a chart with
"stomach pain" or "nervous" written at the top, and
goes off to attend to the next patient. My sad job is
to inform the patient that he or she must describe
the problem again. No doctor wants to hear your
story second-hand, but patients are often bewildered
to find that I know nothing of what they just told the
nurse. Save your breath.

Causes of Earache

Three conditions cause about 98 percent of significant
ear pain. Two are infections of the external and middle ear.

Infections of the External Ear

The external ear is simply the canal that leads to the
eardrum. It's full of germs and wax, which under normal conditions cause no problems. It takes damage to the lining of
the canal to get an infection. Soaking with water does sufficient
damage, so an external infection is also known as swimmer's
ear. Another likely way to do damage is by cleaning your ears
with a cotton swab.

The "big four" for putting money into the pocket of the

medical profession are motorcycles, skateboards, cigarettes, and cotton swabs. You're familiar with the first three, but I see the effects of number four several times a week.

Patients who clean their ears with cotton swabs assure me that they don't stick it in very far. They have the mistaken impression that cotton swabs are only dangerous when they puncture the eardrum. In fact, the eardrum is tough and not easily punctured; if damaged, it usually heals quickly. But the lining of the ear canal is delicate. A swab can easily scrape off a little skin and produce an excruciating infection. Nothing smaller than your little finger should go into the canal. Buy an over-the-counter earwash kit if you want to remove wax.

Infections of the Middle Ear

The middle ear is the space beyond the eardrum that includes those three little bones that you memorized in school: the hammer, anvil, and stirrup. When sounds make the drum vibrate, these bones transmit this vibration across the middle ear to another membrane that activates the auditory nerve. The nerve passes through the inner ear, which isn't involved in this chapter.

The middle ear is normally sterile. Germs from the outside world can't get past the drum, but they can enter through the eustachian tube, the single passage from the middle ear that opens in the back of your nose. Experts theorize that high pressure (more common during colds or allergies) forces fluid back up the eustachian tube and provokes an infection.

Pull your earlobe to get a clue as to which type of infection you have.

In an external infection, the canal is inflamed and tender, so pulling hurts. Pulling is painless in a middle ear infection.

Eustachian Tube Blockage

If both ears hurt, you probably don't have an ear infection.

After all, the left ear is entirely isolated from the right, so only under odd conditions would an organism invade both.

Bilateral involvement is almost always eustachian tube

blockage, the third type of ear pain. When these tubes are blocked (most often by the nasal congestion of a cold or allergy), air is trapped in the middle ear. Pressure builds, so the ears ache. Anyone who flies with plugged eustachian tubes suffers intense pain.

Treatment for blocked tubes is simple: spray your nose with an ordinary nasal spray (Afrin, Neo-Synephrine, Dristan, 4-Way). Wait 5 minutes, then spray again. This projects the spray far back inside the nose where the eustachian tubes open. If you plan to fly with a stuffy nose, *you must spray* before the plane takes off. Do it again before the plane begins its descent.

Drugs for Ear Infection

The best treatment for both kinds of ear infection is antibiotics.

Oral antibiotics are used to treat a middle ear infection. As of 1990 amoxicillin (a relative of penicillin) is the drug of choice to kill the three or four germs usually responsible. I give trimethoprim-sulfamethoxazole (Bactrim, Septra) to patients allergic to penicillin. Some doctors add a decongestant on the theory that it opens the eustachian tubes and relieves pain. I doubt if this works, but there's no harm in spraying your nose. If pain is excruciating, I give anesthetic eardrops. Ask for them if your doctor doesn't think of it.

As usual, when antibiotics are used properly they work wonderfully. An untreated middle ear infection lasts two or three weeks. The right antibiotic reduces this to a few days.

Antibiotic eardrops are used to treat an external ear infection. Pills aren't necessary unless there's a severe infection, but many doctors give them routinely.

Antibiotics don't work at all for a blocked eustachian tube, but you may get them anyway. Doctors produce such dramatic cures treating ear infections that they lean over backward to diagnose them.

It's all right to treat eustachian tube blockage yourself at home by spraying your nose, but see a doctor if it doesn't help.

Eczema and Itching

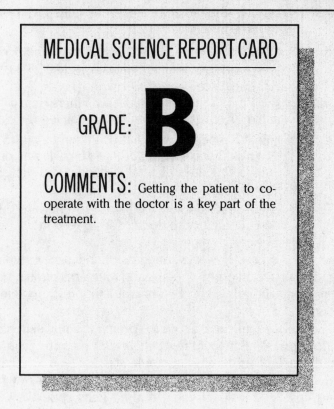

MEDICAL SCIENCE REPORT CARD

GRADE: **B**

COMMENTS: Getting the patient to co-operate with the doctor is a key part of the treatment.

Relentless itching is not merely the hallmark of eczema, *it's the only mark!* You should look on eczema as the mirror image of psoriasis, a disease that produces a vivid skin rash, usually without other symptoms. Eczema symptoms are intense and miserable, but there is no rash.

A skin disorder with no rash? Convincing patients that they have such a condition is tricky, and careless doctors can dig a deep hole for themselves. Take the following dialogue:

DOCTOR: That looks like eczema.

PATIENT: What caused it?

DOCTOR: Scratching.

PATIENT: I try not to scratch, but it really itches. What caused the rash?

DOCTOR: Your skin itched, so you scratched. After a while you damaged the skin enough to produce the rash.

PATIENT: But I didn't imagine this. It was there, and it itched. Could you tell me what caused the rash?.

DOCTOR: What happened was that your skin began to itch. Your skin was normal at that point. It was only after a few days of scratching that you noticed the rash.

PATIENT: Excuse me, doctor, but I don't invent things! I don't come to the doctor for no reason.

And so on. Now the patient is offended. She thinks the doctor has accused her of being neurotic and scratching "for no reason." Experienced doctors use caution in breaking the news.

Make no mistake about it, eczema is a real skin disease *without* a rash. Patients create their own rash in response to the disease. This is easy to understand if you realize how humans behave. Does any part of your body itch now? Stop and think . . . I suspect you'll find an itchy spot. We scratch all the time. Watch a group of people in a theater or restaurant if you don't believe me. However, most of us don't scratch for long, and we don't keep scratching the same place.

Eczema begins as a routine itch. A person with eczema scratches, then goes about his business and, like most of us, doesn't inspect the itchy spot. Only after a day or two does he realize that the itch is persistent and always in the same spot. Then he looks and sees the results: perhaps redness and scratch marks. A few more days of scratching change this redness to oozing and crusting. Long-term scratching makes skin thick and leathery (but still itchy).

The Worst Treatment

"Try not to scratch. . . ." In return for charging large fees, doctors should resist the urge to give stupid advice, but I hear this from otherwise intelligent colleagues in offices down the hall. It's impossible to keep your hands off a patch of eczema. Don't feel guilty.

The Best Treatment

What your doctor should advise is good skin care and cortisone—in that order.

The nerves responsible for itching end a fraction of an inch below the surface. Normally, a thick, moist, healthy top layer of skin (epidermis) keeps minor stimulation from setting them off. In a person with eczema, the skin is abnormally dry and its itch nerves are as hypersensitive as your neighbor's car alarm, so an irritation that would be ignored by normal nerves triggers a burst of itching.

If you don't have eczema, keep this chapter in mind. Sooner or later, you'll need it. As you get older, your skin becomes thinner, drier, less protective, and therefore more susceptible to itching. You might follow my advice now and put off the inevitable day.

Good skin care means hydration (keeping it moist) and protection.

Keeping Skin Moist

The first rule of good skin care is: Stop worrying so much about personal hygiene.

Patients with skin trouble tend to keep themselves meticulously clean, which, like so much self-treatment, is exactly the wrong thing. I can't think of a rash caused by dirt, but soap and water (especially soap) aggravate every skin inflammation. Rubbing oil into already dried skin is another mistake.

Lack of water, not lack of oil, causes dry skin. If you put oil on dry, itchy skin, the result is dry, itchy skin covered with oil. At the end of the day, most of this oil ends up under your fingernails.

The second rule of good skin care is: Hydrate the skin by adding water *then* covering with a layer of oil to keep the water from evaporating.

Don't spend a lot of time choosing the best oil, because oils and creams merely form a barrier over moist skin. That's their only purpose. They don't penetrate. They don't add marvelous things to your skin. They don't nourish your epidermis (remember—it's dead!).

As you might expect, thicker barriers work better. Ointments (greases) work better than creams, and creams work better than lotions. Plain Vaseline is excellent. Primitive tribes covered themselves with animal fat and had smooth complexions. Fortunately, commercial creams work fine most of the time; only the worst victims of eczema and dry skin need an ointment.

Having waded through these rules, you'll understand my skin care program.

- If you shower, get in and out quickly, pat excess water off with a towel, but don't rub yourself dry. Then cover your body with cream. This can be tedious, so you might want to wash every other day, every third day, or even once a week. This routine may damage your social status, but not your health.

- If you bathe, soak for 5 minutes in warm water, then get out and apply cream. Using a bath oil may eliminate the need to apply cream afterward—a big convenience but not so effective for severe cases. Also, it makes the tub slippery and tiresome to clean.

- Stay away from soap. Never apply soap to itchy or inflamed skin. Wash only the parts of your body that need it (hair, armpits, genitals, feet). Soap substitutes may be milder, but dermatologists argue about this. If you must use soap, buy Dove. Experts traditionally look on Dove as the mildest, and some scientific evidence exists in its favor.

Protecting Your Skin

Heat, cold, sweat, chemicals, rough clothes, and ordinary water aggravate itchy skin. Unless you suffer only a local patch of eczema, you must take this into account in your daily activities.

- Always oil your skin after getting it wet, but it's best (except for minimal bathing) to stay away from water. Soapy water is even worse, so anyone with hand eczema must never wash dishes with bare hands. No sooner are these words out than patients assure me that their hands never touch soapy water without protection. They wear rubber gloves. I must break the news that this is the *worst* thing they could do.

- Rubber against flesh produces heat and sweat. Never wear rubber against your skin. Buy thin cotton gloves and put them on first.

- Wear 100 percent cotton next to the rest of your skin, too; never wear wool or artificial fibers. This advice is difficult for the fashion conscious (and people like me who hate ironing), so I allow my patients to experiment with cotton/polyester blends. For those with very sensitive skin, 100 percent cotton is an absolute must. Both sexes must wear pants and long sleeves to protect their limbs from wind and rapid temperature changes.

- Launder clothes in soap, not detergent. Don't use bleach or fabric softener.

- If all this fails, try to modify dry or humid environments with air conditioners and humidifiers. If you can manage it, wintering in warm climates or even moving to California might help.

These things sometimes work, but not as well as taking care of your skin directly. Having seen other doctors or having read popular books, many of my patients have already spent money and been disappointed. As in so many other areas of medicine, there is no substitute for boring work. Even money won't take its place.

How to Use Cortisone

Cortisone doesn't cure anything, but it makes everything feel better. It's perfect for eczema because feeling better cures the problem.

Cortisone works by suppressing your body's inflammatory response, which occurs whenever tissue is damaged. During the inflammatory response blood rushes to the injured area. Fluids, blood cells, and certain chemicals pour out quickly, followed by the first symptoms of inflammation— burning and itching.

The cells and fluid produced during an inflammatory reaction are supposed to attack invading organisms: bacteria, fungi, and viruses. But anything that harms skin causes inflammation: dryness, chemicals, allergies, excessive heat and cold. After inflammation has passed, other cells work to repair injured tissue.

Cortisone doesn't discriminate; it suppresses everything. You can see the danger. If a fungus infection itches, cortisone relieves the itch, but the fungus continues to grow. It may grow more rapidly because the body is putting up less resistance.

Once you have a diagnosis of eczema, you don't have to worry about aggravating an infection, but cortisone's wonderful properties are also responsible for its other side effects. After all, both healing and inflammation result from cell activity and growth. Putting cortisone on skin suppresses cell activity and growth (that's why it helps psoriasis). After long use, skin becomes thin, fragile, and susceptible to damage. When a rash disappears and then returns, I often find that excessive cortisone use is responsible. Treatment consists of stopping the cream to allow the skin to recover.

Using cortisone is especially risky on the face, where skin is already thin and delicate, and in damp areas such as the groin, where the cream is easily absorbed. On the other hand, you can rub cortisone into small, dry patches of eczema for years without getting into trouble, and many of my patients insist on doing just that. But if you take good care of your skin, you might not need cortisone.

Excessive Hair

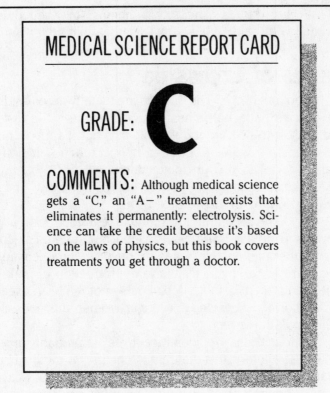

MEDICAL SCIENCE REPORT CARD

GRADE: C

COMMENTS: Although medical science gets a "C," an "A−" treatment exists that eliminates it permanently: electrolysis. Science can take the credit because it's based on the laws of physics, but this book covers treatments you get through a doctor.

Once I had lunch with an endocrinologist, the only one at our large group practice, which employed several hundred doctors. I commented that he must have more interesting cases than he would in private practice. Where they have a choice, patients go to an endocrinologist for obesity, chronic fatigue, or symptoms they believe mean hypoglycemia or a host of glandular disorders. These self-referred patients are almost always wrong, and the average endocrinologist does not delight in such cases. As a highly trained specialist, he prefers "real" diseases.

At our clinic no patient saw a specialist without a referral. Our endocrinologist agreed that he saw fewer inappropriate patients than colleagues on the outside. Except in one category.

"Hairy ladies," he complained. "My schedule is crammed with hairy ladies. Can't you deal with them?"

Causes of Excess Hair

Too much hair? The culprits are usually heredity, drugs, or excessive male hormones. You may believe the last is a good reason to see an endocrinologist, but it's rarely necessary. Almost all women bothered by too much hair don't require a specialist. If your doctor refers you, it's probably because (like so many at my former clinic) he or she finds the condition too frustrating to deal with.

If you're becoming too hairy, take a good look at your mother and aunts. Hairiness runs in families and becomes obvious after menopause, when production of the female hormone estrogen drops faster than the production of male hormones (androgens), so an imbalance—not really an excess—of male hormone develops. Younger women are not entirely off the hook, however.

Among drugs, oral contraceptives are probably the leading cause; switching to a different Pill helps. My medical books contain long lists of drugs responsible for hairiness. I have no reason to doubt them, but I've never cured a woman by stopping a drug, so this must be uncommon.

Sometimes Glands Are the Cause

Rarely, hairiness results from a gush of hormone from a diseased gland or tumor. This condition is serious but also (sometimes) easily cured. These cases are not terribly difficult to diagnose because they show other obvious signs of male hormone activity or virilization—including a deepening voice, shrinking breasts, balding along the temples, and an enlarging clitoris.

More common and less serious are poorly understood ovarian abnormalities that affect some women before menopause. Women with this problem are usually overweight and

Here I'll break my rule about never making statements that patients refuse to believe. Shaving your legs or even a moustache doesn't make hair grow back darker or thicker. It really doesn't.

hairy with menstrual irregularities and infertility. Gynecologists see a fair number and give the same treatment discussed below.

No matter what the cause, the symptoms are unmistakable—moustaches, sideburns, chin hairs, and the general appearance of hair in places where it does not add to your beauty. This is common after age 40 in both sexes, but women complain more, because hair is considered unattractive in a woman except in two locations.

Men are not immune. I'm very annoyed at the thick tufts of hair that began growing from my ears several years ago. I routinely notice this in my elderly patients, but I'm not elderly. Except for asking my wife to cut them short every few weeks, I haven't taken other action, but I genuinely dislike them.

Drug Treatment

Here are the drugs we use in trying to counteract the action of your androgens.

Oral contraceptives. These are a mixture of two sex hormones, an estrogen and a progesterone. Depending on the choice of hormone, a given brand can have a slightly androgenic effect and cause hairiness or a slightly estrogenic effect that does the opposite. Naturally, if prescribing for excess hair, a doctor will try an estrogen-dominant brand. If you only use oral contraceptives for birth control, don't worry about how estrogenic yours are. It's of no importance to most users, and a few experts maintain that it's of no importance to anyone.

PEARL

Hairs never grow where none existed before. They merely become more visible. You notice a moustache when the pale hairs of your lip acquire a dark pigment. It follows that no treatment except destruction makes hairs disappear; when hormones work, they make hair less noticeable.

Spironolactone (Aldactone). This drug is used to treat high blood pressure because it encourages the kidney to excrete sodium and retain potassium, but it also seems to block the action of androgens on hair follicles.

Cortisone (prednisone, Decadron). Cortisone imitates a natural hormone produced by your adrenal gland. When you take cortisone, your body detects this extra hormone and (very sensibly) reduces your adrenal's production. The adrenals of some hairy women produce unnecessary androgen; taking cortisone reduces this, too.

Hairs already present won't fade with this treatment, but future hairs should grow paler and thinner. Wait three months before expecting a change, and give up if there is no improvement in six. And think about electrolysis.

Permanent Removal

Once your doctor has determined that you don't have a tumor or other curable disorder, feel free to find a good, licensed electrologist who works in an office as clean as your doctor's. Ask your friends; few doctors know electrologists.

To destroy hair, the electrologist inserts a fine needle into a follicle and applies a high radio-frequency current (like that in a microwave oven) for less than a second. It is not painless, but neither are many of my procedures, and most patients see it through. Expect to pay $15 to $20 for a session of about 15 minutes. It may take many sessions.

Eye Infections

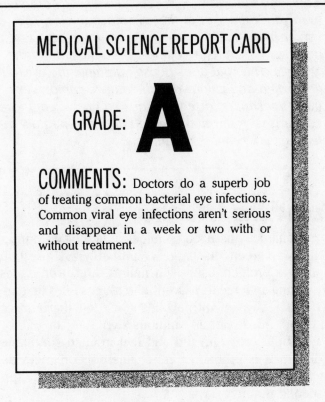

MEDICAL SCIENCE REPORT CARD

GRADE: **A**

COMMENTS: Doctors do a superb job of treating common bacterial eye infections. Common viral eye infections aren't serious and disappear in a week or two with or without treatment.

Doctors sometimes call eye infections conjunctivitis, which simply means inflammation of the conjunctiva. The conjunctiva is the tissue under your lids and the white part of the eyeball. Laymen call the same condition *pinkeye.*

Infection is not the only thing that can irritate the conjunctiva. Allergies, dust, chemicals, and almost any irritant you can think of, including a smoke-filled room, can turn the eyes pink. So how can you tell when you have an infection?

Bacteria that cause eye infections usually originate from your own skin or that of someone else. The conjunctiva resists organisms from the mouth and nose but is surprisingly sensitive to those from the genitals. The cold virus doesn't damage the eye, but gonorrhea and chlamydia, the most common sexually transmitted diseases, cause a nasty conjunctivitis. Viruses from run-of-the-mill upper respiratory infections also cause conjunctivitis.

Diagnosing Infection

Conjunctivitis accompanied by itching or burning and a yellow or green discharge is probably an infection. The conjunctiva protects itself with mucus, and it produces even more during an infection. Overnight, mucus piles up and dries, so you may awaken with eyelids stuck together and covered with crust. This is not an ominous sign.

If both eyes turn red and feel irritated simultaneously, the diagnosis is probably viral or allergic conjunctivitis. Bacteria usually attack only one eye, although they may spread to the second in a few days.

The conjunctivas are not very sensitive to pain, so if your eyes hurt badly, it's probably something else. See a doctor quickly for any eye pain.

The Best Treatment: Antibiotic Ointment

Untreated, bacterial conjunctivitis lasts ten days to two weeks. Treatment with an antibiotic ointment cures it in a couple of days.

The ointment comes in a little tube. To use it, pull your

lower lid forward to create a tiny pocket in front of the eyeball. Squeeze an inch of ointment into the space but don't withdraw the tube. Hold it in front of your eye for 15 seconds while your body heat melts the ointment. If you withdraw it immediately after squeezing, the ointment will follow the tube and end up on your cheek or the floor. After you get the ointment deposited where it belongs, close your eyes and wiggle your eyeballs for a few seconds. Your vision will blur because of the ointment, but this lasts only a minute. Treat the eye every 4 hours for a week.

Although ointment works best, you probably won't get it unless you ask for it. When I give a choice between ointment and eyedrops, almost everyone chooses drops because they're much easier to put in. Most doctors prescribe drops routinely. Drops are fine provided you use them properly—but no one does! Ointment clings to the eyeball better than a watery fluid, so drops should be used every 2 hours instead of every 4. I don't expect a patient to adhere to such a rigid schedule even if he or she swears to do so. Surprisingly, this noncompliance rarely causes a problem. Conjunctivitis clears up even when treatment is inadequate, but I insist on an ointment for a severe infection.

Fungal Infections

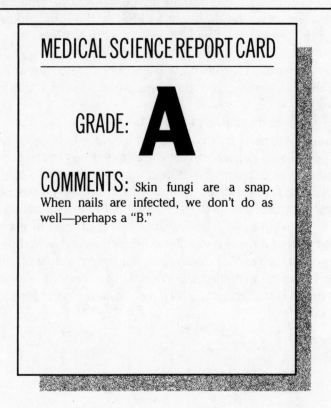

MEDICAL SCIENCE REPORT CARD

GRADE: **A**

COMMENTS: Skin fungi are a snap. When nails are infected, we don't do as well—perhaps a "B."

Fungi are primitive plants; mushrooms are an example. Many fungi grow colorfully on old bread and rotten fruit; others grow on you and me but rarely as vividly. Common human fungi are not invasive; they live on the body surface, taking nourishment from dead skin flakes and natural oils.

My patients with fungal infections blame the family pet, and occasionally they are right. Animal fungi can infect us; so can fungi from the soil and garden, but most human fungi prefer humans and can't grow anywhere else (this is also true of germs, bugs, worms, and other parasites). You catch most fungal infections from another person or even from yourself, since many fungi live quietly on your skin until some event— perhaps excessive heat and dampness—encourages them to multiply.

Diagnosing Fungus

The typical infection starts as a scaly spot with a clear center and a circular raised border. The popular term *ringworm* describes it well. Like all typical descriptions, it fits only a minority of cases. Most fungal infections look like discolored patches of skin. Scales are usually present but sometimes only faintly. In damp areas such as the groin, pink splotches may be the only evidence.

Fungal infections tend to itch—but not very much. A terribly itchy patch on a dry part of your body is probably eczema or a contact dermatitis from an irritating chemical. Fungal infections in dry areas itch mildly or not at all. All bets are off in damp areas between the toes or between the legs.

The Best ℞: Antibiotics

The best treatment for these types of infections is an antifungal antibiotic.

Excellent creams are sold over the counter. The best are miconazole (Micatin) and clotrimazole (Lotrimin, Mycelex).

Fungi grow slowly, but they also die slowly. Be prepared to treat yourself daily for two months. Provided your diagnosis is correct, itching will disappear in a week or two. If you lose interest and stop treatment, you'll feel fine for weeks or even months, but the infection will return.

Experts denounce panty hose, jockey shorts, tight shoes, and all clothing that keeps skin warm and damp—the best environment for a fungus. I will be criticized for not joining them, and I suppose they're right.

Oral Antibiotics

Creams don't work where skin is thick—especially on the feet. Applying creams to itchy areas between the toes makes life bearable, but the fungus remains. It continues to produce unsightly peeling over the soles and heels. Curing these more stubborn infections requires an oral antifungal: either griseofulvin (Fulvicin, Gris-Peg, Grisactin) or ketoconazole (Nizoral).

Fungal infections on the scalp also don't respond to creams. Oral medications work well—perhaps better—than creams for routine ringworm, too, but doctors rarely prescribe them unless creams don't work.

Nail Infections

Patients quickly complain when their fingernails grow yellow, thick, and crumbly, but they are surprisingly blasé when their toenails become as ugly. Perhaps they feel this is one of the tiresome consequences of aging because they notice the same thing in their spouses and relatives. I see this in many, perhaps most, patients who are past middle age.

Nails can't grow old, because they're already dead. A healthy 80-year-old toenail should look no different from an 8-year-old toenail. Many diseases (psoriasis is one) cause thick, crumbly nails, but the most common cause is a fungal infection no different from ordinary ringworm.

Applying poison to the surface of dead nails has no effect. In any case, the fungus also affects the living tissue deep under your skin that gives rise to the nail (just as hair rises from deep hair follicles). Infected nails can be cured only by taking an oral antifungal medication, usually griseofulvin. No antibiotic will reach dead, infected nails, but it will soak into the living nail at the base. As nail grows out, the fungus grows out with it. You must continue on the pill until new, healthy nail grows to the end and the last bit of infected nail is clipped off—then a few months longer. Fingernails take about six months to grow out, toenails at least a year.

Doctors don't like to give powerful drugs for a cosmetic problem, so they are not enthusiastic about treating nail fungi.

That's why many doctors don't bring up the subject when they notice it in their patients. Their reluctance is justified, but if you hate your ugly nails, it's the only good treatment.

The treatment is not perfect. In medical school, I noticed that one big toenail had grown hideously thick and discolored. A dermatologist told me the diagnosis and followed with a long, discouraging discussion of griseofulvin. It was expensive, I'd have to take it for a year, and it often didn't work. Why go to so much trouble for a yellow toenail? Like you, I don't argue with my doctor, so I agreed that it wasn't worth it.

Five years later I had grown tired of looking at that toenail. At the time, I was a resident, so perhaps the knowledge that this was my last year of free drugs influenced me. Griseofulvin gave me a headache for the first week but no problems afterward. There was no improvement for over four months. Then I was delighted to see a small sliver of healthy nail peek out from the base. As months passed, normal nail slowly moved forward, and after a year no ugliness remained.

Three years later the nail looked as bad as ever. Recurrences after treatment are not rare. So I began again. This time the nail looked fine after eight months, so I stopped. A year later the fungus was back. After trying to ignore it for several years, I resolved to make a final effort, so I took griseofulvin for 15 months (even at the wholesale prices I pay, that cost over $30 a month in 1985). Five years later my nails still look fine, but there is no guarantee that this will continue. Still, I'm happy with the results, so I am not as pessimistic as the average doctor. Patients hear my story before having to make a decision.

Gallstones

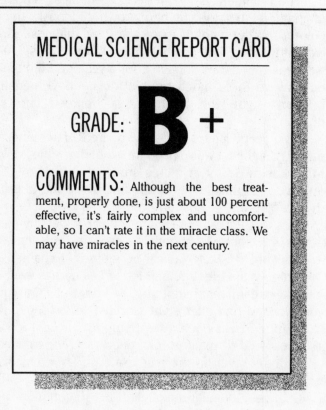

MEDICAL SCIENCE REPORT CARD

GRADE: **B**+

COMMENTS: Although the best treatment, properly done, is just about 100 percent effective, it's fairly complex and uncomfortable, so I can't rate it in the miracle class. We may have miracles in the next century.

Although common (20 percent of women have them), gallstones cause no problems unless they move someplace where they don't fit. It's impossible to predict when this might happen.

Cholesterol makes up most stones in North America. While this is the same cholesterol that clogs our arteries, my chapters on angina and heart attack won't enlighten you on how to prevent or treat gallstones. Gallstones and atherosclerosis are different diseases.

For one thing, gallstones are mostly a problem for women; they have three times the risk of men. Female hormones, which protect against heart attacks, do the opposite for gallstones. Each pregnancy increases the risk. Using birth control pills doubles it.

Women have more fat than men, and stones affect obese women far more frequently. It would be pleasant to be able to announce that eating too much cholesterol or fat leads to stones, but studies don't show this. Overeating in general is responsible. Thin people on high-calorie diets have more stones. Gallstones are rare in primitive tribes and cultures where food is scarce.

Where Stones Come From

Stones form in bile, an oily liquid made by the liver and secreted into the small intestine, where it helps digest fats. Normally, bile doesn't flow directly to the intestine but into the gallbladder, a bag the size of your thumb located under the liver just below your right rib cage. After you eat, signals from the digestive tract force the gallbladder to contract, expelling bile into the intestine as food arrives.

Bile contains cholesterol; bile that forms stones contains too much cholesterol. Water is extracted from bile as it sits in the gallbladder, causing the bile to thicken. This increases the cholesterol concentration still more, and some crystallizes—just as salt crystallizes out of salt water as it evaporates. When the gallbladder contracts, cholesterol crystals flow out with the bile, and no harm results. However, crystals sitting in bile tend to grow into stones. When one grows too large to pass easily through the bile duct, you have something that may or may not lead you to seek a doctor's attention.

Symptom: Pain

When a stone becomes stuck, the gallbladder continues to contract, trying to expel its load of bile. It can't because of the obstructing stone, but it keeps trying. This continuing contraction hurts. It's an intense, gnawing ache as severe as labor pains, felt in the center of the upper abdomen, sometimes on the right and occasionally on the left. After several hours, the stone squeezes through and pops out into the small intestine, ending the agony, although a residual ache may last half a day more. Because food stimulates contraction, most gallbladder attacks occur after a meal, but fatty food doesn't provoke them.

Throughout this century researchers have fed fatty and fat-free meals to gallstone patients and observed who had pain. The results are a tie, but my patients are unconvinced.

Fat has always received a bad press. Our ancestors thought it was sinful. My patients merely believe it is indigestible. In fact, we digest fats as easily as other nutrients and better than carbohydrates. And fats are not the major cause of the digestive complaints that plague humans—gas, constipation, bloating, cramps, nausea. My assurances on this point are in vain. One pleasure of writing is that I can tell the truth without seeing the polite "I know better" smile cross your face.

Best Treatment: Surgery

Provided no tiny stone was left in your bile duct to grow into a painful obstruction in the future, a surgeon who takes out your gallbladder has done you a big favor. You don't need it. Without a gallbladder, bile now flows continually from the liver into the small bowel, but this causes no problem with digestion.

Be warned: If you suffered heartburn, cramps, gas, poor digestion, nausea, bloating, and food intolerance before having your gallbladder out, don't be surprised if these symptoms continue afterward. *Gallstones cause pain.* One out of five women has them, and they do no harm resting quietly in the gallbladder. Patients plagued by other unpleasant digestive symptoms often feel an irresistible urge to have their gallbladder removed, and sometimes their doctors share that feeling. Don't give in.

Medications, Maybe

You've probably heard of drugs that dissolve gallstones. Available since the early 1980s and fairly safe, they don't work very well (grade D+). Treatment costs over $1,000 per year, lasts several years, and dissolves only small stones that contain pure cholesterol and no calcium. (Most stones contain some calcium.) After two years, only 25 percent of the stones have disappeared—not an impressive score when you realize that many recur after treatment stops. Feel free to bring up the subject of medications with your doctor if you face surgery.

High-Tech Solution

You might also ask your doctor about lithotripsy. The lithotriptor is another of those dazzling, million-dollar machines that do wonderful things at enormous expense. Lithotriptors shatter kidney stones with a beam of sound waves. This is now an accepted treatment, which means that your insurance will pay for it. Half a dozen centers around the country are trying to shatter gallstones safely with a similar machine, and I'm sure they'll eventually succeed. At this moment the procedure is still experimental (your insurance won't pay—but if you participate you won't be charged). But when all the questions have been answered, it should be a pretty good (grade B) treatment.

An avalanche of ads has appeared in newspapers and magazines touting "endoscopic" gallbladder surgery in which the surgeon inserts a small instrument through a small abdominal incision and snips off the gallbladder. Despite the vulgar hype, this strikes me as a real advance. It's less risky and uncomfortable than traditional surgery and probably as effective except in patients who are very sick, very fat, or who have had previous abdominal surgery. The major limitation is that most surgeons haven't been trained to use the endoscope. Some have bought one anyway—an expense of well over $10,000. Those that have them, advertise. By the next edition of this book, this chapter may need extensive revision, although I don't see the grade improving.

Gout and Other Pains in a Single Joint

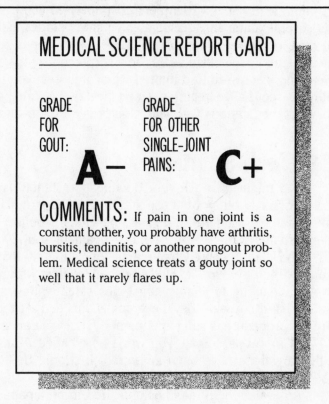

MEDICAL SCIENCE REPORT CARD

GRADE FOR GOUT: **A−**

GRADE FOR OTHER SINGLE-JOINT PAINS: **C+**

COMMENTS: If pain in one joint is a constant bother, you probably have arthritis, bursitis, tendinitis, or another nongout problem. Medical science treats a gouty joint so well that it rarely flares up.

A rich, fat, miserable middle-aged man, his throbbing big toe wrapped in a towel to ward off the slightest puff of air, has been a figure of fun for hundreds of years. This is an accurate picture of a gout victim. Gout is the most masculine of all diseases—except for those affecting organs women don't have. Ninety-five percent of patients are men.

A woman who tells me she has gout is usually wrong. This is also true for many men, because most doctors can't do the best diagnostic test—sticking a needle into a painful joint to extract fluid for examination under a microscope. If the doctor sees crystals of uric acid, gout is certain.

When I ask patients how the diagnosis was made, almost all answer that a doctor drew blood to measure uric acid and found it elevated. Everyone (including the doctors themselves) agrees that this is a poor test. Five percent of adult males have elevated uric acid; perhaps one in ten of those with elevated uric acid develops gout. Despite stern lectures in medical texts and by rheumatologists (specialists in joint diseases), the average internist simply won't stick a needle into a patient's ankle or big toe. They probably never learned how (I didn't).

Causes of Gout

Uric acid is a waste product produced by cells and excreted by the kidney. People with gout have too much uric acid in the blood. Perhaps they produce too much or their kidneys can't get rid of it fast enough. Now and then a shower of uric acid suddenly crystallizes in a joint. No one knows why, but it provokes a violent inflammatory reaction.

Making a Diagnosis

A gouty joint quickly becomes swollen, red, and excruciatingly painful. More than half of first attacks occur at the base of the big toe, and eventually 90 percent of people who have gout suffer in this joint. So an agonizing big toe is better evidence for gout than an elevated uric acid (but not as good as seeing crystals under the microscope). An untreated attack rarely lasts more than a week.

Other common sites in descending order are the instep, ankle, heel, knee, and wrist. Gout practically never affects the shoulder, hip, or back.

After one attack, the joint becomes entirely normal, but repeated episodes produce permanent damage. Doctors rarely treat a patient after a first attack because months or years may pass before the second—but the odds of a second are more than 90 percent.

When Joint Pain Isn't Gout

Telling gout from something else is tricky. A painful shoulder is almost always something else.

A woman with a swollen, painful knee probably doesn't have gout, but a man with a sore knee and high uric acid presents a dilemma that only a needle in the joint can resolve. There is no urgency about making the distinction, because anti-inflammatory drugs help both, but doctors who know exactly what they're treating have happier patients. See a rheumatologist if a single joint gives persistent trouble, and if your family doctor hasn't helped.

Drugs for Treatment

The best treatment for gout is colchicine. Despite this, we rarely use it. Like tar, colchicine is one of the few ancient remedies that works, but don't criticize your doctor for ignoring it. I explain why below.

Nowadays it's fashionable to admire healing methods from other cultures or historic eras. They seem more natural and perhaps less dangerous. This is a mistaken notion. Almost until the twentieth century, healers and physicians never boasted that their drugs were natural. Everyone's grandmother knew about herbs. To earn their fees, doctors had to convince patients that great knowledge and skill went into their potions. Furthermore, if treatment made the patient sick, the healer wouldn't apologize. *That's what he expected! That's what the patient expected!*

Scientists have refined many traditional and folk remedies so that they help without making you sick (usually). Quinine and digitalis are examples, but colchicine defies our skills. Colchicine was originally an herbal remedy made from the autumn crocus or meadow saffron. Scientists isolated the active chemical in 1820, and it's now available in pill form. It will cure your gout as well as it did Benjamin Franklin's, but you won't be as grateful.

At the beginning of a gout attack, a patient takes a dose of colchicine every hour until the pain improves . . . or until

PEARL

Modern science invented the theory that a power-ful drug doesn't have to be dangerous. Sometimes we even use such drugs. Give us credit . . . in other cultures, a patient sick enough to consult a healer expects an unpleasant experience prior to getting better, and the healer tries to oblige. Reading about the medical care in other societies can be a hair-raising experience.

he can't stand the diarrhea, cramps, and vomiting that begin after a few hours . . . or until he has taken the maximum dose.

Patients notice less pain within a few hours and are almost better in half a day. In the past, when no alternative existed, patients got better quickly, and many did not suffer too badly.

The next-best treatment for gout is indomethacin (Indocin), one of the oldest nonsteroidal anti-inflammatory drugs. Some others in this class are Motrin, Advil, Nuprin, Naprosyn, Feldene, Clinoril; all work, but Indocin is the best choice. I prescribe 50 milligrams three times a day for three days, then 25 milligrams three times a day for another four. Patients feel better in less than a day and rarely suffer side effects. If they do experience unpleasant effects, it's usually upset stomach and headache. Indocin works so well that doctors no longer prescribe special diets for gout. Special diets never helped much.

Drugs for Prevention

While nice, relief of symptoms hardly justifies the high mark I award medical science. We earned that by discovering drugs to prevent attacks entirely. Since one must take these drugs every day forever, this is not something to undertake

115

lightly, but I mention the possibility to patients who have experienced a first attack. It doesn't take many more to convince him that this is an experience he never wants to repeat. I urge patients to use these drugs immediately when there's a kidney stone, a common and extremely painful complication of gout. Future stones are worth preventing.

We prevent gout by lowering the uric acid level, most often with allopurinol (Zyloprim, Lopurin). Once the level is reduced to normal, a patient has nearly 100 percent protection against joint attacks and uric acid kidney stones. This is such a marvelous treatment that doctors love to use it, so they use it too often.

Misuse of Allopurinol

If gout doesn't cause your painful joint, taking allopurinol won't make you feel better. It will, however, make your doctor feel better.

The fact is that an abnormal lab test—an elevated uric acid level, for example—makes doctors nervous. Sometimes it means our patient is sick, but not always. Although 5 percent of adult males have an increased risk of gout because of elevated uric acid, most never get it. Experts advise us not to treat elevated uric acid in an otherwise healthy patient.

Experts are wasting their breath. Seeing a high number on a lab slip, many doctors feel an uncontrollable urge to treat it. Personally I prefer treating patients to treating lab slips, but some doctors can't tell them apart.

Deep down, however, they feel uneasy at giving a powerful drug in the absence of disease, so they compromise by using a very low dose—say, 100 milligrams. This dosage of allopurinol is too little to prevent gout but high enough to make the doctor feel better. I see many patients on this dose.

If you're taking 100 milligrams of allopurinol, ask in these exact words: "Doctor, do I have gout?" Doctors rarely lie, so if the answer is yes, you must believe it. But listen carefully. If your doctor waffles, you're taking a drug that treats your lab slip.

Drugs for Nongout Joint Pain

The best treatment for arthritis, bursitis, tendinitis, and other single-joint inflammation is reducing the inflammation.

Once the doctor determines that your pain isn't from a bacterial infection or local injury, a cortisone injection gives quick relief (this works for gout, too, but it isn't done often). As I mentioned in the arthritis chapter, some doctors don't know how to inject a joint, so they prescribe anti-inflammatory drugs instead. These don't work as quickly as an injection, but you should feel better in a few days.

Heart Attack

MEDICAL SCIENCE REPORT CARD

GRADE: **C**

COMMENTS: This grade sounds worse than it is. Today doctors "cure" only a few heart attacks, but this gloomy state of affairs should change rapidly in the face of today's rapidly advancing medical technology. Even today, if you act quickly, our grade jumps to a high "B."

Doctors can't cure the damage caused by a heart attack. We merely keep an eye on you while the heart heals and deal with complications such as abnormal rhythms and cardiac arrest (treatment grade: B) and heart failure when damage is so great that the heart pumps too weakly (treatment grade: D).

Today, however, if you arrive at a well-equipped hospital within a couple hours of the onset of the attack, you stand a good chance of leaving with zero heart damage. Although beyond the experimental stage, the spectacularly complex procedures that can save your heart are still being refined and studied. Not yet available everywhere, they will revolutionize heart attack treatment by the end of the century.

A heart attack is a serious event. Although the incidence has been dropping since the mid-1960s, over a million still occur every year. One-third are fatal, but most deaths occur quickly—before the victim ever reaches the hospital. If the person having the attack lives to hear the diagnosis, the worst is already over. It's a good reason for paying attention to the first symptoms.

Beyond Cholesterol

When a coronary artery becomes plugged, the blood supply to the heart muscle is cut off. The parts that don't receive blood die. If you survive, scar tissue replaces the dead muscle, and life goes on—but a heart with a scar instead of a piece of muscle pumps less efficiently. You don't want too many scars.

What blocks the artery? These days it seems like everyone knows that cholesterol piles up on artery walls, and this buildup (called plaque) seems the obvious culprit. But this is wrong.

Usually a *clot* stops blood flow in a coronary artery narrowed by plaque. As the artery narrows, blood flow grows turbulent as it squeezes through the pinhole opening, and turbulent blood tends to form clots.

This property of blood was a terribly exciting finding 30 years ago. If a clot blocked an artery, doctors reasoned, giving blood thinners would unblock it, thereby preserving the heart muscle. With the announcement of that discovery, some doctors began treating heart attacks with blood thinners; others waited for studies to prove that they work.

Many studies came and went. Some showed that blood thinners helped; others didn't. Overall, the results were unsatisfying.

I don't believe that blood thinners work. They are superb at making blood "thin" (i.e., preventing clots) but poor at getting rid of clots already in place.

But there's better news. Soon after scientists found that clots caused heart attacks, they discovered that those clots didn't stay around for long.

During an autopsy, when pathologists look at a heart even a day or two after an attack, they see a patch of dead muscle, but the artery supplying that muscle is open. This is because the human body doesn't tolerate clots.

After all, a clot is normally an emergency measure. Almost as soon as it forms, the body begins producing substances that dissolve it, and within a few days most clots are gone.

While interfering with clotting is easy (even aspirin does that), dissolving a clot inside a human heart proved a sticky problem. The 1980s finally saw some useful solutions, and this is one of the most exhilarating areas in medicine. You'll learn more further on.

Signs and Symptoms

The textbook description of a heart attack is a severe, squeezing, central chest pain lasting more than 20 minutes, sometimes radiating to the arms, less often to the jaw, neck, back, or upper abdomen. Although this is a mouthful, remembering the adjectives makes your life simpler. *Severe* means just that. A nagging ache is not a heart attack. *Squeezing* tells you that heart pain feels oppressive; many people having an attack insist that what they feel isn't pain but an uncomfortable pressure. *Central* means central; although the heart sits on the left side of the chest, you usually feel a heart attack in the middle. *Twenty minutes* means that short, sharp stabs are not important; pain lasting several minutes may be angina. A heart attack persists.

Don't assume you have indigestion if nausea and vomiting accompany the pain. These symptoms are not rare during a heart attack. Also not rare are weakness, sweating, dizziness, and fear—patients with a heart attack often suspect that something is dreadfully wrong.

Twenty percent or more of heart attacks are painless, a figure that increases with age and the presence of diabetes.

Sometimes the attack passes with no symptoms at all; doctors know this because a scar produces a specific abnormality on the electrocardiogram. Sometimes a person having an attack collapses, becomes breathless, or suffers weakness or an irregular heart rhythm. Don't neglect these symptoms in someone old or feeble.

Dissolving the Clot

The best treatment for a heart attack is a substance that dissolves blood clots—tissue plasminogen activator (TPA).

Everyone with a heart attack should have the clot dissolved as soon as possible, followed by a procedure to open the constricted artery.

TPA (Activase) is currently the best clot dissolver on the market. Humans produce it in minuscule amounts, but genetic engineering has made it easily available. Given intravenously, TPA opens blocked arteries about 80 percent of the time. As experience grows and clot dissolvers become safer, paramedics and other emergency personnel may administer them on the spot. Until that time, it's up to you to get to a hospital quickly.

Other clot dissolvers approved by the Food and Drug Administration are available. The oldest is streptokinase (Kabikinase, Streptase). Not quite as effective as TPA, it's not the best treatment, but you may get it anyway because TPA is *25 times as expensive* as streptokinase! Genetic engineering produces dazzling products, but they don't come cheap.

A single injection of TPA can cost $4,000. Your insurance or prepaid medical plan may find this so hard to swallow that it prefers streptokinase. You may have to insist if you want the best.

Once the clot is gone, another is likely to form unless the coronary artery is fixed. You will be kept on blood thinners until doctors perform a test known as an angiogram that localizes the narrowing, then angioplasty or bypass surgery to eliminate it.

Angioplasty is a clever procedure in which a doctor inserts a thin, flexible tube into an artery in the arm or leg, guides it into the narrow coronary artery, then blows up a small balloon at the end of the tube. This almost always eliminates the obstruction, but it's still not certain how long it takes before it reappears. Angioplasty has only been popular since the mid-1980s. On the other hand, it's much simpler than a bypass (available since the 1960s), in which a surgeon opens the chest and transplants blood vessels from other parts of the body to carry blood around the blocked artery. Given a choice, I'd prefer angioplasty.

The old heart attack treatment of a few days in the intensive care unit followed by a week or two on a regular ward was not cheap. Today's best treatment is no different. Like most highly technical medical advances, the treatment saves lives but not money. It costs about $30,000. Think of this before you sit down to bacon and eggs.

Hemorrhoids

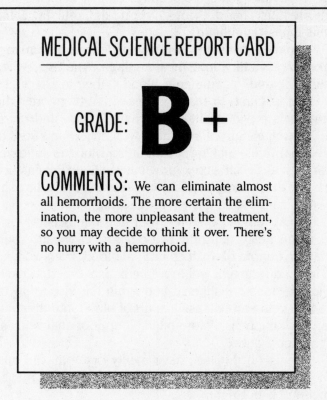

MEDICAL SCIENCE REPORT CARD

GRADE: **B**+

COMMENTS: We can eliminate almost all hemorrhoids. The more certain the elimination, the more unpleasant the treatment, so you may decide to think it over. There's no hurry with a hemorrhoid.

Almost everyone has hemorrhoids, and almost no one knows what they are. Patients tend to believe they're suffering an infection, a tumor, or an injury of some sort, and they usually worry about the implications. I can reassure them. A hemorrhoid is not a life-threatening problem, and it never turns into one, although it can be a major nuisance.

A hemorrhoid is a swollen, flabby vein. Except for its location, it's no different from the varicose veins that plague your mother.

Arteries are thick and muscular because the heart expels blood directly into them at high pressure. By the time blood squeezes through tiny capillaries to nourish tissues, then flows into veins, pressure is almost zero. As a result, veins are thin. They are simply a conduit through which blood travels back to the heart.

Animal veins are well designed, and human veins worked fine until about three million years ago, when our ancestors stood up. Suddenly, blood in their legs faced several extra feet to climb to reach the heart. Furthermore, when an animal gets pregnant, its womb hangs down and out of the way. The full weight of a modern woman's womb rests on her abdominal veins, making it difficult for blood to squeeze past. When bellies of either sex grow fat, abdominal veins bear the load. Too thin to handle this extra pressure, the walls of human leg veins stretch and grow tortuous and painful.

Anal veins also suffer. Your dog's anus is on the same level as his heart; returning blood has an easy path. Your anus lies at the bottom of a tall column of blood. Even worse, when you strain during a bowel movement, anal pressure rises even higher. If you're constipated and strain hard, you may blow a hole in a vein and witness a spurt of blood into the toilet (it's rare, but it happens). More often, your poor anal veins stretch and stretch again.

Veins on the legs have plenty of room, but space is tight in the anus. As veins grow larger you may realize that something is not right.

Signs and Symptoms

Unpleasant symptoms don't always accompany hemorrhoids. Remember, almost everyone has them. But sometimes they bleed or protrude. Patients believe that anal pain means a hemorrhoid, but it usually means a fissure—a tear in the anal skin. A hemorrhoid doesn't hurt unless a clot forms in the vein. Then it hurts a great deal. You'll know it's a thrombosed hemorrhoid if you feel a tender lump on your anus; pain without a lump is probably a fissure. Itching is usually a dermatological problem, less often a hemorrhoid.

The Best Treatment

I'd choose injection for myself if I had to have treatment for a hemorrhoid. Fortunately, my very high-fiber diet puts so little stress on my anus that I'll never be forced to choose. In this form of treatment the doctor injects a caustic chemical that shrinks the hemorrhoid, which later sloughs off. This is a fairly gentle treatment; pain and bleeding afterward are rare. The major disadvantage: It doesn't work well for large hemorrhoids.

Injection is the most popular procedure in Europe but only second in the United States. American doctors prefer banding. Using an ingenious instrument, a doctor (a family doctor if someone teaches him or her) snaps a rubber band around the base of a hemorrhoid. This cuts off the blood supply, so the tissue dies and sloughs away after a week. This isn't supposed to hurt, but about a third of patients have some pain.

Hemorrhoids tend to recur, and new ones appear. Patients may grow tired of repeated trips to the doctor for a clever, not-very-painful procedure that provides only temporary relief. If so, they should consider old-fashioned surgery, which is also the only cure for the largest hemorrhoids. Unlike clever office procedures (others are laser blasting, freezing, and infrared burning; I don't recommend them) no one will ever tell you that hemorrhoid surgery doesn't hurt. Expect sitz baths, stool softeners, and several days in bed taking pain pills.

Nothing clever helps an excruciating thrombosed hemorrhoid, but it disappears on its own if you're patient. Sitting in a tub of hot water helps. After a few days most thrombosed hemorrhoids are gone. If you can't wait, a doctor can inject novocaine, slit open the swollen vein, and extract the clot. This sounds gruesome, but it's not very painful and gives instant relief.

Herpes

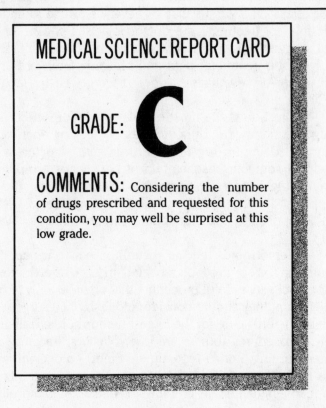

MEDICAL SCIENCE REPORT CARD

GRADE: **C**

COMMENTS: Considering the number of drugs prescribed and requested for this condition, you may well be surprised at this low grade.

Long ago, I was standing in a clinic hallway when a man noticed that I was a doctor. Showing me a few small blisters on his finger, he explained that he had forgotten to ask his doctor about them. Did I know what they were? I told him that they looked like herpes, a minor problem that would clear up in a week. There was no treatment.

A week later the clinic director summoned me to his office to show me a formal complaint. The man had accused me of flagrantly unprofessional behavior by announcing in public that he suffered a shameful sexually transmitted disease.

Media Diseases

It had slipped my mind that we were in the midst of the herpes hysteria. There is always a disease hysteria, happily encouraged by the media. This hysteria is actually an old American tradition. At any given time, Americans are terrified of one particular disease, and no amount of reassurance can reassure them. Now, of course, acquired immune deficiency syndrome (AIDS) fills this role. Although a terrible disease, most of my patients have no reason to fear AIDS, but they fear it anyway.

Although herpes has long attacked every area of the body, especially the lips (fever blisters) and the mouth (canker sores), the late 1960s saw an increasing number of genital infections. By the late 1970s enough of an increase had taken place to provoke media attention and widespread unreason. The years of 1981 to 1984 mark the bounds of herpes hysteria.

"Herpes: The V.D. of the 80's," announced a headline that went on to declare that 20 million Americans were victims and that 500,000 new cases appeared each year. "Incurable, recurrent, and highly contagious," reported the *New York Times*. ". . . an uncontrollable epidemic . . ."

I've forgotten when those quotes appeared, but my article repeating them came out in *Seventeen* magazine in 1982. This was not my first on herpes. As the current media disease, it was a popular topic. *Newsweek* and *Time* featured cover stories; television specials filled the air. Popular interest eventually switched to AIDS, but while it lasted, herpes hysteria produced the usual mass of nonsense and misinformation.

Herpes did not decline with its hysteria; it's as common as ever, but no longer do patients dissolve in tears at the diagnosis. It remains, as always, a tiresome annoyance—with one exception. A pregnant woman may transmit herpes during a vaginal delivery. Herpes in a newborn is devastating, and women suffering an attack late in pregnancy are delivered by cesarean.

127

Cause: A Virus

In response to any viral infection, the body develops antibodies that destroy the invader, and we recover. These antibodies remain in the blood for the rest of our lives and quickly attack the same virus if it appears again. That's why you suffer measles, mumps, chicken pox, and infectious mononucleosis only once.

A herpes infection also produces antibodies, but the herpes virus has a peculiar habit. After the first attack it retreats to nerve cells at the base of the spine, where it remains dormant—sometimes for a lifetime, sometimes for only a few weeks. Coming to life, it travels back down the nerves, kills a patch of skin (producing blisters, then ulcers), then retreats to the spine again and returns to dormancy. Since the virus stays out of the blood, it is safe from antibodies. Fortunately, as time goes on, other body defenses gradually reduce the recurrences. Eventually herpes attacks stop entirely.

Signs and Symptoms

"The earliest warning of an impending herpes attack is a vague burning around the genitals. Nothing is visible at first but the discomfort grows. After two to three days, the pain is intense and there appear one to a dozen shallow ulcers, $\frac{1}{4}$ to $\frac{1}{2}$ inch in diameter. Although they heal in about two weeks, that can seem an eternity. The sores may be excruciating, making urination agonizing. During the first attack the virus is in the blood, so the victim feels tired and feverish, no different from a typical viral infection such as the flu. Once antibodies are present, the virus can't enter the blood, so the only symptom of a recurrence is local pain."

I lifted the above paragraph from an article written during the hysteria, so it's fairly lurid. Although accurate, it describes a severe attack. Most patients aren't so miserable. Some are merely curious about the appearance of tiny scabs on the genitals and are surprised to hear the diagnosis.

One bout of herpes can be tiresome, but recurrences

were the source of its evil reputation. Seventy percent of people who experience their first herpes attack have another within nine months. A smaller number have a recurrence every few months—a miserable affliction. No one knows why this happens. Attacks are triggered by friction from ordinary sex, rubbing, and scratching, or by fevers and other minor illnesses. Many women suffer flare-ups at the same time during the menstrual cycle. Either sex can fall victim during emotional upsets or periods of stress. An important feature skipped over during the hysteria was that recurrences grow less severe and disappear entirely after a few years. On the other hand, it's easy to feel nervous about catching it from a friend. Even during the latent period, some people remain contagious, and we can't predict who.

Medication Can Help

The best treatment for herpes is acyclovir (Zovirax) tablets.

Herpes is incurable, and acyclovir isn't a cure. It slows viral multiplication, so it shortens an attack if taken within a few days of its onset. Afterward the virus becomes dormant and can recur. Taken every day, acyclovir suppresses recurrences, but nothing is gained because they resume as soon as the drug is stopped. It's a useful drug, but if your attacks aren't painful there's no reason to take it.

Tablets came out after the hysteria had passed, but Zovirax ointment appeared at the peak, a year or two before. The publicity was enormous. Patients poured into doctor's offices asking for it. Doctors still prescribe the ointment freely; if they don't, patients ask for it to treat fever blisters, canker sores, and miscellaneous skin disorders.

This is odd when you realize that the ointment is almost worthless. It slightly shortens a first attack, but almost every case we see is a recurrence. The ointment is 100 percent useless for recurrences, as well as for fever blisters and other skin diseases, even if they're herpes. We knew this from the beginning. Both the Food and Drug Administration and the drug company announced it as soon as the drug was approved. But so great was the yearning for something that worked that Zovirax ointment broke all records in becoming a modern folk remedy.

Many patients know deep in their heart that Zovirax *will* help. They look upon a doctor who refuses to prescribe it as eccentric, cruel, or perhaps incompetent. After a few encounters with such patients, many doctors realize that these drugs are fairly harmless, and the pain of prescribing a useless drug is far less than that caused by a disappointed patient. Your doctor wants to make you happy.

High Blood Pressure

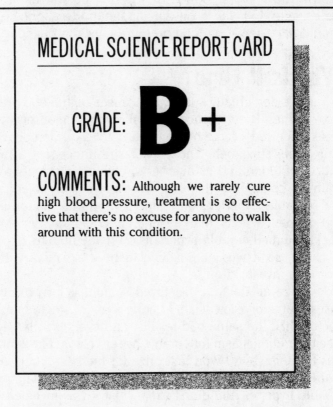

MEDICAL SCIENCE REPORT CARD

GRADE: **B**+

COMMENTS: Although we rarely cure high blood pressure, treatment is so effective that there's no excuse for anyone to walk around with this condition.

Make no mistake about it: High blood pressure is a deadly disease. It wears out your heart, speeds up atherosclerosis, damages kidneys, and blows holes in your arteries.

Nonetheless, if you must have a chronic disease, choose high blood pressure, also known as hypertension. Symptoms won't inconvenience you. Treatment is simple. Best of all, once your pressure is normal, you're normal—meaning that you run the same risk of a stroke, heart disease, or kidney failure as someone who never had it.

Without treatment a 35-year-old man with a slightly elevated pressure (130/90) will die 4 years earlier than a man with a normal pressure (120/80). With a pressure of 140/90, he will die 9 years sooner. At 150/100, he will die 17 years earlier, and 150/100 is only a moderate elevation! Everyone should have a yearly blood pressure check throughout life.

Why Is It High?

We don't really know what causes high blood pressure.

When I left medical school, every person newly diagnosed received a large bottle to carry for a day to collect a 24-hour urine specimen. Then he or she underwent a massive course of blood and cardiac tests, plus an intravenous pyelogram—a complex series of kidney x-rays. The object was to find curable hypertension: tumors, hormone abnormalities, and kidney defects that a surgeon could correct. Medical books claimed curable hypertension made up 5 to 10 percent of cases, so it was unthinkable to treat a patient without a thorough investigation.

Like all doctors, I enjoyed searching for obscure diseases, but after a few years I hadn't found a single one. Other doctors had the same bad results, and even experts began to lose their enthusiasm for curable hypertension. I knew the tide was turning when I won first prize for the best article of 1979 in the journal *Modern Medicine.* It was an essay claiming that curable hypertension didn't exist—that it was invented by experts bored with dealing with a disease they didn't understand. My prize was an all-expenses-paid week for two to Orlando, Florida.

Although curable hypertension does exist, it's less common than we thought. Making the diagnosis is less urgent than lowering pressure, so today we do only simple screening—blood and urine tests. If the pressure doesn't respond to treatment, or a suspicious symptom appears, we search further.

Stress Doesn't Equal Tension

We may not know what causes it, but we know what *doesn't* cause hypertension: tension.

The "tension" in *hypertension* refers to stress on the arterial wall, not emotional stress. High blood pressure is a real disease, not the result of anxiety, fear, or chronic unhappiness. Nervous people don't have a higher risk. Relaxing doesn't lower high blood pressure. Neither do tranquilizers. If a doctor prescribes a tranquilizer for your high blood pressure, he probably doesn't believe you have it. Perhaps he's decided that you're neurotic but prefers to tell you that you have a more dignified disease.

Disease without Symptoms

The only way you can discover if your pressure is high is to take it with a blood pressure cuff.

Educating patients can be discouraging, because the average person has health beliefs that no doctor can budge. The myth that high blood pressure makes you ill is almost universal—even a few doctors think so. Most patients smile politely when I explain about blood pressure, but I can tell they don't believe a word of it. They know that when they have a headache or feel giddy or tired, their "pressure is up." They then take an extra pill or hurry to the doctor—both the wrong actions.

Good Medications

The best treatment is currently an angiotensin-converting enzyme inhibitor (Capoten, Prinivil, Zestril, Vasotec).

Today many blood pressure drugs work by blocking selected regulatory nerves that control your arteries. When I was young, drugs weren't so clever. They didn't block selected nerves; they blocked *everything*.

After 25 years I still recall a funny lecture during a class on hypertension. In the tone of an anthropologist reporting on a strange culture, the professor announced that he would describe "hexamethonium man" (hexamethonium was a powerful drug given in those days to treat hypertension).

Hexamethonium man behaved with enormous dignity, the professor continued. He moved about slowly (otherwise he became dizzy) and spoke carefully (his mental processes were fuzzy). Shaking hands with hexamethonium man was never unpleasant because his skin was always dry (he didn't sweat) and warm (he was pink and warm everywhere because all his blood vessels were dilated). When in public he ate sparingly (to avoid attacks of diarrhea) but drank a great deal (his mouth was dry). Finally, hexamethonium man lived a quiet, solitary life (he was impotent).

A well-treated hypertension patient in your parents' day was not a happy person. With today's drugs, we expect happiness. Side effects still occur, but when they do, we can select a different drug from among a large variety of drug classes (diuretics, beta-blockers, alpha-blockers, calcium blockers, vasodilators, alpha-stimulators, etc.). Sooner or later we'll find one that lowers your pressure without making you feel worse than when your pressure was high (when, as I insist, you felt fine).

Angiotensin-converting enzyme inhibitors are the newest class with the lowest incidence of side effects. In case you're interested, angiotensin-converting enzyme is a chemical that your body produces. This chemical activates a substance in your blood (angiotensin) that goes on to activate another substance (renin) that regulates blood pressure.

Although the best treatment, these drugs are new. That means they are expensive. Rather than start you off on a drug costing a dollar a pill, your doctor may prefer a beta-blocker at a nickel a pill or a diuretic at a penny a pill. If they work, you don't need the best.

Hyperthyroidism

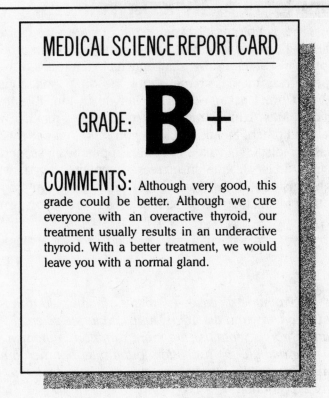

MEDICAL SCIENCE REPORT CARD

GRADE: **B**+

COMMENTS: Although very good, this grade could be better. Although we cure everyone with an overactive thyroid, our treatment usually results in an underactive thyroid. With a better treatment, we would leave you with a normal gland.

Strangely, like thyroid deficiency, hyperthyroidism is usually an autoimmune disease. In an autoimmune disease, the body's own defenses make a mistake and attack an organ. The blood of most people who have an overactive thyroid contains an abnormal antibody called long-acting thyroid stimulator (LATS). This antibody disrupts the pituitary gland, which is responsible for controlling the thyroid gland's hormone output. This disruption causes the thyroid gland to race wildly. No one knows why this happens, but as with all autoimmune diseases, women suffer more than men—their risk of hyperthyroidism is seven times greater.

Symptoms of Hyperthyroidism

The symptoms of hyperthyroidism are mostly the opposite of those of hypothyroidism. (Hypothyroidism produces symptoms of fatigue, dry skin and hair, intolerance to cold temperatures, increased menstrual bleeding, and constipation.) But don't assume that the fatigue of too little thyroid hormone (thyroxine) translates into excess energy when there's too much. Sickness makes you sick, and patients with hyperthyroidism feel weak. They also appear restless, nervous, and tremulous. Despite an increased appetite, they may lose weight. Instead of the constipation and other symptoms of hypothyroidism, they have frequent bowel movements, smooth

PEARL

Autoimmune diseases (diabetes, rheumatoid arthritis, many thyroid disorders, lupus, multiple sclerosis, and chronic hepatitis) are more common in women. As the one glaring exception to the rule that men are more susceptible to disease, this disparity demands an explanation.

According to some experts, women suffer more autoimmune diseases than men because their immune system is actually stronger and more complex. Remember that immune defenses attack foreign organisms that invade the body. Unlike men, women routinely deal with a huge foreign organism inside their body—during pregnancy. To ignore such a large invader requires a sophisticated defense system. Most women handle it well, but the human body is imperfect, so this complicated system is more likely to go haywire than a man's simple equipment.

skin, fine silky hair, heat intolerance, and decreased menstrual bleeding.

Unique signs of too much thyroid hormone are bulging eyes and a fixed stare. If you can see white above the iris when a person is gazing normally, that hints at an overactive gland. A doctor shouldn't be too quick to make the diagnosis; some normal people look that way.

Treatment: Thyroid Destruction

Young, healthy patients are often given drugs that block hormone production. These work well and are fairly safe, but they don't cure the problem and must be taken every day. After a year or two, the doctor stops the drug and hopes that hormone production won't leap up again. About one-third of the time the thyroid begins functioning normally and patients enjoy a remission that may or may not be permanent. If not, permanent destruction is the next step.

Today we destroy the thyroid by an injection of radioactive iodine (RAI). The radiation would be dangerous if the thyroid didn't have a tremendous appetite for iodine and snatch it up as soon as it enters the bloodstream. All the radiation quickly concentrates inside the gland and destroys it. Doctors have used RAI for decades, and it doesn't seem to cause the usual complications of radiation, such as cancer. Nevertheless, we don't use RAI in children, and we like to try drugs first in people under 30.

Experts try to give enough RAI to destroy most of the gland but not all, in the hopes that the remaining portion will produce just the right amount of hormone. Unfortunately, they haven't yet figured out how to do it, so thyroid deficiency develops about three-quarters of the time. This may take decades to show up, so every RAI patient must have a thyroid test regularly.

Before the advent of RAI, surgeons destroyed the thyroid by cutting it out. Surgery is still done, especially in children, and it works fine, but don't insist on it because you're afraid of radiation.

Hypothyroidism

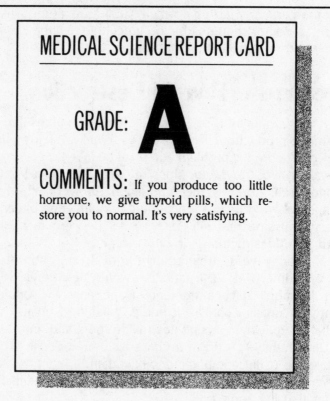

MEDICAL SCIENCE REPORT CARD

GRADE: **A**

COMMENTS: If you produce too little hormone, we give thyroid pills, which restore you to normal. It's very satisfying.

Many laypersons believe that thyroid hormone regulates the metabolism—the thousands of chemical reactions, nerve impulses, muscle contractions, and manufacturing processes that keep you alive and functioning. According to this view, too much thyroid speeds everything up, and too little slows it down. Unlike most popular beliefs, this one is more or less true, but you shouldn't carry it too far. Feeling sluggish is rarely evidence of an inactive thyroid. Giving excess thyroid to someone who is overweight won't help her lose, unless you give enough to make her sick, but sickness from any cause helps you lose weight.

A Disorder of the Immune System

The proper term for the condition in which too little thyroid hormone is produced is *hypothyroidism*. In adults most hypothyroidism is another mysterious autoimmune disorder in which the body's own defenses attack an organ. Another common cause is treatment of an overactive gland, as was explained in the previous chapter.

In the past, iodine deficiency was the leading culprit, but this is rare today. Intelligent readers may guess that iodized salt is responsible for eliminating the problem, and this was true until 50 years ago. Today Americans eat such a variety of food that they get enough iodine from natural sources, especially seafood.

Taking Thyroid Hormone

The treatment of choice for hypothyroidism is thyroid hormone. There is one problem, however. When doctors find a treatment that works wonderfully well, they try to use it as often as possible, so they sometimes use it when it won't work. As a result, thyroid hormone is one of the most over-prescribed drugs in medicine.

Beginning practice 20 years ago, I found a puzzling number of patients (all women) taking thyroid. Questioning revealed that they had once complained of fatigue or difficulty losing weight. The doctor had ordered a blood test, announced that their thyroid was underactive, and given a prescription.

This sounded all wrong. I was especially puzzled when the women insisted that they received thyroid after a single blood test. *No doctor diagnoses a serious, lifelong disease with a single test.* Even hypothyroidism, a relatively simple disorder and one not difficult to track down, requires analysis

139

of several hormones and perhaps an ultrasound or nuclear scan of the gland.

Being an efficient young physician, I launched my own investigation of such patients' conditions. The results usually turned up a normal thyroid. Young doctors enjoy contradicting older doctors, so I was always proud to announce that the patient didn't have thyroid disease and could discard her pills. Then I paused to experience my patient's delight and gratitude. After all, I had just informed her that she didn't have a serious disease. It was always a jolt to discover that this was not good news.

"Then why am I so tired?!" many complained. Or, "Then why can't I lose weight?!"

These are two of the most difficult questions you can ask. Doctors can help (chronic fatigue gets a "C+," obesity a "D"), but this is nowhere near the amazing cure we deliver for thyroid deficiency. Doctors want to cure these conditions as much as patients want to be cured.

Unfortunately, hundreds of disorders besides hypothyroidism produce chronic fatigue. In an otherwise healthy person, psychological stress is by far the leading cause. As for obesity, people who have hypothyroidism don't gain a great deal of weight, although their skin often appears puffy.

Symptoms of Hypothyroidism

Besides fatigue and puffiness, typical symptoms are dry skin and hair, intolerance to cold temperatures, increased menstrual bleeding, and constipation.

The clearest sign is a goiter, an enlarged gland. The thyroid, normally invisible, rests against your windpipe at the base of the neck. Thyroid hormone production is controlled by the pituitary, the master gland located in the brain. Any decline in thyroid hormone production triggers the pituitary to secrete more of its thyroid-stimulating hormone (TSH), which does just what the name implies. Whipped into furious activity by this hormone, the thyroid swells. Sometimes this works in increasing the thyroid's own output. So you can have a goiter and a normal hormone level. Only a test showing a high TSH level will reveal that something is wrong. When TSH fails to prod the thyroid to increase production, you have a large gland but too little hormone.

One expert found an enlarged gland in 93 percent of patients with mild thyroid deficiency, and he formulated the rule: "No goiter, no hypothyroidism."

The Best Treatment: Thyroid Hormone

In the past everyone took "thyroid," an extract of animal glands obtained from slaughterhouses. Although pretty good, the medication contained other parts of the thyroid, and the hormone content varied according to how carefully the company prepared it. Today you can buy pure thyroid hormone (L-thyroxine), and experts prefer it.

Thyroid hormone takes two weeks to work, so if you perk up after a day or two, that's a placebo effect. This means that the drug is working because of the patient's psychological expectation that it will have an effect. This placebo effect often happens when thyroid hormone is given for chronic fatigue in someone with a normal hormone level.

Impotence

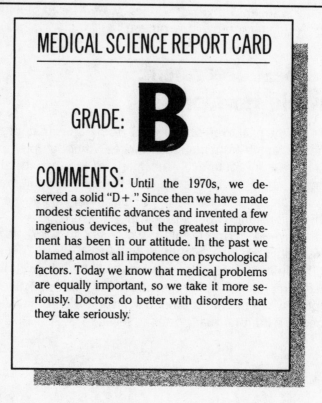

MEDICAL SCIENCE REPORT CARD

GRADE: **B**

COMMENTS: Until the 1970s, we deserved a solid "D +." Since then we have made modest scientific advances and invented a few ingenious devices, but the greatest improvement has been in our attitude. In the past we blamed almost all impotence on psychological factors. Today we know that medical problems are equally important, so we take it more seriously. Doctors do better with disorders that they take seriously.

Although about 100 of my popular health articles have appeared over the past 15 years, I've never written on impotence, because it's a male problem.

Women enjoy reading about health; men don't. Every woman's magazine contains several health-related articles, but years pass before the subject appears in *Playboy, Esquire,* or *Field and Stream.* As a professional writer, I keep in touch with editors of the women's magazines, and they keep in touch with me, but I ignore the men's magazines. They're not interested because (they believe) their readers aren't.

Having said this, I now admit that my record for letters from readers was in response to a single mention of impotence. No other topic has come close. It was not even a whole article. In 1988, *Better Homes and Gardens* published a potpourri in which I discussed half a dozen minor medical advances that readers probably hadn't heard of. In a few paragraphs I mentioned a device worn like a condom that could be blown up with air to produce an erection in someone otherwise incapable. A torrent of letters arrived over the next few months, and even today one or two drifts in every month or so. Almost all writers were married women. It's a burning topic.

The Mechanics of an Erection

What causes an erection? Most people know that there is no bone in the penis (other animals do have one). Many people assume that muscles do the work creating an erection, but muscles don't really come into play until erection is achieved. A penis grows and stiffens because blood flows into it faster than it can flow out. Once the penis is packed with blood, the muscle at the base contracts to cut off blood flow entirely. A penis would become gangrenous if this condition lasted long enough. Fortunately, it doesn't. You can easily see why problems with blood vessels and their regulation (i.e., nerves) are most likely to interfere with an erection.

The Causes of Impotence

In medical school I learned that psychological stress caused 90 percent of impotence and that we should not raise a patient's hopes that he might suffer an easily correctable physical problem. Now doctors agree that physical disorders make up half the cases. We can't reverse all physical causes, but we can help with a great percentage of cases. We also do pretty well with psychological causes.

Psychological Causes

Among the causes of impotence are boredom, depression, fear of aging, impatience, and performance anxiety. Responsible for 50 percent of impotence cases, these causes are probably more common in young men and decline with age.

Impotence from nerve damage alone is not terribly frequent because only nerves near the penis are essential. Most paraplegics can have erections.

When victims of strokes, epilepsy, or Alzheimer's disease are affected, illness or lack of interest is the likely reason.

Physical Causes

Hormonal diseases are often responsible for impotence, and diabetes leads the list. Although impotence is not rare in diabetics, the problem is not lack of insulin or poor control of blood sugar level (at least in the short term) but one of the long-term complications such as peripheral nerve damage or atherosclerosis of arteries near the penis. Psychological causes are equally common in people who have diabetes. I often see a patient whose problem began as soon as he learned that diabetics can become impotent.

When men take estrogens for prostate cancer they may lose interest in sex, but erections are still possible. Similarly, lack of male hormone merely reduces sexual drive and slows erections. It's not essential. Complete impotence is not the result of lack of male hormone, nor is it a normal consequence of aging.

Drug Side Effects

Medications the patient might be taking are the first target of my investigation. Side effects from sedatives, tranquilizers, antidepressants, and blood pressure medications regularly cause impotence, but almost any drug can upset the delicate orchestration of events that leads to an erection.

Substance abuse can create an imbalance of male and female sex hormones that can affect potency. Marijuana lowers the testosterone level. Alcohol, like diabetes, can cause peripheral nerve damage. If alcohol damages a man's liver, it can cause his estrogen levels to rise. In addition, narcotics suppress sexual drive, and smoking interferes with penile blood flow. Clean living definitely improves your sex life.

The Doctor Can Help

Ultimately, your best treatment option is a concerned, friendly, persistent doctor.

Doctors can help most impotence, but one visit rarely does it unless the cause turns out to be a drug side effect. The doctor should take a good history (i.e., ask about your medical problems), explore your sex life, do a physical exam, and order a few (but not many) laboratory tests. Naturally he will check your blood sugar. It's conceivable that impotence might be the first sign of diabetes, but this possibility exists mostly in the minds of those who write medical textbooks. A testosterone level should be one of the tests, but if you receive a testosterone shot on your first visit, you're not getting the best treatment.

Testicular failure causes impotence, and giving testosterone cures it, but remember, *one lab test never diagnoses a serious disease.* If your testosterone level is low, you need other tests to determine why. For all you know, you might have normal testes that have stopped producing hormones because a brain tumor has damaged the pituitary (which controls the testes as well as other glands). It's a far-out possibility, but not the sort of thing you'd want overlooked.

Along with antibiotics and thyroxine, testosterone is another drug that works so beautifully when used properly that doctors love it, so they sometimes use it for disorders that it doesn't help.

If the Doctor Can't Help

A family doctor can solve (or at least explain) most impotence, although it may take a few visits. What then? If the problem is emotional or if a physical problem can't be reversed, plenty of resources exist. Don't worry if your doctor isn't aware of them, because if he isn't, he will quickly refer you to a urologist.

Urologists are surgeons who specialize in the urinary and genital tract. All but a handful are male, so men with sexual problems hurry to them, and many urologists have grown skilled in dealing with impotence. They will perform the same tests as a good family doctor and may add some highly technical ones if they decide to check the nerves or blood flow to your penis. Occasionally they perform surgery to unblock arteries; more often they are the source of mechanical aids—worn or surgically implanted—to produce an erection. When none of their skills is appropriate, they know other resources.

Psychotherapy is the traditional treatment for psychological impotence, but it doesn't work very well (perhaps a "D").

Psychiatrists and other therapists get a "B+" for helping patients with stress, depression, anxiety, and other emotional problems. But they do terribly at relieving the physical disorders that stress aggravates, such as obesity, insomnia, irritable bowels, and impotence.

Trained sex therapists do better—partly through counseling but also by teaching techniques to make sex less stressful. Sex therapy is an area rich in quackery, so don't pick a therapist from the phone book, although you can trust a clinic connected with a large medical center or medical school. See your family doctor first.

Injuries

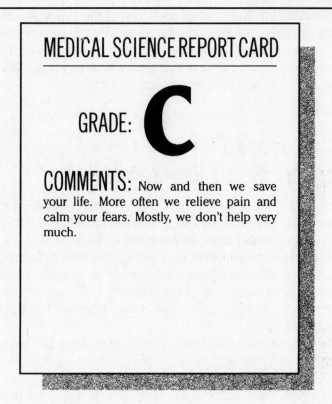

MEDICAL SCIENCE REPORT CARD

GRADE: **C**

COMMENTS: Now and then we save your life. More often we relieve pain and calm your fears. Mostly, we don't help very much.

One summer during medical school when I was on vacation in San Francisco, a friend awoke with an excruciating backache after a day of heavy exertion. She insisted on going to a hospital. As a student I knew nothing about back pain (medical students learn about "important" diseases), but I did know emergency rooms.

"You'll see an intern or resident who doesn't know much more about back pain than I, but he won't call a specialist because you don't have anything dangerous or mysterious," I told her. "He'll order an x-ray, which you don't need.

Then he'll give you pain pills—but not strong ones because he doesn't know you and hates the thought of being tricked by a drug abuser."

She insisted on going anyway. Supported by two friends, she hobbled to the emergency room of the University of California. Several hours later, the same friends carried her out with a prescription for a mild pain pill and the news that her x-rays were normal and nothing serious was wrong. Over the next few days her pain disappeared.

What Doesn't Constitute an Emergency

So what is the best emergency treatment for common sprains, strains, and fractures? you might ask. There is none.

They're not emergencies. If you want to know how to treat injuries, buy a book on sports medicine. I can't explain what to do for each type of injury in one chapter, but the knowledge of what's *not* an emergency will save you enough aggravation, waiting, and expense to pay for this book ten times over.

Injuries to the following parts of the body are not urgent *even if a fracture is present:* fingers, wrists, arms, shoulders, nose, legs, knees, ankles, feet, toes.

A small puncture that might require a tetanus shot *isn't* urgent; you can wait a day or two.

Of course, you must use common sense. A broken bone that protrudes through the skin or a joint that is obviously dislocated requires quick attention. Others may add that pain itself is an emergency; this is hard to quarrel with.

Limping into a crowded emergency room with an agonizing, swollen ankle will not impress the staff. You will wait while more serious problems are seen. You'll wait again while the vomiting child and the man with the bleeding scalp laceration go in. Although both arrived after you and neither problem is urgent, anyone who makes a mess takes priority over someone with a sprained ankle. The staff, after all, must clean the floor.

How to Treat an Injury

Question: What should you do right after an injury?
Answer: Relax. Get some ice. Try to calm down.

A sudden accident in the middle of a pleasant (usually weekend) afternoon is a nasty jolt, but bundling the victim off to the nearest emergency room often makes things worse. An hour without an ice pack will convert a minor, painful injury into a minor, excruciatingly painful injury. Keeping down swelling is a major priority. Swelling may appear anyway, but it's not an ominous sign.

"But is it fractured?" patients invariably ask. Without an x-ray, I can't be sure, but even if a fracture is present, a doctor can't put on a cast until swelling disappears in a day or two.

I followed my own advice ten years ago when I twisted my ankle stepping off the back porch. It hurt badly and swelled vividly, but I believed it was a sprain. After a week of painful limping, I lost patience and went for an x-ray that showed a broken bone in my foot. A cast wasn't essential, but it enabled me to walk without pain. Ever since, my wife tells this story to show how badly doctors take care of themselves, but I suffered no permanent harm.

Why You Need a Family Doctor

If you have a doctor, phone to make sure it's all right to wait until office hours. Don't give up after one call to the answering service. If there's no call back, phone every half hour. Once operators are aware that one caller is persistent, they become very creative in finding your doctor or someone else.

Healthy patients often boast that they need no family doctor. Situations like this make them eat their words. If you don't have a family doctor, getting medical advice after office hours is almost impossible.

Calling an emergency room will get you a nurse. If you tell her about your injury, she will tell you to come in.

She would be foolish to do otherwise because if she is wrong, she will get into terrible trouble. If she urges you to come in, no one will criticize her. As a doctor I often tell someone with a bad injury that it's all right to wait a day or two, but I am paid a great deal more than a nurse to make such decisions.

What Does Constitute an Emergency

If you find yourself dealing with any of these emergency situations, seek medical help immediately.

Possible fracture of centrally located bones. These include the hip, pelvis, spine, neck, skull, and face (except nose).

Lacerations that might require suturing. Believe it or not, suturing is strictly a cosmetic procedure that brings the edges of a wound together to make a thin scar. You would probably want suturing for a fairly small cut on your face, but not for a larger one on the leg. Go have the procedure done as soon as possible. After 24 hours most doctors won't suture a wound because too many germs have settled in, almost guaranteeing an infection below the stitches. See the doctor if you're not sure you need suturing.

Lacerations or abrasions that can't be cleaned. Don't use antiseptics; germs are tough and can tolerate irritating chemicals that will damage your injured tissues. Wash an injury with tap water; use soap and water around the edges. See a doctor if dirt is too firmly ground in to remove. Your body can deal with germs in most wounds, but it can't handle dirt.

Human and animal bites. These usually require careful cleaning and antibiotic therapy.

Burns with blisters, including sunburns. You might treat a few small blisters with antibiotic cream and a nonstick dressing, but larger ones require sophisticated dressings. Dressings and antibiotic creams aren't necessary for a first-degree burn—redness and pain with no blisters. But you may need pain relief if cold compresses or a cooling lotion such as calamine lotion don't help.

Any injury followed by loss of consciousness. A person who becomes unconscious following any type of injury needs immediate attention.

Insomnia

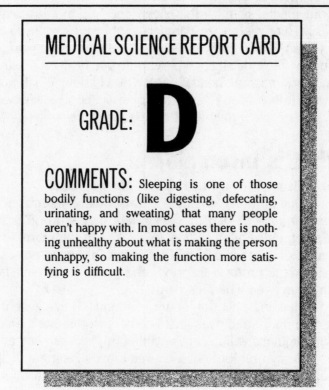

MEDICAL SCIENCE REPORT CARD

GRADE: **D**

COMMENTS: Sleeping is one of those bodily functions (like digesting, defecating, urinating, and sweating) that many people aren't happy with. In most cases there is nothing unhealthy about what is making the person unhappy, so making the function more satisfying is difficult.

A number of my patients worry about sleep and devote much energy trying to get either more or less of it. Even when they succeed, they are not pleased. Partly they are misled by the enormous popular misinformation on the subject. Doctors know more, but our knowledge isn't terribly helpful.

My patients assume that they need sleep. During sleep, they believe, the body disposes of waste, performs repairs, and stores energy for the following day. Actually, no one knows why any living thing sleeps. Some animals never sleep. Some sleep all but a few hours a day. Most humans like 6 to 8 hours, but well-documented cases exist of people who do fine on less than an hour.

There is also a widespread belief that we need sleep for our mental health—that sleep deprivation causes mental illness. To prove this, researchers kept healthy subjects awake for weeks. They got very sleepy, but they didn't go crazy. Naturally, lack of sleep is stressful, but is it more stressful than, say, a nagging headache? We don't know. What it comes down to is that sleep relieves sleepiness. People sleep because they are sleepy. If they don't sleep, they get sleepier.

What Is Insomnia?

Insomnia is a whole family of complaints.

One-third to one-half of insomnia patients actually *sleep normally.* Tested in a sleep lab, they drop off promptly and sleep uneventfully—only to awaken in the morning complaining of another bad night. Some of us have no taste for music, some no taste for food, and many get no satisfaction from sleep even when it's normal.

Sleeping pills don't cure insomnia. They cause it, producing a poor-quality rest that I call oblivion rather than sleep, but insomniacs will accept anything in place of lying awake.

In my opinion, habit causes most sleeping difficulties, though it's straining to call this insomnia. Early in my career when patients complained that they couldn't fall asleep, I told them to stay out of bed until they felt sleepy. When they awoke and couldn't get back to sleep, I told them that it was time to get up. This advice got a very bad reception.

Since the only known purpose of sleep is to relieve sleepiness, why stay in bed if you're not sleepy? Humans are the only animals with this peculiar behavior. No animal would dream of resting unless it felt like it. Many problems arise because every individual requires a different amount of sleep. Two percent of the population feels best with more than 10 hours. Many people do fine with only 5 or 6. The elderly don't need less sleep, but the quality of their sleep often declines.

Although too chic a word for my taste, *biorhythms* explain some sleeping problems. Many body functions wax and wane throughout the day. Examples are body temperature, hormone secretion, and blood pressure. Even hunger and sleepiness tend to occur at the same time, no matter how inconvenient that may be. A person may crave a midnight snack but feel no urge to eat breakfast.

Many insomniacs would sleep normally if they synchronized bedtime with their body rhythm. Unfortunately, it may be telling them to get sleepy at 3:00 A.M. and to wake up at 11:00 A.M. If they go to bed at the usual time, they are doomed to lie awake until their biorhythm enters its sleepy phase.

Depression and worry cause sleep problems. As an intern I was familiar with the bleary-eyed look of colleagues who had been up all night. Most of my insomnia patients don't look this way, although they complain bitterly of lack of sleep. They don't dread daytime sleepiness so much as the hours of lying awake, alone with their thoughts.

Psychiatric disorders produce disturbed sleep. A typical depressed person awakens late at night and can't get back to sleep, but *everyone* wakes up several times a night during normal sleep. Usually we drop off again and forget it happened. Sometimes we stay awake for a while.

Most of us treat these episodes as a minor annoyance, but it's an ordeal for every insomniac. They become bored. They brood about how sleepy they'll be the following day. But mostly they worry about their problems; life seems terribly difficult in the middle of the night. We all pass such nights now and then. Those who do it regularly end up in the doctor's office.

In my experience, most patients don't take sleeping pills in order to be wide awake the next day. They want to assure themselves of oblivion during the night.

The Best Treatment: Acceptance

Prescribed by a doctor, acceptance as a treatment for insomnia earns a "D." Patients don't come to the office to hear this kind of advice.

But it works reasonably well if you do it. I'm an insomniac. I always wake up several times a night; usually I go back to sleep, but once or twice a week I don't. When 15 minutes has elapsed, I say to myself, Here I go again. And I know several hours will pass before I get to sleep. So I make myself comfortable, turn on the radio, or strike up a conversation with my wife (that rarely works). Or, just like you, I worry about my problems.

To make things worse, I make a wee-hour hotel call three or four times a month. (I'm the hotel doctor for Los Angeles.) The call guarantees insomnia; besides the time spent on the call, it always takes 2 hours to get back to sleep. On top of that, I get many phone calls that don't require a hotel visit. Unless the conversation is completely satisfactory, that knocks me into insomnia. Among guests that keep me awake are those who don't want to pay my fee (not unreasonable; at these hours it's high) and those who assure me that they don't require my services but will call back in a few hours if they don't get better.

How do I deal with this? I don't. Sleeping late is difficult; my biorhythms demand early rising. Sometimes I take a nap, but that's risky; a long nap assures insomnia the following night. Even if I approved of sleeping pills, I couldn't take them, for fear of getting a hotel call. Mostly my insomnia doesn't interfere with my life—and I'm definitely not a serene, tolerant person.

A bowel movement every three days isn't necessarily constipation, fat thighs aren't obesity, and most of what patients call insomnia is tiresome but not a disease. You've heard the old saw: "If it isn't broken, don't fix it." Doctors don't do well treating inconvenient bodily behavior that isn't a real malfunction. But that doesn't mean you shouldn't see a doctor. Remember my rule: See a doctor if you feel bad. Don't worry about having a significant disease. A good doctor makes almost everyone feel better.

If your doctor can't do much for your sleeping problem (despite repeated visits—one visit never counts), ask for a referral. Sleep specialists are terribly clever, and if your insurance will pay, you'll have a fascinating time with their machines and sleep labs.

Irritable Bowels

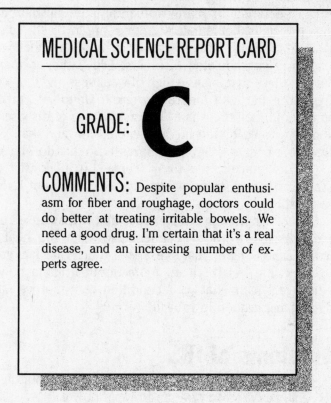

MEDICAL SCIENCE REPORT CARD

GRADE: **C**

COMMENTS: Despite popular enthusiasm for fiber and roughage, doctors could do better at treating irritable bowels. We need a good drug. I'm certain that it's a real disease, and an increasing number of experts agree.

Irritable bowel syndrome (IBS) is the most common digestive disorder. Perhaps 20 percent of Americans have complaints, although most don't see a doctor. It's also the leading reason for referral to a gastroenterologist, which is peculiar because the disease is not life-threatening and treatment isn't complicated. Specialists see so many cases because family doctors grow frustrated.

Stress Factor

Hyperactive and hypersensitive intestinal muscles are responsible for the unpleasant symptoms.

Three times as many women as men suffer from IBS. To me this hints that female hormones are involved. To others it points to stress. Almost everyone maintains that women suffer more stress-related disorders. Old-fashioned men and women believe that this is a sign of weakness and that women suffer more because they are weaker. Up-to-date men and women hold that stress is a universal cause of disease scandalously ignored by the medical profession and that women suffer more because they are oppressed. What do I believe?

Stress makes everything worse, but it doesn't cause anything. Treating stress makes you feel better, but it doesn't cure anything.

Back when everyone believed that stress caused ulcers, we didn't have a good treatment. Now that we heal them quickly, experts agree that stress isn't much of a factor. Time is on my side. As we learn more about irritable bowels, I predict we'll learn that your condition can improve *without* reducing aggravation in your life.

Symptoms of IBS

If you're not satisfied with the behavior of your digestive tract, chances are you have an irritable bowel.

Constipation is a sign, but so is diarrhea, because the hypersensitive colon is unpredictable. In fact, a typical victim has alternating periods of one or the other. Other irritable bowels simply twitch without changing stool behavior; these patients suffer cramps and bloating (despite the universal belief, gas doesn't cause painful bloating; abnormal bowel contractions are responsible). Anything that stimulates the digestive tract, such as caffeine or anxiety, makes symptoms worse, and women suffer more in the second half of their cycle—after ovulation and before menstruating.

Abnormal contractions change the appearance of stool. It may exit as thin as a pencil, in individual pellets, as hard as raw potatoes, as soft as mashed potatoes, or covered with mucus. These signs—including mucus in your stool—are not ominous. My patients worry about mucus, whether it appears from the throat, nose, or anus, but it's a normal response to irritation.

The Fiber Factor

The fiber fervor peaked in the mid-1980s, and today you're less likely to hear that roughage will make your life wonderful. Nonetheless, Americans eat too little fiber, and a high-fiber diet is nutritious.

Don't expect fiber to cure IBS, but it helps. The low-residue diet of the average meat-and-potatoes man or of the woman who watches calories (and avoids carbohydrates) produces too little stool for the normal colon to handle. A twitchy colon has even more trouble. Eating indigestible fiber gives the colon the satisfyingly large residue it expects. Remember that it's a huge organ—the diameter of your fist and 4 feet long. It needs the work.

Only plants contain fiber; you find it in fruits, vegetables, and grains (but not juices). Meat and dairy products

---

PEARL

If you know what your stool looks like, you have irritable bowel syndrome.

I discovered this rule, and it's a good one despite two limitations. Older people preoccupied with constipation don't qualify, and anyone violently ill looks closely into the toilet. With these exceptions, it's almost infallible. When patients below retirement age and in reasonable health give me a detailed description of the color, consistency, and contents of their stool, I know what I'm dealing with.

---

contain almost none. Cooking has little effect on fiber, so raw foods aren't better. I'm not going to tell you how much fiber to eat, because I disapprove of people who measure or count things in their food. But here's a rule that might prove helpful: You'll know you're eating enough fiber when your stool floats.

Once your diet contains enough fiber to keep your colon busy, abnormal muscle contractions won't produce so much distress. Constipation and diarrhea will improve; painful cramps will diminish. The effect of fiber on bloating is unpredictable. If bloating is accompanied by painful cramps, it should get better with increased fiber intake. If bloating is followed by gas and flatulence, increased fiber may make it worse. Fiber gives you gas.

Medications That Help

Some patients improve enough by increasing fiber intake that life becomes tolerable. I give antidepressants to the rest.

Most patients who get antidepressants aren't depressed, but the dose that helps irritable bowels isn't large enough to treat depression. No one is certain why antidepressants help, but low doses are useful for many ongoing pain disorders such as headaches and low back pain. They work on depression by altering nerve function in your brain, but similar nerves regulate muscle function elsewhere, so there may be some crossover.

Medical science has gone as far as we can go in the dietary treatment of IBS. I predict that drugs will take us to the next stage by acting on the brain and altering hormones in some beneficial way. Early research shows that gonadotropin-releasing hormone—which is made in the brain and regulates a woman's menstrual cycle—dramatically improves irritable bowel symptoms. Although the research is preliminary, the hormone looks hopeful.

The IUD

IUDs (intrauterine devices) are as old as barrier contraceptives. Arabs traditionally placed pebbles inside the uterus of female camels to prevent pregnancy during long journeys across the desert. Women in past eras inserted small pieces of wood, metal, pewter, or glass for contraception as well as abortion.

Modern IUDs existed for most of this century, but they remained obscure until the 1950s, when researchers grew interested in population control and developed a host of new contraceptives. Early IUD rings, bows, coils, springs, and loops resembled instruments of medieval torture and occasionally produced that effect when inserted. Later devices such as the Lippes loop were less uncomfortable, but all present the same tiresome problems. Any foreign object placed in the uterus acts as a contraceptive. Larger objects give better contraception but produce more cramps and bleeding. Smaller ones feel better but provide less protection.

Twenty years ago researchers began adding small amounts of medication to small IUDs and found that this practice vastly increased their protective power. The two medications used in current IUDs are copper (Cu-7, Tatum-T) and progesterone (Progestasert). Released inside the uterus, these medications aren't detectable in the blood.

Widely Used . . . for a Reason

Amazingly enough, IUDs are more popular throughout the world than the Pill.

Not only that, they protect against pregnancy as well as the Pill—and probably better. In theory, oral contraceptives give complete protection, but in actual use, medicated IUDs have a slightly lower pregnancy rate.

The side effects of IUDs are more tolerable than those of the Pill. Women given birth control pills are *more likely* to discontinue them after a year or two than those given an IUD.

If I make IUDs sound wonderful, let me assure you that I don't consider them more wonderful than pills or barriers— but not less wonderful, either. They have good points and bad points, but the bad points have been exaggerated.

My patients are certain that IUDs cause terrible pelvic infections and sterility. They remember the Dalkon shield, a disastrous IUD that caused serious problems and gave the rest a bad name. The truth is that FDA-approved IUDs create only a slightly increased risk of infection and perhaps no increase at all in women with a single sexual partner. Like the increased risk of blood clots from oral contraceptives and the increased chance of pregnancy with barrier contraceptives, these are genuine problems that you should be aware of. There is no such thing as a method that is absolutely safe.

The Only Choice

The best IUD is the Progestasert.

This choice is easy because it's the only one available in the United States. Copper IUDs are probably as good, but the Dalkon shield lawsuits frightened the manufacturers into withdrawing copper IUDs from the U.S. market. They are still widely used in Europe and Canada.

Low Back Pain

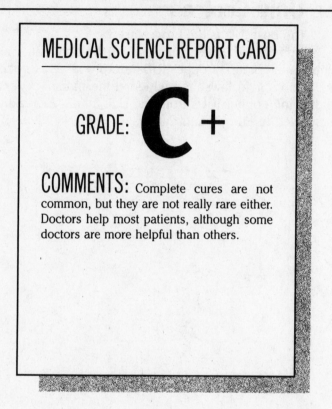

MEDICAL SCIENCE REPORT CARD

GRADE: **C**+

COMMENTS: Complete cures are not common, but they are not really rare either. Doctors help most patients, although some doctors are more helpful than others.

Eighty percent of us suffer a severe backache at least once during our lives. It's the leading cause of job absenteeism and disability. Some of this is avoidable. Before your doctor can help you get rid of back pain, however, he'll have to get a handle on what's causing it. There are several possibilities.

Cause: Strain

Walking upright is a balancing act. The upper body sits so symmetrically on the base of your spine that it takes little strength to hold it there. This is fortunate, because back muscles are too weak to do the job. They work nicely making the fine adjustments we need to change posture, but forcing them to carry weight is asking for trouble. So muscle strain is the leading cause of back pain in young people (and probably later, too).

When pain is especially bad, many people worry that they might have a slipped disk. Most parts of your body shrink or stiffen as you age, including the rubbery disks that cushion each vertebra. When stressed, a disk may break; it doesn't really slip. If a broken piece presses a nearby nerve, you suffer what is known as sciatica—named after the sciatic nerve. Sciatica is back pain that shoots down the leg. Surgery sometimes cures a slipped disk, so see an orthopedist when sciatica is intolerable; otherwise try treatments I discuss later.

Osteoporosis is much in the news lately; arthritis is hardly in the news at all. Both get too much blame for back pain, but they deserve some.

As we age, our bones tend to become gradually thinner and more fragile. This condition is osteoporosis, and *it's painless.* However, fragile bones break, and fractures hurt. When osteoporosis weakens a vertebra to the point where it can't support your body weight, the vertebra collapses. Called a compression fracture, this condition is painful, but it heals. That's why you can't blame a compression fracture for chronic back pain.

Old joints become worn and rough, so they hurt when they rub together. You have plenty of vertebral joints, so arthritis can cause low back pain. It's not certain how common this is because diagnosis is difficult. (A discussion appears in the chapter on arthritis.) I suspect that most low back pain in the elderly is simple muscle strain.

Don't mistake low back pain for a kidney infection, as so many of my patients do. Kidney infections make you ill, and kidney pain occurs in the midback, not lower down.

163

PEARL

In your quest to get at the cause of your pain, don't be too eager to have your back x-rayed. Most causes of back pain don't show up in the pictures.

When a radiologist looks at an x-ray and sees bones with rough edges, the report will mention arthritis. There is less there than meets the eye; it simply means "old bones." As we age our bones grow rougher, and an x-ray shows this. This happens to everyone, including people with no pain, so "arthritis" on an x-ray doesn't mean diseased bones any more than wrinkles on your skin mean skin disease.

Back x-rays can detect collapsed vertebrae, bone cancer, and congenital abnormalities, but they aren't useful for spotting simple muscle strain, a ruptured disk, or arthritis. They don't even detect osteoporosis until it's severe.

Getting Relief

The first treatment for low back pain, no matter what the cause, is rest, heat, and the passage of time. Over-the-counter ibuprofen (Advil, Nuprin, Medipren) relieves pain as well as anything doctors are likely to prescribe. Since 90 percent of backaches disappear within a few weeks no matter what the treatment, there's no urgency about seeing a doctor before then. Chronic or recurrent pain is another story.

The best treatment for chronic back pain is a concerned, friendly, persistent doctor. A good family doctor helps almost all chronic back pain provided he or she puts in the effort—and the patient does the same.

Expect a thorough examination and, although not necessarily on the first visit, x-rays. These are often normal even with chronic pain, but *sometimes* they make the diagnosis—especially if you have a compression fracture.

After the examination, the doctor should tell you why your back hurts and what to do. If your backache is caused by muscle strain, you should hear about proper posture and beds, the safe way to lift and sit, and an exercise program. If he reaches into a drawer and hands you a "back sheet" take it and say "thank you." But give a demerit if he doesn't go over the information item by item. These handouts contain excellent but general advice. They don't, for example, tell you how many of which exercises to do and how often. If your doctor doesn't plan an exercise program for you, ask for one.

Before leaving, *you should know your next appointment,* because the doctor will want to know how you're doing. Give another demerit if you don't get one, but go back in a month unless you're entirely better. As long as your doctor is trying (and you're following instructions), keep going back if the pain persists. A good family doctor makes life tolerable for almost everyone with chronic back pain and refers hardly anyone except those that may need surgery. At least, that's the way it should be.

In an ideal world, family doctors help most back pain. In real life, many run out of gas too early, but patients are too passive to nudge them. I'm amazed at how many people go through life with a miserable backache, seeing the doctor for a prescription renewal and a few reassuring words, but never undergo a thorough investigation to get at the real cause, followed by an aggressive trial of therapy.

PEARL

Low back pain is not one of medical science's triumphs. A minority of victims remain persistently unhappy, but don't assume you're among them until you give us a chance.

Can a Special Doctor Help?

As long as your doctor shows an interest, offers advice, and (most important) keeps giving return appointments, don't despair. *Specialists have no wonderful secrets* for dealing with common problems like this. Let your doctor give it his best shot. You'll get a referral if it doesn't work. Feel free to mention a referral if the doctor hasn't much to offer. Doctors who don't want to treat back pain jump at the chance to send you somewhere else.

Where will this referral take you? Traditionally to an orthopedist, a specialist in bones and joints. If you have a crippling ruptured disk, this is the surgeon who can remove it. If a ruptured disk is not your problem, ask for a referral to an orthopedist who has a particular interest in the *nonsurgical* treatment of back pain. Otherwise, he may have even less interest in helping you than a mediocre family doctor. (This advice will certainly outrage a few orthopedists leafing through this book, but it's true. Orthopedists are surgeons. Surgeons enjoy surgery—or if that's not possible, they prefer problems they can solve fairly quickly. If they didn't they wouldn't go into surgery.)

You might ask for a referral to a doctor of physical medicine (also called a physiatrist) if one is available.

Be careful! Don't confuse a physiatrist with a physical therapist. People do it all the time, and it's one of the few things that make physiatrists really upset. A doctor of physical

PEARL

If you have a common problem, go to a doctor who enjoys treating common problems—a family doctor. If you think you'll get better care for your sore throat from an ear, nose, and throat specialist than from a family doctor, think again. It'll be worse!

medicine is a genuine physician who has been to medical school, then served several years of residency training like other specialists.

Physical medicine means, literally, the treatment of disease by physical methods—heat, cold, water, electricity, or mechanical apparatus. If you know someone crippled by an accident or stroke, a doctor of physical medicine supervised the rehabilitation. He or she treats injured muscles, bones, and nerves, using medical science to aid whatever natural healing powers remain. Doctors of physical medicine produce few dramatic cures, but they enjoy what they do. They are patient and persistent, and they help almost everyone. Don't go if your back has hurt for a week or even a month. But when even the best family doctor throws in the towel, a doctor of physical medicine may have something to offer.

Lyme Disease

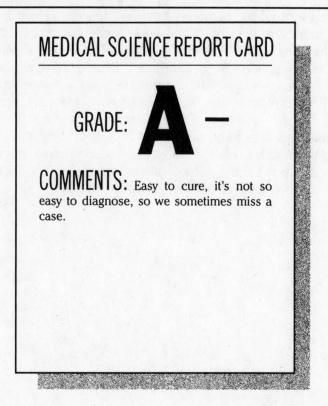

MEDICAL SCIENCE REPORT CARD

GRADE: **A −**

COMMENTS: Easy to cure, it's not so easy to diagnose, so we sometimes miss a case.

AIDS has broken all records for public hysteria for the excellent reason that (unlike past media diseases) it's a major public health problem. If not for AIDS, Lyme disease would be the media favorite. It's new, strange, and occasionally serious. A fair amount of nonsense has appeared in print, so several of my patients have already insisted on a test despite my assurance that Southern California is not a Lyme area.

An Old Disease

Like most new diseases, Lyme disease is not really new. Once doctors began looking, we found it everywhere in the world, but it may be a recent arrival in North America. The *Lyme* in Lyme disease is the suburban area around Lyme, Connecticut, where in 1975 pediatricians began seeing children with fever, rash, and multiple joint pains. Ordinary viral infections cause these symptoms, but only for a few days. These children were sicker than expected for a viral infection, although not sick enough to be hospitalized.

When doctors realized that their patients weren't recovering quickly, they scratched their heads and consulted their textbooks to find a diagnosis. Mostly they decided they were seeing juvenile rheumatoid arthritis. Common in adults, rheumatoid arthritis is rare before adolescence and harder to diagnose because blood tests that identify it are usually negative in children.

Each pediatrician in Lyme saw only a few cases, so they didn't realize what was happening, but a mother learning that her child has a serious disease doesn't keep the news to herself. Many were surprised to find other mothers with affected children—39 in all, plus a dozen adults with similar symptoms. Alarmed at the high incidence of a rare disease, the mothers called the Connecticut State Health Department. An investigation concluded that this disease was something new, and I began reading journal articles about "Lyme arthritis." As we learned about other symptoms, the name changed to Lyme disease.

Cause: Tick Bites

A tick that calls attention to itself rarely dies of old age, so most go about their business quietly. Less than a third of patients with Lyme disease even remember a bite.

The germ responsible is *fastidious*, a medical term meaning finicky and difficult to grow in the laboratory. So seven years passed before researchers proved that it was a member of the genus *Borrelia*—a mildly obscure group of corkscrew-shaped germs that cause diseases common in poor parts of the world but not in the United States.

Only a few species of tick carry Lyme disease and then only if they have lived on an infected wild animal. Furthermore, a tick goes about its business slowly, so removing it quickly will probably prevent transmission. The best way to get rid of a tick is to grab the head (never the swollen stomach) with tweezers close to the skin and pull steadily upward. Don't worry if some skin comes out at the same time, and don't be upset if a piece of the head remains in the skin. Wash the area with soap and water and leave it alone. See a doctor if the area grows red and painful or if a rash appears.

Lyme Signs

Three days to a month after the bite, the germs multiply enough to reveal themselves as a red dot around the bite area. This expands to a red blotch, often with a clearing center like a bull's-eye; sometimes the center becomes raw or covered with blisters. The redness is not painful or particularly itchy and fades in a few weeks.

Usually (but not always) the rash is accompanied by fatigue, headache, body aches, fever, and chills—symptoms no different from those of the flu. These also disappear in a week or two even without treatment.

Eighty percent of victims skip the next stage. Weeks to months after the first illness, 20 percent develop neurological symptoms such as meningitis (a frightening name, but mostly it means a bad headache), temporary paralysis of certain nerves such as those of one side of the face, numbness, and burning pains. Sometimes the germs damage nerves regulating the heart, causing irregular beats, palpitations, and dizziness. Once again, these symptoms generally last a few weeks.

About half of untreated patients develop arthritis one month to two years after the bite. Pain and swelling typically attack larger joints, most commonly the knees. If you have a swollen knee for no clear reason and live in an area with Lyme disease, remind your doctor. These symptoms last a few weeks but recur repeatedly for several years before disappearing. The most unlucky 10 percent continue to have recurrences and can suffer permanent joint damage.

Diagnosis Is Difficult

Treating Lyme disease is easy; making the diagnosis isn't. The rash is hard to miss when present, but it's faint one-third of the time. Other early symptoms are useless as a diagnostic aid, and no lab test helps during early stages. Detecting antibodies to Lyme disease proves that you have had it, but it takes at least a month for your body to generate them.

Fortunately there are things to go on besides symptoms. It's a summer disease, with 90 percent of cases appearing from June to September. A flulike illness during the winter is probably the flu. More important, many parts of the country don't have Lyme disease. Almost all cases occur in three areas: the northeastern coast (mostly New York, New Jersey, Connecticut, and Massachusetts), the upper Midwest (Minnesota and Wisconsin), and the Pacific Northwest (Northern California and Oregon). Although it is spreading, Lyme disease remains rare except in the Northeast; your doctor should know when it becomes significant in your area.

The best treatment for Lyme disease, once you have a diagnosis, is the antibiotic doxycycline.

A three-week course of several common antibiotics works fine in the first stage and fairly well in the second stage, but it cures only half the cases that go on to arthritis.

Menopause

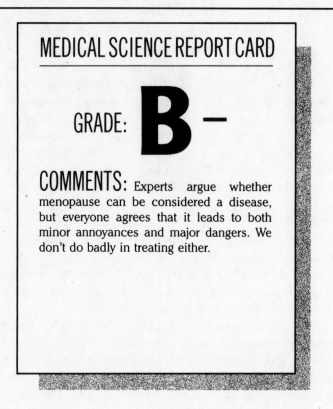

MEDICAL SCIENCE REPORT CARD

GRADE: **B –**

COMMENTS: Experts argue whether menopause can be considered a disease, but everyone agrees that it leads to both minor annoyances and major dangers. We don't do badly in treating either.

Menopause means the end of menses. Most women experience this between age 50 and 52, although it can occur from the early forties to midfifties. Better nutrition in the twentieth century has reduced by several years the average age that girls begin menstruating. It has also delayed the onset of menopause. Before 1900 women generally experienced it three to four years earlier.

What Happens

Menopause occurs when the body produces too little estrogen to create the uterine lining that must be shed every month.

Around age 35 a woman's ovarian estrogen production begins a slow decline that continues well past retirement age. Menopause occurs at some unpredictable point during this time frame. For several years before, periods may become erratic, so doctors wait until a woman past 45 has had none for over six months before pronouncing her postmenopausal. Remember this rule, because *bleeding after menopause is always abnormal* (unless you're taking estrogens) and should always be brought to the attention of a doctor.

Hot Flushes

No particular symptom accompanies the exact moment of menopause. Some unpleasant symptoms, such as hot flushes, may occur even before. Most take time to develop.

The typical hot flush follows this pattern: a sudden reddening over the head, neck, and chest followed by intense body heat and concluded by profuse sweating. Most women experience them for a year or two, but a minority must endure this distressing symptom for more than five years. Associated with a surge of pituitary hormones, a flush is accompanied by a jump in skin temperature and cooling deep inside the body. We can measure this physical effect, although we're not sure why it happens.

Bone Loss

Osteoporosis is the most serious consequence of declining hormone production. To a certain extent, osteoporosis is another tiresome consequence of aging. Both sexes slowly lose calcium from their bones, beginning around age 35. After a few decades, bones become fragile, fracturing after a fall that would merely bruise a younger person. In advanced cases, bone simply collapses from normal stress. This is why old

PEARL

Only 20 years ago, a wise old professor assured my medical school class that symptoms never accompany a drop in estrogens. When patients complain, he added, we should search for physical illness or emotional stress. Asked for proof, he cited underdeveloped countries and primitive tribes. Primitive women, he explained, zip through menopause, grow old, and die without a peep about hot flushes, insomnia, depression, or other fashionable complaints. We understood his point—that modern, indolent, overfed women had too much time to brood about advancing age and worry about loss of their "femininity."

Nowadays we know that primitive men don't pay much attention to primitive old women, so no one knows what bothers them. Primitive cultures with their high-fiber diets, active lifestyle, and lack of stress are wonderfully flexible examples of healthful living; no matter what the current health fashion may be, no one will contradict you if you cite them.

women suffer compression fractures of the vertebrae and literally shrink in height.

Bone loss happens faster in women, especially in the ten years after menopause. Old women suffer more fractures than old men partly because female bones are smaller to begin with and partly because women get less exercise and eat less calcium when young, so their bones are already less dense when osteoporosis begins. But mostly women lose bone because their estrogen level drops following menopause. White women suffer more bone loss than black women for unclear reasons (they may have smaller bones, but a racial difference in bone loss rates definitely exists). Cigarette smokers lose bone faster than nonsmokers.

One in three women fractures a hip if she lives long enough. This is a catastrophic event—worse than a heart attack. One-third of women who break a hip are dead in a year. Most of the rest remain disabled. One in three women also fractures a vertebra after age 65—not so disabling but very painful.

Other Effects of Menopause

Long-term lack of estrogen also shrinks and thins the tissues that depend on it—mostly the vulva and vagina. As a result a woman may experience itching, pain during sex, and painful urination. Popular mythology to the contrary, estrogen deficiency does not cause redistribution of your fat, loss of muscle tone, sagging breasts, or wrinkles.

My gynecology texts published as late as 1977 state firmly that psychological problems (not menopause) produce insomnia, fatigue, headaches, inability to concentrate, anxiety, and depression. My 1990 text treats the subject with more caution, and so do most doctors today. Studies are hard to interpret because getting rid of hot flushes with estrogens is easy, and every woman feels better without them. Giving estrogens may also produce a vague tonic effect and improve memory.

The Best Treatment: Estrogens

For decades a health-conscious woman going through menopause endured hot flushes and uncomfortable sex in the belief that estrogens did more harm than good. The reluctance to take estrogens seemed reasonable at the time. Her doctor probably warned her of the cancer risk. Since oral contraceptives caused blood clots, experts cautioned, estrogens given to treat symptoms of menopause might do the same. Not only that, men given estrogens to treat prostate cancer suffered a dramatic increase in heart attacks; the doses were larger than a woman would have to take, but this was ominous news.

Beginning a decade ago, experts began changing their minds. The massive death and disability toll of osteoporosis exerted a major influence—especially after studies showed that women given estrogens had far fewer fractures. The worry about blood clots and heart disease was laid to rest when studies showed that *women* on estrogens had fewer, not more, heart attacks.

Estrogen users definitely have more uterine cancer. While easy to diagnose and treat early, it's an obvious draw-back. The good news is that experts now believe that the risk is eliminated by giving progesterone for part of each cycle. There is no evidence that hormones increase the risk of other types of cancer.

Risk versus Benefits

Today most doctors, myself included, believe that the benefits of estrogen outweigh the risks.

The major benefits of estrogen therapy include *fewer broken bones* and *fewer heart attacks.*

The chance of a woman not on estrogens dying of a hip fracture is 1 in 60; the chance of a woman on estrogens dying of uterine cancer is 1 in 20,000. Only estrogens slow

---

PEARL

Don't hold your breath waiting for doctors to an-nounce that the cancer risk from estrogen therapy is zero. Scientists can never prove the negative, e.g., they can never prove that bananas do not cause cancer.

---

osteoporosis and reduce fractures. Getting plenty of exercise may help; taking extra calcium (by itself) doesn't help.

In the area of heart attack reduction, new research has produced such spectacular results that doctors are reluctant to believe them. For example, in a recent study, 2,300 women receiving estrogen had one-third the deaths from cardiovascular disease than a similar group of women not receiving the therapy. Since cardiovascular disease is by far the leading killer of women, these results could represent a revolutionary development.

Estrogens greatly slow bone loss, but they never make bone stronger. Since the fastest loss occurs in the decade after menopause, I advise treatment as soon as menopause takes place. When you stop taking estrogens, osteoporosis makes up for lost time, so you should probably continue indefinitely.

Menstrual Cramps

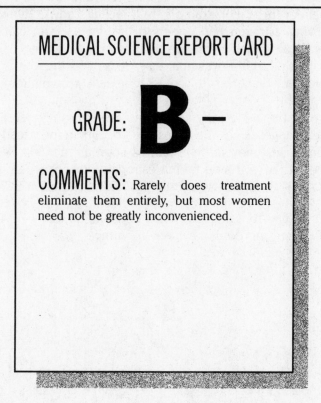

MEDICAL SCIENCE REPORT CARD

GRADE: **B −**

COMMENTS: Rarely does treatment eliminate them entirely, but most women need not be greatly inconvenienced.

By *menstrual cramps* I mean the aching low abdominal pain often radiating to the back and thighs that periodically affects most women from their midteens until menopause. Pain usually begins a few hours before bleeding and diminishes by the second day of full flow. Consider it menstrual cramps if it's your usual monthly pain; new or different pain or any pain that gets worse over several months is something else and worth a trip to the doctor.

Why Cramps?

Despite the association of cramps with bleeding, they are not related.

You can have little or no bleeding but severe cramps, and vice versa. However, you can't have cramps without ovulation.

When a girl menstruates for the first time, it should be painless.

Called menarche, this first period occurs around age 13. The appearance of periods merely means that a girl's estrogen and progesterone levels have increased enough to produce an adult uterine lining that must be shed now and then. Her cycle hasn't matured enough to enable her ovaries to eject a monthly egg. Ovulation begins a year or two after menarche, so a girl may begin feeling monthly discomfort around age 15 (and, as some consolation, notice that her periods are more regular). When cramps and bleeding begin *simultaneously* in a young girl, it suggests a structural problem such as a tight cervix that prevents blood from escaping. Menstrual discomfort at an early age should be mentioned to the doctor.

Who Cramps?

Who suffers pain and discomfort during menstruation, and who doesn't?

- Overweight women suffer more, athletes less.
- Women with regular periods suffer more than those who are irregular.
- Women who flow less than three days have less pain than those who flow longer.
- Women whose mothers suffered badly *don't* have more cramps than average. This myth dates from the old days when doctors believed that menstrual problems were mostly psychological. Now that we can explain them and provide good treatment, we've changed our minds about your mother's influence.

Cause of Cramps

The ovaries' production of the hormone progesterone following ovulation stimulates the uterus to produce prostaglandins, a family of hormonelike substances with a variety of actions, many of which have pain as a side effect. In the uterus, prostaglandins force muscles to contract and blood vessels to constrict, actions that cut off the blood supply to the uterine lining so that it dies and sheds every month. Vigorous prostaglandin activity is painful.

This excellent theory seems to explain why most women suffer cramps, and it certainly explains why certain kinds of medication provide relief.

The Best Treatment: Prostaglandin Inhibitors

Most common pain remedies inhibit the body's production of prostaglandins. A fairly good inhibitor, aspirin was the best treatment in the past (grade: C). Acetaminophen (Tylenol, paracetamol, Anacin-3) has no inhibitory action and doesn't help.

The introduction of ibuprofen (Motrin, Rufen, Advil, Nuprin, Medipren) in the 1970s represented a major advance. It inhibits prostaglandins more efficiently than aspirin and is now the mainstay of therapy. Others of the same class (nonsteroidal anti-inflammatory drugs or NSAIDs), such as Naprosyn, Anaprox, Feldene, Clinoril, and Tolectin, cost more but work equally well. They're worth a try if ibuprofen doesn't help.

Scoring 80 percent on a test earns you a "B −" in most schools, and that's how well the NSAIDs perform. Twenty percent of women aren't satisfied. To them I offer birth control pills. Suppressing ovulation prevents the prostaglandin surge entirely, so the Pill works better than NSAIDs, but it's too much drug for a problem present only a few days per month. Try NSAIDs first.

Mental Illness

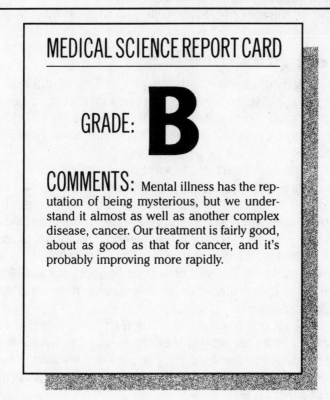

MEDICAL SCIENCE REPORT CARD

GRADE: **B**

COMMENTS: Mental illness has the reputation of being mysterious, but we understand it almost as well as another complex disease, cancer. Our treatment is fairly good, about as good as that for cancer, and it's probably improving more rapidly.

Mental illness is caused by brain disease, an actual physical abnormality. When lungs are diseased, you cough or gasp for breath; diseased joints also hurt; and when nerves that control your mental processes are diseased, you hurt just as intensely. Having mentally ill relatives increases the risk of mental illness, so heredity is as strong an influence as with many physical diseases.

This view of mental illness is not a personal observation or wisdom drawn from years of clinical practice, but the truth.

Studies of the brain in the mentally ill turn up real abnormalities. And treatment can correct those abnormalities. Psychotherapy remains important, but the great advances in treating mental illness over the past generation have come from our ability to correct brain malfunctioning, mostly with drugs.

Brain Abnormalities

Depending on the brain process that's affected, you may suffer a disease of mood (depression, mania), a disabling anxiety (panic, obsessive-compulsive behavior), an addiction problem (alcoholism), or overall disorganization (schizophrenia).

Although most doctors are now treating mental illness as a disorder of the brain, you don't often hear mental illness described as brain disease. Faced with a deep human belief, the truth does not often prevail. We smile on hearing that other cultures believe evil spirits or demonic possession causes mental illness. We are more scientific; we believe that stress is responsible, or that an unhappy childhood, intolerable marriage, or difficult life leads to a breakdown or other severe psychiatric illness.

I look on stress as the modern equivalent of evil spirits: the belief in an all-pervasive badness that threatens everyone and overwhelms some of us. People who no longer believe that severe stress causes strokes or heart attacks still think it leads to mental illness.

Being unhappy is definitely not healthy. But when I say that "stress makes everything worse but doesn't cause anything," it applies to mental as well as physical disease.

Some experts theorize that a stressful environment—divorced parents—or a catastrophic event—loss of a spouse or job—triggers psychiatric illness in someone already susceptible. In studies, patients usually recall a significant negative life event that preceded their psychiatric illness. I don't know how much of this theory to believe, because my patients are all convinced that something significant preceded almost any physical illness: They see an argument with a wife hours before a heart attack or a dash through the rain two days before pneumonia as significant. People who suffer a catastrophe of any kind look for a cause and usually find one.

The Value of Psychotherapy

Besides medications, which vary depending on the disorder, the best treatment for mental illness is education.

By *education* I mean psychotherapy. I say "education" to impress on you the trivial difference between how a good doctor talks to patients with physical versus psychological illness. When I discuss a low-cholesterol or low-calorie diet, patients know that they must leave my office and apply this information (most fail, but they try).

When I use psychotherapy, my techniques aren't much different. As an example, let's consider a patient with a panic disorder who is frightened of crowds. I always ask the patient to tell me the worst thing that would happen if she went into a crowd. Almost always, the answer is that she doesn't know; she's just afraid. Eventually I'll persuade her to mention some possibilities. She might say that people will laugh or touch her. After talking we both agree that this is very unlikely. I have taught this patient something she didn't know, at least not consciously: Nothing awful will happen if she goes into a crowd. But now, just as with the problem of cutting back on cholesterol, she must apply what I've taught her. Patients with mild panic disorders may succeed in facing that crowd unaided; others require drugs. Panic disorder, like other mental illness, is a real physical disease and sometimes requires physical treatment in the form of drugs. (In fact, drugs work better in panic disorder than in high cholesterol, and for treating obesity, drugs are almost useless.)

What I'm saying is that psychotherapy works, but *it doesn't make life easier!*

A good therapist (meaning any good doctor) teaches you about yourself, shows how your behavior causes you unnecessary pain, and gives you a more accurate picture of reality (e.g., strangers won't laugh at you; friends won't hate you if you refuse to do them favors). But once the door shuts after a session, all the things that make you nervous are just

183

as nerve-wracking. That's why psychotherapy has a bad reputation and why some people seem to spend their lives on the couch. They are waiting for the therapist to make life easier. But all he or she can do is teach that frightening actions (talking to the opposite sex, dealing with a boss, going into crowds) won't produce a catastrophe. The patient must decide to take the action, and it's still frightening.

Psychotherapy alone works fine for mild emotional problems, but serious mental illness requires more. Mental illness is not a sign of weakness any more than a heart attack is. Will power won't control overwhelming feelings or thoughts. Mental illness is as painful and disabling as cancer or arthritis; if you and your doctor don't look on it as a real disease, you won't get the best treatment.

Migraine Headache

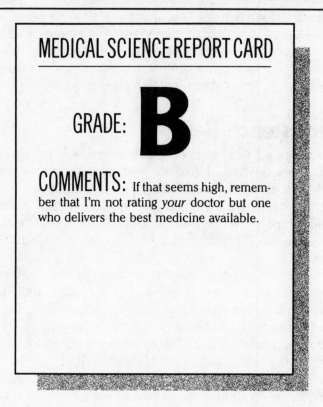

MEDICAL SCIENCE REPORT CARD

GRADE: **B**

COMMENTS: If that seems high, remember that I'm not rating *your* doctor but one who delivers the best medicine available.

Ten million Americans have migraine; most are women and almost all began suffering in their teens or twenties. Almost all are suffering too much because the average doctor doesn't take advantage of the best treatment. Mostly this is the doctor's fault. We love solving problems on a single visit, but we can hardly ever do that with migraine. Like psoriasis, low back pain, and high blood pressure, migraine requires long-term effort. Doctors can help almost everyone, provided they're persistent and insist on seeing the patient again and again.

Working in hotels and walk-in clinics, I see innumerable migraine sufferers who are receiving adequate treatment. Now and then these people visit their doctor, complain of their headaches, and receive a good treatment plus the advice to return if it doesn't help. This approach is bad because follow-up treatment is especially important in migraine.

If you have migraine that's not well controlled, you *must* leave the doctor's office knowing the exact date of your next appointment. If you don't, something is wrong.

Persistence Helps

When I treat someone with migraine who has at least one attack a week, I like to give appointments every two months. It may take half a dozen visits before the patient agrees that her symptoms are tolerable (the patient, not the doctor, decides this). Then I see the patient every year because a certain number experience a slow return of migraine symptoms.

Some assertive patients quickly let the doctor know when treatment stops working, but most are unwilling to bother him until a headache becomes unbearable. This state of affairs invariably occurs at night or during a weekend, so they see an unfamiliar doctor in an emergency room or walk-in clinic. By morning the pain is gone, so it seems less urgent to inform the family doctor. Almost all migraine can be helped a good deal, but either the doctor or the patient must make a continuing effort.

What's a Migraine?

No one knows exactly what causes migraine, so we can't blame stress. Although stress can trigger migraine, a lot of people under stress *don't* get them. Many experts say migraine affects certain personality types—neat, compulsive people who are preoccupied with detail. I don't believe this.

Stress makes everything worse, but it doesn't cause anything. As for personality types, sickness affects your personality, not vice versa.

We do know what happens during an attack. Migraine is classified as a vascular headache, meaning that blood vessels cause the pain. During a migraine, certain arteries in the head become exquisitely tender, and each heartbeat stretches their walls, aggravating the pain. That's why a migraine throbs. Usually only a single artery hurts, so a typical attack affects one side of the head. The temporal artery is probably the most common culprit. It runs up the side of the head, and you can feel its pulse about an inch in front of your ear.

While a throbbing, one-sided headache describes a typical migraine, "typical" symptoms are no more common than in any other disorder. Bilateral migraines occur. Throbbing pain occurs at the onset, but after a few hours scalp muscles join in the general misery, so a generalized, steady ache may take over.

I haven't mentioned the dramatic flashing lights or other visual excitement that sometimes precedes a migraine. That's because it's so rare; only 10 to 15 percent of people with migraines experience these.

Nausea and vomiting as well as light intolerance accompany a typical attack, but sometimes these symptoms are missing. They can accompany *any* severe headache.

The Best Treatment

An artery in the throes of migraine is abnormally relaxed and flabby, so that each heartbeat makes it balloon out agonizingly. If you can stiffen the walls of the artery so that it doesn't respond to the heartbeat in an inappropriate way, pain will diminish.

In the end the best treatment for migraine is drugs. Artery-stiffening drugs have been around for centuries.

Caffeine Can Help

The oldest artery-stiffening drug is a natural remedy, if you can consider caffeine in this light. You're probably familiar with the headache it causes rather than the one it helps. They're related. Caffeine stiffens blood vessels, so that if you're a heavy coffee drinker and skip a cup, your chronically stiff blood vessels relax abnormally, and you feel an annoying, throbbing vascular headache that disappears like magic with more coffee. Caffeine also helps vascular headaches that aren't caused by caffeine withdrawal. It doesn't do much for a full-blown migraine, but I urge patients to try a few cups of coffee to relieve lesser migraine.

Take Ergots Early on

Ergotamine, the mainstay of good migraine therapy, works very well if used properly, and not so well otherwise. Unfortunately, improper use is too frequent.

Another natural product, ergots have been known for thousands of years—but only as a poison. They are derived from a fungus that grows on rye, and throughout history have caused mysterious symptoms that have only recently been explained. Too much artery stiffening shuts off blood flow, so one symptom of ergotism is burning pain in an arm or a leg. In the Middle Ages this peculiar pain was called Saint Anthony's Fire. Only in 1920 did chemists isolate ergotamine from the fungus. Doctors soon discovered its usefulness in treating migraine.

Ergotamine is combined with caffeine in the most popular migraine remedy, Cafergot. The proper dose is two pills at the first hint of an attack and two more every half hour until six are taken. Using it like aspirin (two every 4 hours) doesn't work as well. You must get the ergot into your body quickly, in an adequate dose, and before the migraine is full-blown. Cafergot is also available by suppository. The rectal route is not better, but it is useful if the drug makes you nauseous.

Plain ergotamine works faster when delivered by an inhaler or in a pill dissolved under the tongue. Take one puff or one pill every 5 minutes to a maximum of six. Although you're supposed to start using the drug at the first hint of a migraine, ergotamine also works after the headache is under way, but much more slowly. It may take 5 or 6 hours. Only an injection works quickly, perhaps within 15 minutes. Doctors don't inject ergotamine very often because they are accustomed to Demerol or morphine, which work as well.

If, like too many migraine victims, you have no doctor to call when a headache strikes, you find yourself in a clinic or emergency room under the suspicious eye of a doctor who wonders if you're a drug abuser. Under the circumstances, even if that doctor does decide to give you a narcotic, he's likely to give too little. Ask for ergotamine.

When patients tell me that ergotamine doesn't work for their migraine, I generally find that they don't really have migraine. When they tell me that the medication makes them violently ill, I take them seriously. Ergots have powerful side effects, especially on the digestive tract, but both doctors and patients tend to give up on them too quickly. By adding anti-nausea drugs and changing the means of administration (rectal to inhaler to under the tongue) most patients find a route that's tolerable. You may have to endure some stomach upset in exchange for stopping the headache.

If you have migraine and you're getting a pain medication (Tylenol with codeine, Empirin, Darvon, Fiorinal), either you don't have migraine or you're not getting the best treatment. While fairly good for tension headaches, *pain medication is bad therapy for migraine!*

Prevention of Migraine

When migraines occur often, perhaps once a week despite the best treatment, you and your doctor should think about adding a different class of medication to prevent the headaches before they occur.

The decision is up to you. If migraines are becoming tiresome, you may decide it's worthwhile to take a drug every day to reduce their frequency—and you *must* take these preventive drugs every day.

You already know that drugs to treat migraine pain tighten the arteries. Drugs that help prevent migraine seem to make the arteries less sensitive to whatever it is that makes them relax and pulsate in the first place. There are literally dozens of different prophylactic medications!

- Three different classes of drugs usually used to treat high blood pressure (they have less effect on the pressure of those who don't have high blood pressure, and they help desensitize arteries)

189

- Low-dose antidepressants (good for many sorts of chronic pain)
- Nonsteroidal anti-inflammatories (the same medications used for arthritis and menstrual cramps)
- Low-dose ergotamine combinations
- Certain antihistamines (Periactin)
- Drugs that block certain nerve transmitters (methysergide, monamine oxidase inhibitors)

You need to realize how many drugs there are, because it's essential for you and your doctor to *keep trying!* It may take months or even years (at two months per drug) to find one that works for you. Don't give up! Don't let your doctor give up!

Biofeedback Basics

So many best treatments in this book are drugs, that I'm sure I will be criticized for neglecting natural methods. *Natural* usually means commonsense, traditional, or vegetable. Healers have used them for thousands of years; occasionally they work, but rarely as well as drugs and other "unnatural" methods developed over the past century.

Biofeedback has a reputation as a natural therapy. Although touted as a cure for everything from high blood pressure to warts, it isn't. But you may be surprised to learn that it is an accepted treatment for chronic headaches. Training sessions teach patients to relax muscle groups or blood vessels—something usually beyond conscious control. Provided trainees are carefully selected, most have fewer and less severe headaches. Ask your doctor if biofeedback training is appropriate for you.

Despite the fact that it's a natural method (i.e., without drugs) don't assume that biofeedback is cheaper, easier, or more effective. It's not (grade: C). Sessions are not cheap. Trainees must have the discipline to concentrate intensely and practice every day. Most successful patients still need some medication. Nevertheless, biofeedback can be genuine help for both migraine and tension headaches.

Muscle Aches (Fibromyalgia)

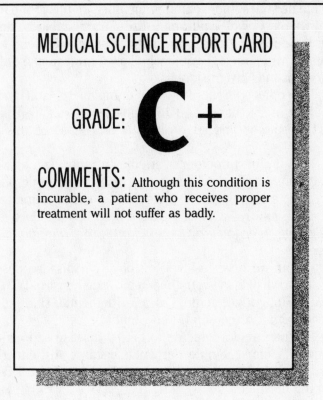

MEDICAL SCIENCE REPORT CARD

GRADE: **C+**

COMMENTS: Although this condition is incurable, a patient who receives proper treatment will not suffer as badly.

Fibromyalgia is not a sexy disorder; you won't read about it in magazines, and I don't recall a book on the subject. I suspect that most readers, including those who have fibromyalgia, know nothing about it. Unfortunately, this is also true of many doctors, but one should expect this ignorance of any malady with no laboratory or x-ray abnormality, which strikes mostly women. It is the most common disorder seen by rheumatologists. Eighty percent of those who have it are women.

Cause: Sensitive Muscles

Fibromyalgia belongs to a group of "twitchy" disorders, in which parts of the body react too vigorously to stress or even to normal stimuli. Familiar members of this group include the irritable bowel syndrome, insomnia, migraines, and tension headaches. Victims of one twitchy disorder tend to have others. This is true of people who have fibromyalgia, only their major miseries are muscular.

People with fibromyalgia complain of stiff and sore shoulder, neck, back, and hip muscles. Almost all patients don't sleep well and suffer chronic fatigue. Does this sound familiar?

In the past doctors referred to fibromyalgia as psychogenic rheumatism (i.e., aches and pains in neurotic people).

Here's a medical secret: Having a vivid name for your disease is always a plus. Doctors perk up at adjectives like *malignant, infectious, acute, virulent, toxic, fulminant,* or *venereal.*

You are never as well off having a disease described with a word like *tension* (headache, premenstrual), *psychogenic* (pain, cough, itching), *senile* (dementia, skin growths), or *degeneration* (cerebral, bony, retinal).

When doctors decide to take a disease seriously, they change its name. Senile dementia became Alzheimer's disease; hysteria became conversion disorder; moron became learning disabled.

During the 1970s researchers into psychogenic rheumatism detected two abnormalities that turned up again and again.

The first was tender points at specific sites in the body—including points on the neck, shoulders, hips, elbows, and knees. Patients don't notice these points until a doctor feels them during an exam. The diagnosis is certain when more than ten are present.

The second was nonrestorative sleep in over 75 percent of cases. People with fibromyalgia sleep through the night but wake up unrefreshed and tired. Researchers measuring their brain waves during sleep find a particular type of disruption in their pattern. Knowing that a distinct brain wave abnormality exists helped convince doctors that fibromyalgia is real.

Getting a Diagnosis

The best treatment is exercise and antidepressants, but you won't get either unless your doctor knows that fibromyalgia exists.

You'll be surprised to learn that a doctor doesn't have to understand many ailments in order to treat them. (A hundred causes exist for a cough and a sore throat. With an effort we could find each one, but we rarely try because it wouldn't affect what we do.)

Doctors have no shortage of tired female patients with aches and pains, and our treatment as a whole rates a solid "D." Prescribing the usual anti-inflammatory drugs (Motrin, Naprosyn, etc.) helps fibromyalgia only marginally because its pains are from muscle spasm, not inflammation. Tranquilizers and sleeping pills only make nonrestorative sleep worse. Finally, if you hear that your symptoms are the result of "stress" and that reducing stress will help, you are hearing a doctor who has nothing to offer.

If you think your doctor has missed the boat, show him this chapter, but don't expect too much. Doctors rarely appreciate patients who announce their diagnoses, because they're usually wrong. However, now and then one of my patients comes in with a brilliant idea. So if the symptoms of fibromyalgia match what you've been experiencing, go ahead and show this chapter to your doctor. Give the doctor half a dozen chances to help. Then if you still aren't getting any relief, see a rheumatologist. Proper treatment doesn't require a specialist, but it does require someone who has at least heard of the disorder.

Exercise for Pain Relief

Athletes and women in physically demanding jobs don't complain to me of chronic fatigue with or without aches, so I feel strongly that flabby muscles trigger fibromyalgia. Patients who exercise have less pain and sleep better.

Beware of experts who tell you that exercise is fun. Many healthful activities are not fun; regular, repetitious exercise is one of them. I jog half an hour five days a week to keep fit, but I find it not quite as entertaining as shaving—and I gave that up in 1977. More organized activity such as aerobic exercises to music is fun at first, but this still requires four or five sessions a week, and the dropout rate is high. On the other hand, sports are certainly fun. Confining them to weekends won't put you in condition, but if you can play something vigorous like tennis, racquetball, or basketball more frequently, that's excellent. However, this requires organization and the cooperation of friends, which is hard to sustain.

Nowadays I always explain to patients that exercise is work. The continuing benefits are wonderful, but earning them requires stubborn persistence.

Patients with aches and pains ask about massage, chiropractic manipulation, acupressure, and acupuncture. I answer that they work fine, but relief is always temporary. You must have these treatments forever. Exercise is better. Besides relieving pain, it lowers the risk of heart attacks and prevents osteoporosis, and it's cheaper. But it's also (except for acupuncture) much less enjoyable.

Medications That Help

Antidepressants help the sleep disturbance of fibromyalgia better than any other class of drug, but no one knows why. Since the dose is only ⅕ to ⅒ of that used to treat depression, the benefit has nothing to do with improving your mood. As it happens, low-dose antidepressants work well in a host of difficult maladies that include chronic pain, insomnia, and muscle spasm among their symptoms.

Amitriptyline (Elavil, Endep) and imipramine (Tofranil, Janimine) are the most common antidepressants, but a dozen others work as well. Even at low doses, side effects are annoying, especially drowsiness and a dry mouth. Different members of this class of drugs affect patients differently, so try several before you decide if they will be of any help to you.

Obesity

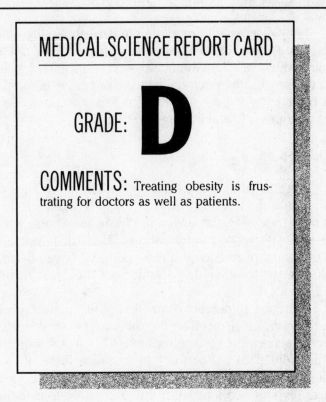

MEDICAL SCIENCE REPORT CARD

GRADE: **D**

COMMENTS: Treating obesity is frustrating for doctors as well as patients.

A few months after finishing internship, I worked for a "diet doctor." Calling him this is an exaggeration because he was basically a general practitioner who used a great many gimmicks to increase his income.

It's not easy to get rich practicing good medicine. On the fringes, a plastic surgeon specializing in cosmetic procedures or an orthopedist with a thriving sports medicine clinic earns well over half a million a year, although he or she must work hard. An ordinary surgeon who doesn't specialize in lucrative cases can easily make several hundred thousand—again by working hard. But no amount of work enables a family doctor to match this income unless he has a gimmick: something to bring in large numbers of patients who *don't* see the doctor.

Any disease that requires regular trips to the office for tests, counseling, or injections—anything done by office staff earning much less than the doctor—can be a gimmick. Almost all fad diseases that doctors like me disapprove of require this sort of care: hypoglycemia, Epstein-Barr infections, Candida, food allergies, clinical ecology problems.

Fat Wallets

Weight control is a major gimmick in which a doctor can make a great deal of money for little work. Let me add that many doctors specializing in obesity aren't quacks. There even exists a specialty organization of bariatric physicians that strikes me as professional and scientific. I have no great objection to patients seeing such doctors, but their results are not superior.

Perhaps 10 percent of my first boss's patients came for weight control. All received diet pills and a weekly injection of human chorionic gonadotrophin (HCG), a hormone popular in the early 1970s because it "melted away fat." (HCG is still available, but it doesn't work anymore; all miracle diets and diet drugs stop working after the books that tout them stop selling.) Except for a quick monthly chat with the doctor, the patient normally saw only the "nurse" (actually a clerk) who handled the weekly shots, weighing, and exhortations about sticking to the diet.

The program worked brilliantly the first month. Almost everyone lost 10 to 20 pounds. Naturally, patients were thrilled. Then the diet pills lost their effect, and hunger returned. Some patients lost a bit more weight, but almost no one continued losing after a few months. To my amazement, patients kept returning. Many continued weekly visits for six months or a year with no results or even while experiencing a climbing weight. Some dropped out only to return later. That first month was a powerful draw.

Rules for Weight Loss

Later, in a legitimate clinic, I worked very hard with obese patients but never used pills or hormones. I photocopied diets, menus, exercise programs, and health tips and passed them out liberally. I held counseling sessions and lectures. Patients filled out diet diaries and counted how many times they chewed. During an attempt at behavior modification, they ate in the same spot with the same utensils at the same time every day.

Compared with the diet doctor, my patients spent less money and lost just as much weight. They did not, however, lose more. My program worked fine the first month, not so well after, and mostly not at all after six months. I recall only a few patients who went from fat to thin—all were men who had had a heart attack.

Long experience has led to Oppenheim's rules of weight loss:

- Losing up to 20 pounds is easy. Everyone loses quickly when they cut their calorie intake. Most people can tolerate a few weeks of hunger as the pounds melt away; if not, diet pills work fine at curbing the appetite. Never spend money to lose the first 20 pounds.

- Losing more than 20 pounds is hard. The body takes a month or two to adjust to a decreased calorie intake. Then it stubbornly resists more loss.

- Keeping weight off is even harder. Patients deceive themselves with the fantasy that if they could only reach their weight goal, their happiness would sustain them. This doesn't happen. Almost everyone who loses weight regains it. Only about 5 percent don't. These few have undergone the same profound internal change of heart that enables another minority to swear off alcohol or hard drugs.

Blame Nature

Nature *wants* you to be fat. For most of our existence humans have been hunters (or scavengers of the kills of other hunters). And hunting animals have to be gluttons.

Prehistoric men might spend days searching for food. During this time they starved. Once the kill was made, they had to compete with other interested predators and deal with the lack of a way to preserve food. It was crucial to eat as much as possible as fast as possible. Those who gobbled best had the best chance of surviving until the next kill. For thousands of generations, humans did their best to get fat. They rarely succeeded because there was too little food and it took too much exertion to get it, but they tried.

Today we don't risk starvation between meals, so overeating is no longer a useful trait, but our bodies are still geared for it. We don't drink when we're not thirsty, but eating when we're not hungry is perfectly natural. When we go on a diet, our brain insists on sending hunger signals even when our intake is adequate. Evolution is slow. It hasn't caught on that we don't need to gobble extra food and store it away in the form of fat.

Join a Support Group

The best treatment for obesity is joining Weight Watchers and similar groups.

I'm cheating in recommending these groups, because they aren't really a medical treatment, but doctors' counseling, educational groups, and diet booklets have a poor record (except, of course, for the first 20 pounds). Organizations like Weight Watchers earn a "C"—not terrific but an improvement over what you can expect from the doctor.

Look for a self-help group with two qualities: (1) It charges nothing or an amount you can afford indefinitely, and (2) you can belong *forever!*

These weight-loss groups are not much different from Alcoholics Anonymous—a gathering of people suffering a chronic problem, which great effort can control but never cure.

Dieters should never expect to lose their craving for food. They should associate with other dieters to provide mutual support and encouragement or simply to find others who want to talk about what will always be a subject of intense interest.

Drying out (i.e., locking an alcoholic away from drink for a month or two) never works. It's equally true that dieting doesn't work. No matter how much you lose after a few months on a diet, your problem isn't solved. People who stay thin understand that they're on a diet for the rest of their lives. Most people can't accept this bleak view, but most obese people never get thin and stay thin. Only 5 to 10 percent of those who join a good diet group succeed; Alcoholics Anonymous has a similar success rate.

Five to 10 percent of all fat people is a lot of people, so many do succeed, but it's hard. I wish I could write something more optimistic. An author can retire after one successful diet book, but I doubt if Doctor Oppenheim's program would play well on the late-night talk shows.

Painful Testicle

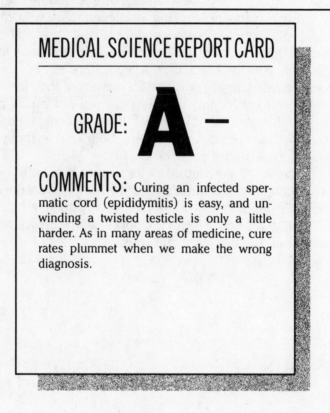

MEDICAL SCIENCE REPORT CARD

GRADE: **A –**

COMMENTS: Curing an infected spermatic cord (epididymitis) is easy, and unwinding a twisted testicle is only a little harder. As in many areas of medicine, cure rates plummet when we make the wrong diagnosis.

The only thing that epididymitis and twisted testicle have in common is that they both cause pain, often excruciating pain.

It's tricky to write about two unrelated disorders in the same chapter, but men can't tell what's causing their pain, and even doctors have trouble telling one from the other. When doctors are successful, we can cure either disorder; when we're not, a patient sometimes loses a testicle.

Oddly enough, neither disorder affects the testicle itself but rather its appendages. Painful things rarely happen to the testis itself.

Germs Cause Epididymitis

High pressure during urination or sexual intercourse forces urine backward from the urethra through the prostate and into the spermatic duct. If urine is infected, epididymitis will follow. No one has ever proved that this is exactly what happens, but it sounds reasonable.

In younger men, infecting organisms are mostly those found in run-of-the-mill sexually transmitted diseases: gonococci and chlamydiae. Older men can blame germs from prostate and urinary tract infections.

Once the doctor diagnoses epididymitis as the cause of testicular pain, a course of antibiotics brings quick relief.

Nature's Design Flaw

The cause of a twisted testicle (medical term: *torsion of the testes*) is yet another of nature's clumsy design defects.

Embryology is fascinating, and here's a small lesson: Everyone starts life looking female. Until two months after a baby begins developing in the womb, ovaries and testes look identical; each are located in the abdomen, where the future ovaries will remain. But they soon begin to change, and the testes slowly descend through the abdomen, finally leaving during the eighth month and settling into the scrotum. Hanging outside the body keeps the testes cooler than the rest of you. This is essential for the continuation of the human race: Sperm die at body temperature, so a man with undescended testes remains sterile.

Even in their exterior location, the testes still remain connected to the abdomen. Sperm and secretions travel through a tube up into the belly before reversing themselves and flowing back down and out the penis. The testes themselves awkwardly hang from a cord that delivers their blood supply. Hanging so freely, the glands can twist back and forth. Now and then one testis twists too far and can't untwist again. In its twisted position, known as torsion, the blood supply to the testis is cut off.

Perhaps one man in 200 suffers a torsion. Teenagers make up most of those who go through this painful experience, but it's not rare in young adults. The incidence drops after 30. You might think that activity provokes twisting, but half of cases occur during sleep; cold weather also increases the risk. Most likely local muscle contraction twirls the testis beyond a point of no return.

Surgery May Be Necessary

My first encounter with torsion of the testes occurred at the Beverly Hills Hotel, where a guest's ten-year-old son was suffering abdominal pain and vomiting. Despite the boy's discomfort, my exam left me puzzled because his abdomen was soft and painless. Only after he mentioned that the pain traveled lower did I look and discover a red and swollen testicle. Rather than wait for the father to call a cab, I drove them to the UCLA medical center myself.

After several hours and much debate among urology residents and professors, the child was sent out with nothing more than pain medication. He was suffering torsion of the appendix of his testis. Like the appendix you're familiar with, this testicular appendix is a piece of useless tissue that occasionally causes trouble. No harm results when *it* twists, and pain goes away in a few days. Although the source of about one-quarter of acute scrotums in boys, it takes an expert to decide that surgery isn't necessary.

Diagram for Diagnosis

The right testis twists clockwise, the left counterclockwise, so a skillful doctor can untwist them and relieve pain without surgery, but this is never a permanent solution.

Don't be a hero when pain begins. Torsion cuts off the blood supply; after 24 hours most testes are dead and must be amputated. Surgery within 6 hours saves almost all. The surgeon will also tighten the opposite testis to reduce the risk of a future torsion.

How can you tell whether you have torsion or epididymitis?

Generally speaking, torsion happens quickly, and infection of the epididymis develops over a day or two. This is the "typical" behavior, so don't bet on it. One-third of torsions develop gradually, and epididymitis can explode. Think of torsion if, as in the example above, abdominal pain and vomiting are prominent.

Since epididymitis spreads from a urinary infection, experts say you can expect a penile discharge, urinary discomfort, and even fever with this disorder. I rarely find these symptoms, however.

These are only hints. In either case you must see a doctor—and quickly—if you experience painful testicle.

Panic

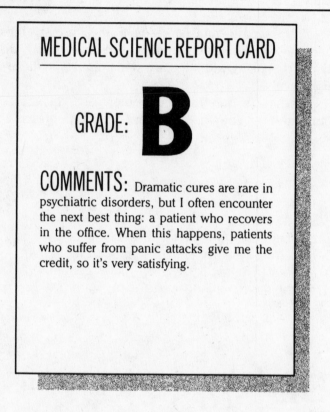

MEDICAL SCIENCE REPORT CARD

GRADE: **B**

COMMENTS: Dramatic cures are rare in psychiatric disorders, but I often encounter the next best thing: a patient who recovers in the office. When this happens, patients who suffer from panic attacks give me the credit, so it's very satisfying.

Typically someone is doing something ordinary such as shopping or working at a desk when she (three times as often as he) becomes overwhelmed by fear. The knowledge that nothing frightening has happened only makes it worse. She wonders if she is going crazy. She breaks out into a sweat; her heart pounds, and she struggles to breathe; she may believe she is having a heart attack.

Panic from Nowhere

People having a panic attack tend to end up in emergency rooms, but a patient arriving at my office is easy to diagnose. Most are under middle age so it's easy to rule out heart disease. Once I've done this, I sit back, adopt a calm, sympathetic expression, and do nothing. I never give impossible advice ("relax...," "pull yourself together ..."), and neither should you if you encounter a person having a panic attack.

The patient is always desperate to know what's happening. I explain that it's a panic attack (other doctors may call it an anxiety attack, but *anxiety* lacks dignity; a patient in such pain deserves a serious word). She always asks why it happened. I answer that no one knows, but that it isn't her fault; it comes out of nowhere. She always asks me to do something. I answer that nothing can be done, but that she will feel better soon; in fact, she is feeling better already. This is always true, because attacks rarely last more than an hour.

Isolated panic attacks are fairly common, and many pass without a doctor's involvement. Many never recur, but once someone suffers a second and knows she may have a third, the effect is devastating, far more than migraine, angina, or almost any physical pain. A person will do *anything* to prevent another attack. Many become frightened of places where the attack occurred. Agoraphobia (fear of open spaces) and other phobias are not simply weird eccentricities; they are often desperate efforts to avoid panic attacks. Some victims are afraid to leave home.

Cause: Brain Disease

Freudian psychoanalysis explains that deep, unresolved conflicts burst to consciousness in a panic attack. This explanation seems less than valid when you realize that attacks can occur during dreamless sleep. Freudian considerations aside, researchers find distinct abnormalities in the brains of people prone to these attacks. One area of the brain—the locus ceruleus—seems to control certain emotions; when stimulated, it causes anxiety. Panic attacks may be a form of epilepsy in which the locus ceruleus discharges violently.

Other factors also seem to contribute to panic attacks— especially brain chemicals known as neurotransmitters. We know this because drugs that control panic affect nerve transmission. In fact, they are the same drugs used for depression, so the disorders are probably related. Over half of patients with panic attacks also suffer major depressions.

How Much Panic?

There's nothing mysterious about the panic of a panic disorder. It's the same fear we feel in real danger, and it provokes the same gush of adrenaline—a hormone governing your "fight or flight" reaction. Adrenaline makes your heart race and your muscles tighten and tremble; it dilates your pores to make you sweat and your bronchi so that you breathe more quickly. Although essential for emergency action, these physical responses are terribly upsetting if you're sitting quietly over dinner.

PEARL

Musicians, actors, and public speakers worry that adrenaline released by stage fright will interfere with a performance. If so, they can take a drug to prevent it. The same beta-blockers (Inderal, Tenormin, etc.) that treat high blood pressure and angina also help stage fright. But don't get your hopes up; these drugs block the symptoms caused by adrenaline (pounding heart, trembling, sweating, difficulty breathing). They don't ease the fear itself, so they're of little use in panic disorders.

Antidepressants Help

The best treatment for panic attack is Clomipramine.

This is a newer antidepressant, but the older ones also work well—80 to 90 percent of people can expect good results. Alprazolam (Xanax), a relative of Valium, works even better, but it's stubbornly addictive. Patients feel uneasy and anxious when the drug is withdrawn, although only a minority get their panic attacks back. I don't recommend it, but many other doctors do.

Drugs quell panic attacks but not the phobias left in their wake. These require intense counseling and behavior modification therapy in which people are gradually helped to confront the situation that frightens them. Family doctors rarely want to spend the time. Treating phobias has become a sub-specialty among psychiatrists; people who need help should ask for a referral.

Pneumonia

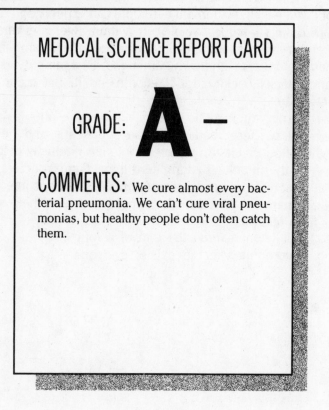

MEDICAL SCIENCE REPORT CARD

GRADE: **A –**

COMMENTS: We cure almost every bacterial pneumonia. We can't cure viral pneumonias, but healthy people don't often catch them.

Pneumonia is an infection in the lung itself. Doctors make the diagnosis by seeing a patch of fluid on a chest x-ray where normally they would see the transparent air of healthy lung. One can suspect pneumonia just from listening with a stethoscope because breath sounds crackle as they bubble through the infected fluid, but an x-ray is more accurate. Before the advent of x-rays doctors diagnosed pneumonia by listening to the chest, and I still do on hotel calls.

Misplaced Germs

Most of the germs that cause pneumonia originate in the victim's mouth, dwelling there harmlessly until some accident allows them to travel where they don't belong.

Beyond the larynx, your bronchial tubes and lung are sterile. Since no one is perfect, you regularly aspirate saliva and bits of food back past the larynx, but this provokes coughing, which expels most of it. The remainder sticks to your bronchial tube mucus, which slowly moves upward to the throat to be swallowed.

In a healthy nonsmoker, pneumonia probably occurs during an upper respiratory infection that blunts these defenses. Cigarette smoke and alcohol both poison the bronchial lining, so smokers and drinkers suffer more pulmonary infections. Age, unfortunately, impairs lung defenses. Before the antibiotic era, pneumonia was called "the old man's friend," because it often marked the end of a long illness. Today a good pneumonia vaccine exists; everyone past 65 should have it.

Pneumonia Symptoms

Pneumonia announces itself with cough and fever, sometimes with chest pain and difficulty breathing. Don't assume that it's pneumonia if you cough up mucus. A bad cold produces plenty of mucus, while some pneumonia coughs are dry. Do suspect pneumonia if your cough is bad and you feel really sick.

Doctors love to read about pneumonia, but encountering it in the office is less exciting. We love reading about it because so many different pneumonias exist, caused by different organisms, producing different (but unfortunately overlapping) symptoms and x-rays. Doctors love tracking down the specific cause of any disease, and it's important that we do so; only with a definite diagnosis can we choose the best treatment.

Diagnostic Difficulties

The need for an accurate diagnosis is especially true for pneumonia, as different antibiotics are given for different forms of the disease.

Sadly, despite all the miracles of modern medicine, science isn't much help in finding the specific germ responsible for an individual's pneumonia. A doctor takes a medical history to look for these kinds of clues.

- Pneumococcal pneumonia typically arrives suddenly, with shaking chills, severe cough, and high fever.
- Hemophilus pneumonia typically attacks middle-aged drinkers and smokers.
- Mycoplasma pneumonia affects younger adults, producing a nagging, dry cough and low-grade fever.

Since these are "typical" symptoms, no sensible doctor relies on them. Listening to the chest, looking at the x-ray, and ordering a blood count also provide hints but no proof. To find the germ causing a particular case of pneumonia, the doctor must do just that—find the germ. This is not easy.

Why Do a Sputum Culture?

Many doctors order a sputum culture in which the patient hacks and spits into a cup, which is sent to the laboratory, smeared on a culture plate, and incubated for a day or two. The technician then identifies the bacteria on the plate. When I was a medical student 20 years ago, experts agreed that this was a terrible test because it's almost impossible to keep harmless mouth germs from mixing in the sputum and confusing the results. Experts still frown on the sputum culture, but doctors order it anyway because it's the only simple test that might find a germ.

An aggressive doctor can bypass the mouth by sticking a needle directly into the throat to extract sputum—or even directly into the lung—but this is rarely done unless the patient is sick enough to be hospitalized. Most doctors order a sputum culture. Others treat without one.

Treatment: Antibiotics

Erythromycin is the best treatment for mycoplasma pneumonia, a second choice for pneumococcal pneumonia, and sometimes effective against *Hemophilus* and other bacteria. Like all shotgun therapy, it's not the best for everything, so be grateful that pneumonia in a healthy adult is rarely life-threatening.

The typical course of erythromycin for pneumonia lasts two weeks. You must also have a repeat chest x-ray after six weeks to make sure the pneumonia has disappeared. If you don't get one, you haven't had the best treatment.

Prostate Enlargement

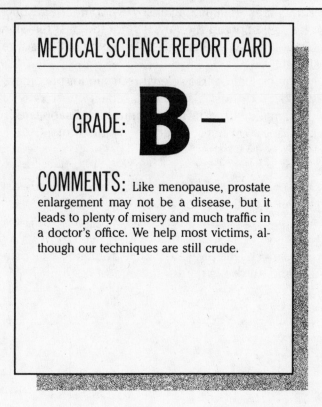

MEDICAL SCIENCE REPORT CARD

GRADE: **B –**

COMMENTS: Like menopause, prostate enlargement may not be a disease, but it leads to plenty of misery and much traffic in a doctor's office. We help most victims, although our techniques are still crude.

If any organ proves that the human body teems with design flaws, the prostate wins hands down. Nature made a foolish choice in locating it, then compounded the mistake disastrously by making it behave in a way that's exactly opposite from every other sex gland.

The prostate envelops the urethra at the junction where it exits the bladder—a terrible location. Why couldn't it sit off to one side like the ovary?

A man's urine flows through a tube no thicker than a

pencil running down the center of the prostate, an active sex gland. This location just begs for trouble because anything that makes the gland swell—infections, drugs, injuries—obstructs urine outflow.

To make matters worse, the prostate swells with age. This swelling begins around age 45; 30 years later, 90 percent of men have substantial enlargement. Not everyone with a large prostate suffers enough to require medical care, but there are enough that a drug to keep prostates small would devastate the urological profession.

Cause: Hormones

Experts believe that a man's androgen (male hormone) level drops faster than his estrogen (female hormone) level as he gets older. Eventually he suffers a relative excess of estrogen that stimulates prostatic tissue. However, some male hormone must be around for this stimulation to occur. (When a grown man is castrated, his prostate shrinks. A eunuch keeps a small prostate and all of his hair to the end of his life.)

Drugs that block estrogen or androgen are surprisingly feeble at shrinking large prostates. In theory they should work. This lack of effectiveness probably means that there's something we don't know.

Signs of Trouble

A man is usually in his fifties or sixties when the first symptoms of prostate trouble appear. At first he notices his urinary stream growing narrow and weaker. Although this is the first outward sign, obstruction is already advanced.

You can think of the bladder as similar to the heart; both are hollow, muscular organs that must expel a fluid regularly. Like the heart struggling against high blood pressure, the bladder faced with a narrowing urethra thickens and enlarges to overcome resistance. The bladder may carry on for decades or even forever, but when it reaches the limit of its strength, a man notices that something is not right.

As obstruction increases, he finds himself straining for

several seconds before urine appears, then straining to maintain the flow. He may stop and rest several times before finishing. Eventually, without realizing it, he doesn't empty the bladder completely. As this residual urine increases, the bladder fills to capacity more quickly, producing the urge to urinate, so he may find himself hurrying to the bathroom every few hours, more often at night. By this time, most men have seen a doctor, but a few stoics struggle on until the bladder surrenders completely.

Why Treatment Is Necessary

Early in my internship an ambulance deposited an elderly gentleman at my emergency room. According to relatives, he had grown more and more lethargic throughout the day and finally lapsed into a semicoma. I examined him, expecting to find signs of a stroke or severe infection. Nothing abnormal turned up except for his barely conscious state. Puzzled, I consulted the resident physician, who did a quick exam and informed me that I had missed a swollen bladder. In the future, he added, I shouldn't confine my search to the usual area in the low abdomen. This patient's bladder reached above the belly button. The nurse inserted a catheter. Two quarts of urine flowed out, and the man woke up.

This was acute urinary retention. Don't wait for it.

The Best Treatment: Surgery

Be happy that you live in the twentieth century. Inconvenienced by an enlarged prostate, our founding fathers had no choice but to carry around a thin metal tube, the purpose of which you can guess. Late nineteenth-century surgeons found some patients willing to undergo castration, but this was never popular.

Today you are most likely to have a transurethral resection of the prostate (TURP), an ingenious procedure during which the urologist inserts a sophisticated piece of optical equipment known as an endoscope into the penis and cuts away the obstructing tissue. It's the most common operation for men 65 and older.

A TURP works perfectly 90 percent of the time; the death rate in the hands of an experienced surgeon is 1 in 250. If this seems high, remember that patients are often in their seventies or eighties.

The most frequent severe complication is permanent urinary incontinence, which occurs less than 1 percent of the time. Impotence occurs in about 10 percent of patients, and at least 40 percent become sterile because they ejaculate backward into the bladder after the surgery.

Alternatives to Surgery

Clearly, the surgery is far from ideal, and plenty of new ideas are in the works.

As I mentioned above, hormones have been a disappointment, but several common blood pressure medications modestly reduce obstruction. Although used more in Europe than the United States, all are available here, so ask your doctor for a trial. They are terazosin (Hytrin), prazosin (Minipress), and phenoxybenzamine (Dibenzyline).

For several hundred years, doctors have threaded a balloon inside the penis and blown it up to stretch the narrowed urethra. This procedure seems absurdly simple, but disaster follows if the balloon expands too much or in the wrong place.

Urologists now have the instruments to control the balloon more accurately, and interest in this treatment has blossomed. A few urologists insist that a 10-minute balloon dilatation works beautifully. Most patients feel better afterward, but measurements show surprisingly little improvement in urine flow. No one knows what the long-term consequences of a dilatation are, and many urologists insist that it's worthless. I genuinely don't know what to think, but it seems fairly safe, and I'd have one before going on to a TURP.

Psoriasis

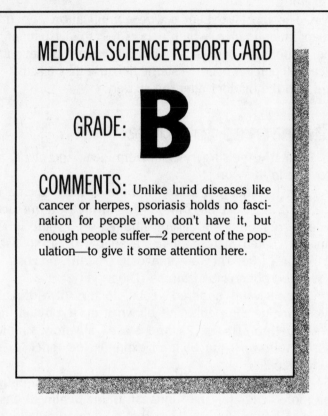

MEDICAL SCIENCE REPORT CARD

GRADE: **B**

COMMENTS: Unlike lurid diseases like cancer or herpes, psoriasis holds no fascination for people who don't have it, but enough people suffer—2 percent of the population—to give it some attention here.

No one knows why it begins, but what happens afterward is easy to explain. In a person with psoriasis the skin cells multiply wildly.

Normally a cell in your skin's outermost layer (the epidermis) begins life a fraction of an inch below the surface. As days pass, it slowly moves upward and dies, but it remains with you for several weeks as part of that tough protective layer (the surface of your skin is really dead tissue). Then it falls off. Your skin's surface is falling off all the time, but you rarely notice. A healthy skin cell takes four weeks to complete this cycle. *A psoriatic cell takes less than four days!*

Pink, but Not Healthy

Because psoriatic cells zoom upward before they have time to die, the surface turns a living pink. Because the cells fall off so quickly, silvery scales and flakes cover the skin. When I see a pink patch of skin covered with scales, I'm pretty sure of the diagnosis.

Psoriasis prefers the elbows, knees, scalp, genitals, and buttocks, although a bad attack can affect any area. Luckily, the face is not a common site, so you're probably unaware of how many of your acquaintances suffer from it. Also luckily, itching is not a common symptom. The worst part about having psoriasis is simply how it looks. Patients avoid the beach or any recreational activity in which they must dress lightly and expose a mass of red, scaly patches. This isn't really necessary.

The Doctor Can Help

The best treatment for psoriasis is a concerned, friendly, persistent doctor. This is no platitude. A disinterested doctor can do a fine job of treating you for strep throat, tuberculosis, a broken arm, or an ulcer. He or she merely gives the correct prescription or instructions, and you must be sensible enough to obey.

Psoriasis requires more. A lifetime disease, psoriasis wears out its victims. They grow tired of dealing with it. Perhaps they're willing to rub on a cream a few times a day, but otherwise they want to get on with their lives. Unfortunately, when ignored, psoriasis smolders on, but patients tend to adapt to their disfigurement. Sometimes their lives become very constricted.

Time and again, I've seen a patient wander into a walk-in clinic to refill a cortisone cream. Looking under his clothes, I see a mass of red, scaly plaques. Doesn't he want to get rid of these? I ask. Usually the patient agrees that he's worse than usual, but he blames it on running out of cream. He's probably wrong.

A family doctor can treat all but the worst psoriasis—and keep a patient's skin clear most of the time. But except for the mildest cases, *it takes an effort* from both parties. Much of the doctor's effort goes into education, inspiration, and nagging.

Fresh psoriatic patches are easier to treat, so they must be attacked early. Small stubborn patches or large sheets will eventually disappear—but rubbing on a cream won't do it. Life is unfair, and life has been slightly more unfair to a person with psoriasis, but medical science allows most to live a normal life provided they put in some extra, boring work.

Beyond Cortisone Cream

The best psoriasis treatment starts with cortisone, but only the mildest cases clear completely. So many other good treatments exist that I can't spell out what's best, but I can tell you something equally valuable: when to suspect that you're *not* getting the best.

When your psoriasis hasn't responded completely to cortisone, it's fine if the doctor prescribes stronger creams, but if after several visits for more concentrated creams, the doctor simply encourages you to keep applying them, *find another doctor.* I'm constantly irritated to discover family doctors who won't devote the same energy to controlling chronic skin disorders that they spend on high blood pressure or heartburn.

Treating Plaques

Here are other excellent treatments you should know about. Unless you have a very mild case, your doctor should use them. None requires a dermatologist.

Creams won't touch an old, thick plaque, but it should melt away if the doctor injects cortisone directly into it.

Rubbing cream onto acres of dry, scaly plaques is a waste of energy. It won't penetrate. You can overcome this barrier by applying cream, then wrapping the skin in plastic overnight. For even better penetration, you must get rid of the scales and soften the plaques. Your doctor should instruct you on various creams and baths that accomplish this.

Tar Treatment

Even the laziest doctor encourages patients with psoriasis to sunbathe or lie under an ultraviolet lamp. This sometimes helps, but it helps more if you sensitize your skin first by applying tar. If you have persistent psoriasis and you don't know about tar, something is wrong with your doctor-patient relationship.

Tar is one of the few ancient remedies that really work. Until the advent of cortisone, patients with moderate to severe psoriasis were regularly hospitalized in special wards, bathed and painted with tar day after day between exposures to light. Within a few weeks plaques melted away and stayed away for months. This is still done for the most recalcitrant cases.

In the past, tar was coal tar, which the local gas works was happy to sell rather than dump into a nearby river. It was black, smelly, and noxious to use. Today drug companies have developed tar ointments and bath oils that are almost odorless, almost colorless, and almost easy to use. But they require more effort than simply rubbing on a cream, and the doctor must provide some explanation and cheerleading.

Tar is important. If you use cortisone cream regularly for a few months, your plaques will grow less and less sensitive. More potent creams will help for a while, but very potent creams are amazingly expensive and have unpleasant side effects. Applying cortisone in the morning and tar at night keeps plaques sensitive and clears your skin faster.

As I'll repeat throughout this book, specialists have no secrets. A good family doctor treats psoriasis no differently from the average dermatologist, so give him or her a chance. If you're referred to a specialist, either you have a particularly severe case or your family doctor hasn't the patience or interest. Dermatologists do have access to many complex treatments and poisonous drugs, but you will only see them after a trial of the therapy I discuss above. Most patients never need them.

Sexually Transmitted Diseases

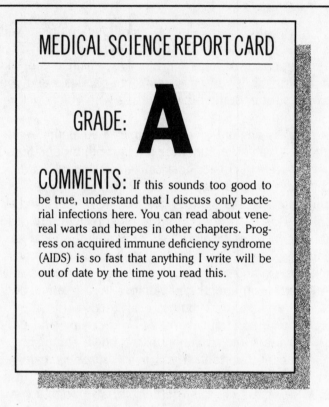

MEDICAL SCIENCE REPORT CARD

GRADE: **A**

COMMENTS: If this sounds too good to be true, understand that I discuss only bacterial infections here. You can read about venereal warts and herpes in other chapters. Progress on acquired immune deficiency syndrome (AIDS) is so fast that anything I write will be out of date by the time you read this.

Life was simpler in the good old days when we called them venereal diseases (a term derived from Venus, the goddess of love), and only five existed. Even better, three were so rare we never saw a case, but every student learned the names—chancroid, granuloma inguinale, and lymphogranuloma venereum. That left syphilis and gonorrhea, old reliables that had been around for centuries. By the late 1940s penicillin cured both, so doctors assumed that these two diseases were on their way out.

PEARL

We can never wipe out a disease by curing it.
    Polio remains incurable. Common and frighten-
ing until a generation ago, immunization has made
it a curiosity today, and many doctors wouldn't rec-
ognize a case if they saw it. We can cure syphilis
and gonorrhea, but wiping them out is not on the
horizon.

Something odd happened during the 1960s. New venereal diseases began appearing. Herpes was a well-known
skin disorder, but genital infections were almost unknown
when I saw my first case in medical school. In those days
chlamydia were a family of microorganisms that caused parrot
fever, trachoma (the commonest cause of blindness in Africa),
and other obscure diseases that American doctors found only
in medical textbooks. Then suddenly chlamydia became the
most common of all sexually transmitted diseases.

Besides new diseases, we have discovered plenty of
old favorites in an unfamiliar role. It turns out that sex is the
best way to transmit a host of ailments, from influenza to
warts. Hepatitis and cervical cancer are no less venereal diseases than syphilis and gonorrhea.

Some experts blame the sexual revolution for an explosion of diseases, but this is only part of the explanation,
because the three old-timers (chancroid, etc.) mentioned
above remain obscure. I suspect that nature is acting as im-
partially as it normally does. Nature treats all organisms
equally, so it assumes that bacteria and viruses have as much
right to life as humans. When doctors manage to suppress a
disease, nature notices the vacant territory and encourages
another organism to take up residence. This may sound discouraging, but medical science is keeping up.

Although AIDS has driven other sexually transmitted

221

diseases from public attention, they are still with us. Most are more of a threat than AIDS is to large segments of the population—especially women—and several are spreading alarmingly.

Syphilis Stays On

Syphilis, a major menace for centuries, is still with us— 70,000 reported cases a year, with an even larger number going unreported.

Until the antibiotic era, syphilis provoked as much public hysteria as AIDS does today. Many people panicked at the sight of a pimple, fearing that it was the earliest sign. Advanced symptoms—insanity, blindness, heart disease, paralysis— seemed somehow more terrible if they were the result of syphilis than of other diseases. As with AIDS, pregnant women who were infected passed syphilis on to their babies, with catastrophic results. Another gruesome parallel was the popular feeling that syphilis offered a moral lesson. Pitiful though a person suffering the ravages of the disease might be, many believed that he was getting what he deserved.

Signs of Syphilis

Traditionally, the first symptom of syphilis is the chancre—a painless ulcer that appears (usually on the genitals) a few weeks after bacteria enter the skin, persists a few weeks, then quietly heals. Weeks to years later the advanced form of the disease begins, and it can attack any organ. In the past, thick medical texts discussed this single disease. Doctors and even whole hospitals specialized in treating it. Syphilis was the leading diagnosis of inmates in insane asylums. Since the advent of penicillin, advanced cases of syphilis have dropped by 98 percent—a genuine medical miracle. But there is still plenty of syphilis. Homosexuals make up half of reported cases, so they are at especially high risk.

Diagnosing and Treating Syphilis

Early diagnosis remains a problem. Chancres are easy to miss. According to one study, 42 percent of heterosexual men were diagnosed at this stage; among homosexuals the rate was 23 percent; among women a mere 11 percent. Fortunately, a sensitive blood test exists. It's required for a marriage license, often done routinely on hospital admissions, and should be performed on all pregnant women. Everyone with multiple sexual contacts should have the syphilis test regularly.

Still, penicillin remains the best treatment.

Penicillin pills never work. One injection of a long-acting penicillin treats the early form of the disease nicely. If a doctor suspects you've had it longer than a year, you should get three injections, once a week for three weeks.

Gonorrhea: Far from Gone

Gonorrhea, too, continues to be very much with us. It is our most common reported communicable disease (chicken pox is next). Although two million cases per year make it far more frequent than syphilis, gonorrhea has never provoked the same dread. Perhaps it should, because it can be very destructive, especially in women.

Symptoms of Gonorrhea

Most men infected with gonorrhea notice a painful penile discharge within a week of exposure. Untreated, this discharge lasts an average of two months; abscesses, arthritis, meningitis, and other complications can occur but often do not. From 5 to 10 percent of affected men experience no symptoms at all, but they are still contagious. Both men and women may be infected in the throat or anus—again producing either pain or no symptoms at all.

Women suffer a greater variety of symptoms. They may dismiss common ones such as a vague discharge or painful urination as a vaginal or bladder infection. In 15 percent of cases, the disease spreads to the uterus and fallopian tubes, producing abdominal pain and fever. This pelvic inflammatory disease (PID) may require hospitalization and often leads to sterility. Gonorrhea in women is more likely to spread throughout the body—to skin, liver, heart, joints, and so on. As in other sexually transmitted diseases, pregnant women pass it to their babies. Finally, half of all women who become infected experience no symptoms. Besides infecting others, they still suffer tubal damage and infertility.

The Best Treatment: Ceftriaxone

Forty years ago a small injection of penicillin wiped out gonorrhea like magic. Gradually the bacteria that cause gonorrhea grew more resistant, forcing doctors to give larger and larger injections, then two large injections. About ten years ago some bacteria learned to produce penicillinase, an enzyme that inactivates penicillin. The bacteria were then completely resistant. Massive penicillin still works most of the time, but ceftriaxone is less painful. If doctors keep sprinkling antibiotics over their patients like confetti, we can expect more and more germs to develop this sort of resistance.

Although ceftriaxone is fine for gonorrhea, everyone who gets this disease must also receive treatment for chlamydia.

Treating Chlamydia

Chlamydia infections are not reportable. Otherwise, at three to four million cases per year, they would lead the list of sexually transmitted diseases, dwarfing herpes, gonorrhea, and syphilis combined. Despite these figures, chlamydia receives little publicity, probably because its immediate symptoms are not as unpleasant as those of the others. Yet it causes more permanent harm than do the others, especially (again) in women.

Signs of Chlamydia

Infected men have a penile discharge similar to gonorrhea but usually less severe. Following infection it takes longer for the discharge to show up—weeks to months. Severe infections cause sterility; more often the attack is so mild that men ignore it.

As with gonorrhea, many women with chlamydia suffer annoying vaginal or urinary discomfort but they may also experience no symptoms. If pregnant, they may transmit the infection to the baby. Finally and most ominously, the infection can spread upward to produce PID.

While chlamydial PID causes less pain and fever than gonorrhea, the results are equally bad. The first attack leaves 12 percent of victims sterile; the second raises this to 33 percent; the third to 50 percent. Sexually transmitted diseases and infertility have been growing in tandem. Today 20 percent of young American couples are affected; one-quarter of infertile women have had PID. In addition, damage from PID can lead to persistent abdominal pain, menstrual irregularity, and a vastly increased risk of ectopic pregnancy (pregnancy in the fallopian tubes requiring emergency surgery). A chlamydia test should be a routine part of a woman's health care—as routine as a Pap smear.

The Best Treatment: Doxycycline

Taken twice a day for a week, doxycycline is very effective. Doxycycline is a convenient form of the antibiotic tetracycline, which works as well but must be taken four times a day. Having tried tetracycline myself, I feel strongly that only the most compulsive person can take a medicine so often for more than a few days.

In the presence of gonorrhea, it's impossible to diagnose a chlamydial infection, and chlamydia is so common and destructive that we don't want to overlook it. As a result, the best treatment for gonorrhea *requires* a course of doxycycline in addition to ceftriaxone. Without it, you're not getting the best treatment.

Sinus Infections

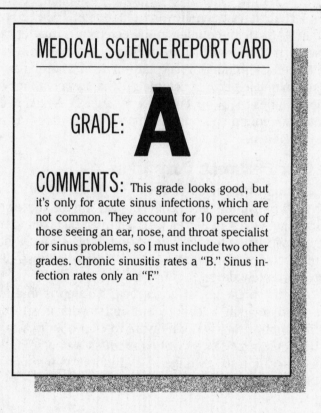

MEDICAL SCIENCE REPORT CARD

GRADE: **A**

COMMENTS: This grade looks good, but it's only for acute sinus infections, which are not common. They account for 10 percent of those seeing an ear, nose, and throat specialist for sinus problems, so I must include two other grades. Chronic sinusitis rates a "B." Sinus infection rates only an "F."

Sinuses are empty spaces in your skull—four on each side. They are probably an extension of the nose. All are lined by the same mucus-producing tissue, and all connect to the back of the nose through small openings.

As long as the sinuses drain into the nose, they rarely cause trouble. Even a bacterial infection has trouble getting started because it provokes an outpouring of mucus that washes it away. Viruses also provoke mucus flow, but the mucus doesn't dislodge them because they live *inside* your cells.

Obstruction Causes Problems

When a sinus outlet blocks up, you quickly realize that something is not right. Almost anything that produces irritation or swelling of the nasal lining can obstruct a sinus.

- The common cold and other viral infections (the most frequent)
- Allergies
- Sudden pressure changes (as in swimming, diving, flying)
- Smoke, fumes, and temperature changes—mostly in those with a sensitive nose
- Nasal deformities

Sinus Signs and Symptoms

Air and mucus can't escape from a blocked sinus, so pressure builds up. The oppressive, swollen-headed feeling that accompanies a bad cold should make you think of sinus congestion. Although unpleasant, it's not serious and goes away along with the cold.

The lining of a plugged sinus can't easily fight off bacteria, so occasionally germs settle in and grow. This increases pressure still more, so people with sinus infection feel severe, often excruciating pain over a *single* sinus. Bacteria produce pus, which may ooze from the sinus and flow out *one* nostril. This is acute sinusitis.

Just as germs almost never infect two ears at the same time, they prefer a single sinus. Generalized head pain is not evidence for a sinus infection. Mucus pouring from *both* nostrils points to a bad cold, not a sinus problem.

A few unfortunates have repeated or poorly treated infections that permanently damage the tissue, allowing bacteria to burrow in and become walled off. This chronic sinusitis may reveal itself as a postnasal drip with occasional hoarseness and coughing, plus a flare of acute sinusitis every year or two. These symptoms are only aggravating, so a patient may go for years without the correct diagnosis. She may assume that she has an allergy, a persistent cold, or a smoker's drip. *Pain is not a typical symptom.* Contrary to the popular belief, recurrent headaches are not a common sign of chronic sinus infection.

Treating Sinus Conditions

The best treatment for sinus congestion: decongestants.
The best treatment for acute sinusitis: decongestants.
The best treatment for chronic sinusitis: surgery.

Sinus Congestion

Sinus congestion is an upper respiratory problem for which doctors give unnecessary antibiotics, so home treatment is the wisest course. In any case, no decongestant requires a prescription. Oral drugs (Sudafed, Sine-Aid, Sinarest, Drixoral) may work, but topicals work better.

Use a nasal spray. Drops roll over too small an area and might not strike the sinus opening as they dribble through.

The proper technique for using a nasal spray is to spray each nostril, then wait 5 minutes. This gives the nasal lining time to shrink. Now spray again. This penetrates far back to the sinus openings.

Don't use a nasal spray more than twice a day or for more than a week. After this time, topical decongestants lose effectiveness and begin to have a rebound action, producing more, not less, stuffiness.

Acute Sinusitis

Victims of acute sinusitis are anxious for an antibiotic, but this is not the primary therapy. Once the infected sinus can drain, pain disappears and the infection clears up. (Any infection caused by an obstruction goes away once the obstruction is relieved. That's why draining a boil cures it without antibiotics.)

Acute sinusitis requires a nasal decongestant plus local heat and steam. Although antibiotics aren't mandatory, almost every doctor gives them. Rarely, when obstruction is stubborn and pain unbearable, the doctor punctures the sinus to relieve the pressure.

Chronic Sinusitis

Ear, nose, and throat specialists manage chronic sinusitis. As long as symptoms remain tolerable, a patient may get along on decongestants, plus antibiotics for the occasional flare-up. A minor procedure that irrigates the infected sinus can produce a long remission. The only permanent solution is surgery to scrape away the infected tissue and establish permanent drainage.

Strokes

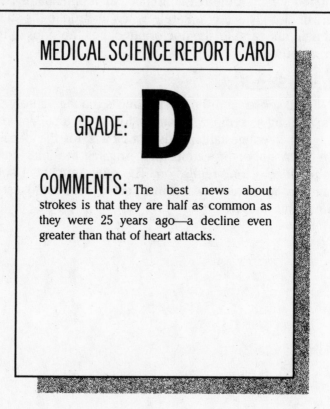

MEDICAL SCIENCE REPORT CARD

GRADE: **D**

COMMENTS: The best news about strokes is that they are half as common as they were 25 years ago—a decline even greater than that of heart attacks.

We can credit the dramatic decline in strokes to better control of high blood pressure, by far the leading risk factor. A person with even the modest elevation of 160/95 runs six times the risk of someone with normal pressure. Smoking, a high cholesterol level, and diabetes also increase the risk, but not as strongly as for heart attack.

Although both stroke and heart attack have similar causes—a clogged artery—providing treatment is easier in the heart than in the brain. Giving a clot dissolver would be disastrous if the stroke was the result of bleeding—and so far it's impossible to rule this out in the early stages. Heart bypass surgery works; bypassing blocked brain arteries is popular, but unfortunately studies don't show dramatic benefits. I'd classify this surgery as experimental. This doesn't mean that you shouldn't agree if your doctor suggests it, but get a second opinion.

Stroke Prognosis

Question: What is the leading cause of death in someone who has recovered from a stroke?

Answer: A heart attack.

Since heart attack is the leading cause of death in the United States, it means that having a stroke doesn't put you into some kind of special, doomed category. Once the stroke heals, you have a dead area of the brain, but this probably won't shorten your life because most of the brain (unlike your heart) isn't necessary for day-to-day living.

What Causes Strokes

Three different scenarios describe almost all strokes.

In one a blood clot forms in a brain artery, blocking the blood supply to a portion of the brain. Clots make up over half of strokes.

An embolus is also a clot but one that forms elsewhere (usually in the heart), breaks loose, and lodges in the brain. Emboli make up about 30 percent of strokes.

Hemorrhage, bleeding into the brain, occurs in the remaining 15 percent. Although it's reasonable to blame high blood pressure for ruptured arteries and hemorrhagic strokes, clots are also more common in people who have hypertension.

Stroke Symptoms

Like most old disease terms, *stroke* is more colorful than today's medical description (ischemic cerebrovascular disease) but also more inaccurate. A stroke is not often a dramatic event.

Fainting and intense dizziness are two symptoms that I

231

hear about quickly. If the person who faints is elderly, the family is certain that it's a stroke, but I've never seen a stroke that began with fainting. Now and then a stroke patient is dizzy, but I've always found another obvious sign in addition to dizziness.

The most common symptom is paralysis that occurs without pain. Most often, a patient simply awakens in the morning unable to move one side of the body. Next in frequency, I encounter speech difficulty. A young person who talks gibberish has probably taken drugs. In the elderly, this probably means damage to the speech areas of the brain. Less common symptoms are blindness (always one-sided, never complete), numbness on one side of the body, permanent lack of coordination (inability to walk or even sit up), and loss of an intellectual ability—to talk, understand speech, read, or write.

When any of these symptoms disappears in less than a day, it's not a stroke but a transient ischemic attack (TIA), perhaps from a clot that temporarily blocks an artery, then vanishes. Sometimes the source is obvious—a clot in a vein or the heart. Even if a TIA doesn't have an obvious source, a doctor will try to prevent further TIAs by prescribing a drug, most likely aspirin, to discourage clotting.

Despite popular belief, headache isn't typical of most strokes because, although full of nerve tissue, the brain contains no pain nerves.

While the brain itself can't feel pain, surrounding tissues are very sensitive, so if a stroke begins with hemorrhage over the surface, it causes an excruciating headache. A sudden headache in someone who doesn't usually have them is an emergency no different from chest pain.

See a doctor if you experience any change in sensory or mental functions—difficulty seeing or hearing, numbness, clumsiness, unsteadiness, or confusion. Although any of these symptoms may mean a stroke, they're usually something else.

Best Treatment

Support is an uninspiring word for the observation and assistance doctors provide until nature takes its course and heals the brain damage. But support saves lives and prevents disability. We nourish the patient, try to prevent infections and bedsores, and keep the limbs mobile—a paralyzed muscle shrivels unless this is done. After the worst is past, controlling high blood pressure and other risk factors and perhaps prescribing a blood thinner make a recurrence less likely. Only rarely do we "cure" a stroke—by surgically repairing a leaky artery or removing a clot.

The services of a doctor of physical medicine (not the same as a physical therapist) are essential even before a patient leaves the hospital. Although the damaged area of the brain doesn't get worse, a stroke-weakened arm or leg continues to weaken unless it's used and exercised. If you see someone with a bent, withered limb that can't be straightened, blame incompetent medical care, not a stroke.

Within a few months almost everyone regains some strength and other abilities. When this doesn't happen, it's likely that something not connected with the stroke has happened: a heart attack, a damaging pneumonia or other infection, bedsores, or muscle deterioration from absence of physical therapy.

The most malignant complication of stroke is despair. Waking up paralyzed is not as painful or frightening as suffering a heart attack, but after the initial shock almost everyone feels overwhelmed by the knowledge that he or she is crippled. This depression passes, and it's treatable, but everyone—family and patient as well as the doctor—must realize that this emotional response is almost guaranteed.

Tension Headache

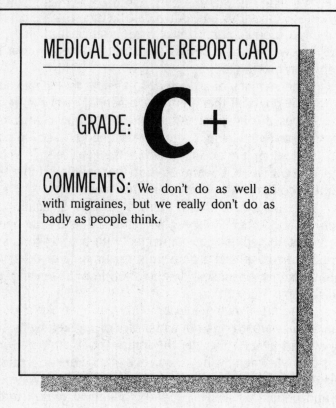

MEDICAL SCIENCE REPORT CARD

GRADE: **C+**

COMMENTS: We don't do as well as with migraines, but we really don't do as badly as people think.

Ninety-nine percent of tension headaches go away without a doctor's intervention. Occasionally a patient complains that she gets several each week. Questioning, I find that during her entire adult life, she's had headaches that go away promptly when she takes aspirin, Tylenol, Advil, Nuprin, or another over-the-counter drug. After making sure that these are simple tension headaches (by asking questions; tests are hardly ever necessary), I reassure her and try to impress her with *how lucky she is!*

No one is perfect, and tension headaches are evidence of this. Almost everyone gets them. If they don't greatly interfere with your life and go away when you take a pill, give yourself a pat on the back. Life would be tiresome if the pills didn't work.

Why Tension Equals Headache

A prevalent myth has it that any bad headache is a migraine.

Actually a tension headache can be every bit as painful. Both types run in families and both can be triggered by stress or menstrual periods.

But why should muscle tension cause pain in your head and not, for example, your chest or thigh? The answer lies deep in evolutionary history and shows that nature, for all its beauty, works slowly and clumsily.

For several hundred million years, our animal ancestors walked on four legs. As explained in the chapter on low back pain, nature hasn't yet adapted the human body to an erect posture.

Watch an animal. Notice what happens when something makes it nervous. *It raises its head* to check the surroundings for danger. Since the human head is already on top of the body, we can't raise it, but nature hasn't gotten the message. When humans grow nervous, their neck muscles pull on the skull. This accomplishes nothing except to cause a headache, but nature won't catch on for at least another ten million years.

Tension Headache Symptoms

The traditional tension headache hurts in a band around the skull from forehead to upper neck, but conditions don't always produce classic textbook symptoms. Patients tend to tell me that their head hurts all over, a bad description to give your doctor.

Doctors don't like to hear that "everything" is wrong. Be specific. Tension headaches can hurt in specific areas and can even throb like a migraine.

Treatment with Antidepressants

Pain drugs are the best *home* treatment for the tension headache, but if a doctor gives you prescription pain medication such as Empirin, Darvon, or Fiorinal, you aren't getting the best tension headache therapy. I see many patients who are receiving only prescription painkillers for their headaches, and some seem satisfied. But their satisfaction is partly because they assume that nothing else is available.

If you get a prescription refill for pain-relief medication more than once a year, you probably need an antidepressant. If you take headache medication several times a week, you need an antidepressant. If you have a nagging headache almost daily, and a bad one every few days, you definitely need an antidepressant.

Small doses of antidepressants are frequently used to treat pain. The medications have a number of effects on the body besides relieving depression, and the doses that bring pain relief are far below those required to help relieve depression. In the case of tension headache, there may well be a depression connection, however.

Chronic, nagging headaches signal depression more often than we think. Certainly, my tension headache patients feel that they are under stress and seem less satisfied with their lives than most. Another bit of evidence is that the usual starting dose for pain relief (25 milligrams of Elavil or Tofranil—only ⅙ of the minimum dose to relieve depression) is sometimes not enough. So doctors must raise the dose again

236

and again, sometimes to the full amount required to treat depression before the pain goes away.

Long-term prevention of tension headache and migraine requires the same persistence and experimentation—and often the same drugs (see the chapter on migraine).

Headache Questions

You sometimes worry that your headache is something other than a migraine or tension headache. Here are some of the conditions my patients worry about—and my usual answers.

High blood pressure?   Probably not. People with hypertension have no more headaches than those with normal pressure. The only way to tell if your pressure is elevated is to take it with a blood pressure cuff. This is one of those scientific facts that people have a hard time believing. My patients with high blood pressure suspect that their pressure is up whenever they have a headache. They're wrong.

A sinus infection?   No. An acute sinus infection is excruciating and localized to one sinus area. It quickly brings a person who has it to the doctor. A chronic sinus infection produces a postnasal drip or nasal discharge but little pain. Sinus disorders rarely cause long-lasting or recurrent headaches.

PEARL

When headaches drag on, the distinction between muscle tension and vascular (or migraine) grows less clear, and chronic headaches are probably a mixture. Popular writers tend to ignore this (to be fair, so do doctors), but you should be aware so that you don't overlook any treatment.

Eyestrain? People with chronic headache often have their eyes checked, but to no avail. Eyestrain pain occurs while the eyes are straining and goes away when they relax.

Something more serious? Perhaps an x-ray will show what's wrong? No test proves that what you have is migraine or tension headaches. Doctors make the diagnosis by listening to your history and doing an exam. If you have migraine or tension headaches we won't find anything out-wardly wrong. In my experience, if a headache victim pesters the doctor long enough, he or she will receive a dazzling high-tech experience such as a CT or magnetic resonance scan. The results will be normal. I never order one unless something doesn't seem right.

I become suspicious that something else is going on only when the medical history isn't typical. For example, when the pain is different or when it's the first severe headache in someone who never has headaches. Naturally, I investigate if the physical exam turns up something abnormal such as weak-ness of one part of the body.

Everyone with a new or unfamiliar headache should see a doctor to discuss it and be examined. If everything points to a migraine or tension headache, that's almost certainly what it is.

Throat Infections

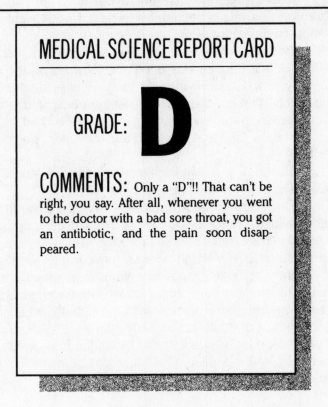

MEDICAL SCIENCE REPORT CARD

GRADE: **D**

COMMENTS: Only a "D"!! That can't be right, you say. After all, whenever you went to the doctor with a bad sore throat, you got an antibiotic, and the pain soon disappeared.

A few years ago my sister phoned to complain about a distressing encounter with a doctor. She had been worried about a sore throat and painful lump that appeared under her jaw. (I would have explained that it was a swollen lymph node that would disappear in a few days.) After an examination, the doctor announced that she had a throat infection and wrote a prescription for an antibiotic.

"It's probably a viral infection, isn't it?" she asked. The doctor agreed.

"I've heard that antibiotics don't work for viral infections. Is that true?" my sister continued. This was tact. She knew my vehement opinions on the subject.

"That's true, " he answered defensively. "But this keeps it from turning into a bacterial infection. I don't want you to develop complications."

"But why would one infection turn into another infection? Does that happen very often? I get viruses all the time."

By now I was loving this story. A wise doctor would have agreed that my sister didn't need an antibiotic and torn up the prescription. But admitting a mistake is hard.

"I've decided that you need this antibiotic. Do you want it or not?"

"Doctor, I just want to know about this lump in my neck. The infection doesn't bother me."

"Don't worry about the lump. Take the prescription— or don't take it. It's up to you." He shoved the prescription into her hand and stalked out of the room. Naturally my sister was upset. Although his behavior was inexcusable, one should understand the doctor's point of view. Undoubtedly he had given antibiotics to hundreds, perhaps thousands, of grateful patients suffering viral infections. Undoubtedly he no longer felt the twinge of guilt doctors feel when we do something we shouldn't. Suddenly a patient had reminded him—a flustering experience that caught him off guard. A quick-witted doctor would have handled this better.

Cause of Throat Infection

"I'm sure it's strep," patients with a particularly painful throat tell me. Strep throat is the only common throat infection we cure (grade: A+). My heart leaps with joy when I see a case, because I can dispense with my why-antibiotics-don't-work explanation, give penicillin, and know in advance that my patient will be genuinely grateful. But I rarely see such cases. Strep, a bacterial infection, is largely a disease of children. Almost all sore throats in adults are caused by viruses.

At one time I worked for a student health service on a large university campus. Since almost every patient was under 30, serious diseases were rare, but people with sore throats came in droves and usually left with an antibiotic. After a year on the job I became so frustrated by this overprescribing that I decided to do the scientific thing and prove that this wasn't necessary. So I laboriously read through the laboratory records to collect results of all the throat cultures over a 2½ month-period. Incidentally, you may think a throat culture detects whatever germs grow in your throat, but you'd be wrong. The usual throat culture only checks for the presence or absence of beta strep, because that's the only common infection we can treat.

My results on 1,016 student throat cultures: 4.9 percent beta strep. These results are more amazing when you realize that we didn't do throat cultures on every student with a sore throat—only those in whom we suspected strep. All the doctors admired my findings, but no one changed their prescribing behavior. Doctors are as human as their patients. They will quickly break a bad habit that produces unpleasant consequences, but there are no unpleasant consequences for giving antibiotics for sore throats.

Symptoms of Throat Infection

Throat pain, sometimes with swollen neck glands, is a sure sign of infection. Lymph glands normally swell when the body is fighting a nearby infection, so this is not ominous and no reason to see a doctor.

If coughing accompanies the sore throat, the chance of strep is almost zero, because strep is purely a throat infection. Don't get too excited if you see white spots on your tonsils. While these occur in strep, they also appear in viral infections. Even the severity of pain doesn't point to something that requires an antibiotic. In my experience, infectious mononucleosis ("mono"), a viral infection that antibiotics won't touch, hurts even worse than strep.

Gargles Are Best

The best treatment for an infected throat is one your mother probably used—gargles.

Use salt water if you're stoic. Stir a couple of teaspoons

of salt into a glass of water. It tastes terrible but works fairly well, and it's cheap. Commercial gargles, lozenges, or sprays (Chloraseptic, Sucrets, Cēpastat) are not so appetizing either, but they contain mild local anesthetics that help. For bad throat pain, ask your doctor for a prescription gargle containing xylocaine. It will certainly numb your throat.

Never gargle with aspirin. Aspirin works in the blood-stream by blocking certain pain receptors; it's not a local anesthetic. In fact, it damages any tissue it touches.

When to Seek Help

See a doctor if your sore throat is severe and accom-panied by a fever but *no cough*. By all means, go if you're generally miserable and want advice (try the phone first if you have the sort of doctor who can be reached). Doctors help almost everyone they see, but "help" for a sore throat may mean an unnecessary antibiotic.

Toxic Shock

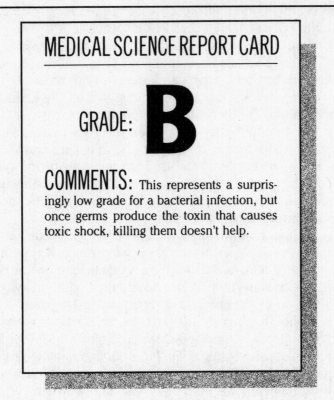

MEDICAL SCIENCE REPORT CARD

GRADE: **B**

COMMENTS: This represents a surprisingly low grade for a bacterial infection, but once germs produce the toxin that causes toxic shock, killing them doesn't help.

It seems like yesterday that frightening reports of young women dying of a mysterious disease filled the newspapers. The year was 1979. Only two years later, herpes replaced it as the most newsworthy disease. Yet toxic shock was never common: There were 1,000 cases out of 35,000,000 women at risk during the peak year of 1980, but no one should suffer such a devastating and preventable disease.

Cause: Staph Germs

Toxic shock syndrome is caused by a toxin released by the common germ *Staphylococcus aureus,* which normally lives on the skin or in the nose or vagina. Most of the time you and your staphylococci live in peace, but if you've ever had a boil, you've experienced a typical staph infection. More rarely, these bacteria cause pneumonia and other serious infections. While any staph can induce a boil, most can't produce toxic shock. Only a few strains give off the toxin that's absorbed into the bloodstream to produce the disease.

How could such a familiar germ give rise to a new disease? And why did it strike young, menstruating women? Since 97 percent of victims used tampons, suspicion quickly fell on them. Furthermore, a wave of new, highly absorbent tampons had recently come on the market. By 1980 doctors had confirmed their suspicions.

Tampons were the culprit. All provide a focus for infection, but the risk rises as absorbency increases. Any germ can grow in the fluid absorbed by a vaginal tampon; most are harmless because they do not invade the body. Staphylococci also remain in the vagina, but their toxin is absorbed.

Once scientists pinpointed the problem with tampons, they realized that toxic shock syndrome was not new. It has struck whenever staph grow in large enough numbers: in skin, surgical, and childbirth infections and as a complication of influenza, pneumonia, and other respiratory disease.

Tampons encourage bacterial growth, as do other materials placed inside the body. People with nosebleeds have gotten toxic shock from their nasal packing; a few cases have occurred in women using the contraceptive sponge and diaphragm.

Toxic shock is not subtle. It begins suddenly with high fever, muscle aches, vomiting, and diarrhea, usually accompanied by a generalized "sunburn" rash. Consider these symptoms a medical emergency. The 4 percent death rate results from the "shock" in toxic shock, a disastrous drop in blood pressure, which can lead to kidney or respiratory failure.

Best Treatment: Support

Support, in this case, means giving intravenous fluids to replace losses, controlling fever, and keeping blood pressure up. We also give antibiotics. While they have no effect on the illness itself, they seem to reduce recurrences—which once affected 30 percent of patients. With the precautions we observe today, the risk of recurrence is now about 5 percent and almost zero in nonmenstrual toxic shock.

Preventing Toxic Shock

Now that we understand toxic shock, it's fairly easy to prevent most cases. Here's what you can do.

- Use the lowest absorbency tampon that meets your needs.
- Change it every 6 hours; don't leave it in overnight.
- Don't use a tampon for minor discharges.
- Don't leave a sponge in more than 30 hours.

Once the facts were known and the most absorbent tampons taken off the market, toxic shock faded from the news, but it's still with us. Several hundred cases occur each year, including some deaths, mostly in young women, although nonmenstrual toxic shock now makes up a quarter of cases.

Herpes hysteria replaced toxic shock as the top media disease in 1981 and was in turn displaced by acquired immune deficiency syndrome (AIDS) in 1984. AIDS still preoccupies my patients, whether or not they are at risk. Certainly the young women in my practice worry more about AIDS than toxic shock. Yet, unless they inject drugs, their chance of toxic shock is greater.

Ulcers

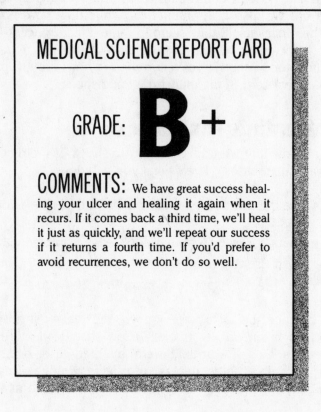

MEDICAL SCIENCE REPORT CARD

GRADE: **B**+

COMMENTS: We have great success healing your ulcer and healing it again when it recurs. If it comes back a third time, we'll heal it just as quickly, and we'll repeat our success if it returns a fourth time. If you'd prefer to avoid recurrences, we don't do so well.

You get an ulcer when acid eats a hole in your stomach or (more commonly) in the duodenum—the beginning of the small intestine just beyond the stomach.

The popular belief that too much acid causes ulcers is probably wrong. Some people with a duodenal ulcer have a high acid secretion rate, but others don't. Stomach ulcer patients have *less* acid than most. More likely, ulcers appear when something weakens the protective coating over the digestive tract, permitting acid to damage the tissue. Researchers in most cases don't know why this coating is damaged. Of course, corrosive drugs damage the barrier; aspirin users have a high risk of stomach ulcers. Cigarette smoke, which damages so many parts of the body, does the same to your acid barrier. Smokers experience twice as many ulcers, slower healing, and more recurrences.

Some people are born with a tendency to ulcers. Those with type O blood have a high rate of duodenal ulcers; type A blood leads to more stomach ulcers.

Stress doesn't increase the risk. Nervous people and air traffic controllers don't suffer more. Nor do those who eat a poor diet.

Ulcers Ache

"Burning upper abdominal pain relieved by food and antacids" describes the typical ulcer. Medical texts and popular writers repeat it. So do almost half of my patients. Not everyone experiences relief after eating. However, almost all ulcers hurt in the upper abdomen. If food brings on the pain or makes it worse, you probably have something besides an ulcer.

The Best Treatment: Sucralfate

Sucralfate (Carafate) is a drug that in the presence of acid, turns into a thick paste that sticks to any damaged tissue. You've heard of other digestive remedies that coat the stomach, and you may believe that milk does the same. In fact, if you swallow any of these, they form a puddle in the lowest part of the stomach. Only sucralfate really coats it. After six weeks of treatment, over 80 percent of ulcers heal.

Sucralfate is my best choice because it acts locally inside the digestive tract. It's not absorbed, so side effects are rare. Although fairly popular, sucralfate is not the choice of most American doctors, who tend to prefer traditional drugs that enter the bloodstream. To treat ulcers, they often choose an H_2 blocker (Tagamet, Zantac, Axid, Pepcid), which suppresses secretion of stomach acid. These are a safe class of drugs that heal ulcers as well as sucralfate, so don't be upset if your doctor prescribes them.

Neutralizing Acid

Ulcers heal of their own accord. Even without treatment, 50 to 70 percent are gone in six weeks.

Keeping acid away increases the percentage. Plain antacids work as well as the latest drugs, but most doctors gave them up in favor of newer remedies. Don't be too eager to buck the trend. The correct dose is 2 tablespoons at 1 and 3 hours after meals, at bedtime, and whenever pain occurs. This is an inconvenient number of doses that produces a fair amount of mild digestive upset. Don't assume it's cheaper, either; taking more than 14 tablespoons of antacid a day runs into money.

Vaginal Infections

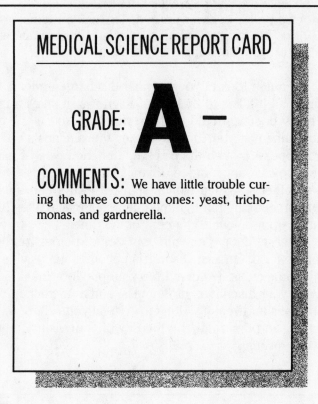

MEDICAL SCIENCE REPORT CARD

GRADE: **A** –

COMMENTS: We have little trouble curing the three common ones: yeast, trichomonas, and gardnerella.

Vaginal infections are one of the minor disadvantages of being a woman. Men don't have similar urethral infections, although they may harbor organisms that inconvenience their partners.

How can you tell when you have a vaginal infection? Here are a few helpful guidelines:

- All that itches is not a vaginal infection. In fact, a long-standing itch probably isn't. It's more likely a local irritation from soap or other chemical—or even from chronic scratching.

- A simple discharge *can* be a sign of infection. And it doesn't have to itch, burn, or smell.
- A bad odor is never normal. The usual vaginal secretions hardly smell at all. However, I discourage patients from smelling themselves too closely.

A quick look at your vaginal discharge under a microscope is all it takes to make the diagnosis. It takes a minute, and every doctor should perform this test. You won't get the best treatment if your doctor makes the diagnosis without a microscope. Although the discharge of each type of infection has a "typical" appearance, this visual evidence is as unreliable as other so-called typical signs. I always guess what I'll find before looking through the microscope, and after 20 years I'm still wrong about 20 percent of the time.

Please, cooperate with your doctor before you head to the office for diagnosis. Diagnosis becomes impossible if you slip in some cream left over from your previous infection. This converts your discharge into a mess, and a microscopic exam of a mess is unrevealing. Don't try to treat yourself for a vaginal infection, and don't douche the day of your visit. We want to see your discharge.

PEARL

I'm mystified by the number of patients who complain of a bad odor but don't have one. This is invariably true of those who tell me that they have bad breath.

During my day I see a fair number of patients whose feet, armpits, and other areas smell bad. Almost always, these patients don't mention it. Those who are quick to apologize for their smell often don't have one.

Microscopic Invaders

Vaginal infections arise from a number of troublesome microbes.

You Catch Yeast from Yourself

A common fungus that normally lives quietly in the vagina is responsible for yeast infections. Sometimes it multiplies when you take antibiotics that kill the neighboring bacteria that compete with it. Sugar nourishes yeast, and I've diagnosed a few diabetics whose first symptom was too many yeast infections. Sugar from their urine was fueling the infections. Doctors still warn women on birth control pills to expect more yeast infections, but studies of low-dose pills don't find any such increase.

Everyone denounces tight pants as a factor in yeast infections. It seems reasonable to join them, although little evidence exists to back this up.

Yeast infections itch. A discharge may or may not be visible. When visible, it usually looks like cottage cheese. A normal vaginal discharge can also look cheesy, so don't make the connection unless you also itch.

The best treatment for yeast is an imidazole cream or suppository.

For such a lucrative market, many drug companies are scrambling to patent a version slightly different from all the rest. You can now choose from miconazole (Monistat), terconazole (Terazol), butoconazole (Femstat), clotrimazole (Gyne-Lotrimin, Mycelex), and econazole. All are equally effective.

Trichomonas Is Contagious

You catch trichomonas from someone else. It's a genuine sexually transmitted disease. Men hardly ever show symptoms, but if the doctor doesn't treat the woman's sex partner at the same time, she is soon reinfected.

Other vaginal organisms lie quietly under the microscope, but trichomonas microbes swim about energetically. An extensive infection fills the slide with round, wiggly organisms. I used to like educating patients by showing them what

251

PEARL

Women with a discharge usually announce that they have a yeast infection. They never tell me they have gardnerella, although it makes up nearly half of vaginal infections. Yeast comes in second at about 30 percent.

I see under the microscope, but I no longer do this with trichomonas because the sight horrifies too many.

Trichomonas produces a discharge that may or may not smell bad. It usually itches but rarely as intensely as yeast.

The best treatment for trichomonas is metronidazole (Flagyl, Protostat).

This is an excellent antibiotic that works against many germs and is one of the few that kills amoebas, trichomonas, and other protozoa. Twenty years ago we prescribed one pill three times a day for ten days. Then we discovered two pills twice a day for a week works as well. Now we know that eight pills taken at once works almost as well, so that's the most popular course.

Your sexual partner must take the same course of treatment. *The doctor should give you two prescriptions!* Insist on it. Never let the doctor get away with saying, "Tell your husband to see his doctor. . . ." It's a complete waste of time. Doctors are rightly uneasy at giving prescriptions to people they haven't seen, but sexual partners of trichomonas patients are the exception. Every one of them requires metronidazole; zero require a test. Don't leave without two prescriptions!

Gardnerella: A Germ

Gardnerella may normally live in the vagina, but infections aren't as well understood as the two above. In the past, when we understood gardnerella infections even less well, we called them nonspecific vaginitis. Although having more sex increases the risk, gardnerella is also common in virgins, so we're not sure how they arise.

Gardnerella provokes a discharge that may smell fishy. If it doesn't, I add a drop of potassium hydroxide to the slide and then smell. A fishy odor confirms the diagnosis.

The best treatment for gardnerella is again metronidazole.

Eight pills at once doesn't work as well here, so we give two twice a day for a week. In the past, doctors routinely treated sexual partners, but studies showed that this doesn't affect the recurrence rate. Habits are hard to break, so many doctors still do it. I treat the man only if my patient's infection keeps coming back.

Warts

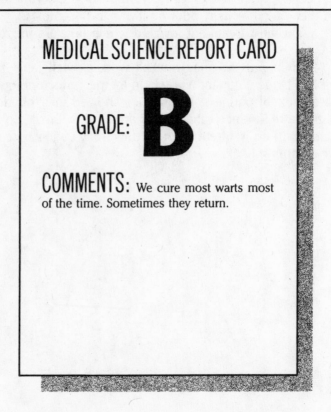

MEDICAL SCIENCE REPORT CARD

GRADE: **B**

COMMENTS: We cure most warts most
of the time. Sometimes they return.

Trivia question: Can you name the only human tumor definitely caused by a virus?

Answer: Warts.

Tumor simply means a swelling of abnormal tissues, but cancer is also abnormal tissue, so a wart is a part of the cancer family. Fortunately, a wart is benign—meaning it doesn't invade nearby tissues or spread throughout the body like internal malignancies. Scientists are certain that viruses cause many human cancers, but so far only the wart virus is a proven culprit.

In case you've never seen one, a wart is a bump with a rough surface like a cauliflower. A tiny wart may be smooth, but any larger, smooth bump is probably something else.

Warts are painless except where they press other tissue. Plantar warts on the bottom of the foot are painful because the pressure of walking forces them to grow in rather than out.

You Can Catch Warts

Like other viral disorders, warts are contagious, although the incubation period is long: from a month to a year after exposure. They spread by direct contact and from combs, razors, swimming pools, and locker room floors. Scratching, picking and biting your own warts spreads them, and sex passes them between the partners' genitals.

Although my patients are skeptical about this, be assured that no wart lasts forever. One-quarter disappear within six months, half within a year, two-thirds in two years. This is why I encourage anyone with warts in safe areas (not the face or genitals) to use over-the-counter remedies. These don't work well, but they help pass the time, during which many warts fade away on their own.

Like other infections, warts are attacked by your body's immune system. Some people seem naturally resistant, but people who have AIDS (acquired immune deficiency syndrome), leukemia, and other immune deficiencies become more susceptible. Finally, as the years pass, your body grows more resistant. Warts are common in teenagers and fairly rare by middle age. If you're past 50 and think you have a wart, it's probably a seborrheic keratosis, otherwise known as a mature age spot.

The Best Treatment: Destruction

Popular writers (many with an M.D.) tell you how to charm away warts by positive thinking, spells, hypnosis, and suggestion. They may also recommend a gentle salve that shrinks warts on contact. Go ahead and try all of these treatments. No one dies of warts, and these remedies are harmless.

Traditional healing techniques (psychic energy, herbal

potions) have been around for thousands of years and fulfill a deep human need. In my younger days I would denounce them as superstitious nonsense—and then watch a politely superior smile flicker across my patient's face as I confirmed his or her belief that doctors are narrow-minded and unspiritual. I hated that expression! Now that I am wise, I never attack popular health beliefs unless they are positively dangerous or unless I can offer something much better. Medical wart treatment works better than folk remedies, but it's mildly uncomfortable and not so superior that I urge patients to have it.

The Means of Destruction

You cure a wart by destroying it. Scientists are working on more clever methods such as vaccines and other ways to stimulate the immune system, but the results are unimpressive. Be skeptical if you read about a new injection that melts them away. Such announcements appear regularly in popular magazines.

The current state of the art of wart destruction is far from impressive. You destroy a wart by:

- Burning it
- Freezing it
- Pouring a corrosive chemical on it
- Cutting it out with a sharp instrument
- Blasting it with a laser

When many treatments exist for a problem, none are terrific.

Prepare for a Long Haul

You *must* be philosophical about warts. They have infinite patience. They will take terrible abuse, lay low for a time, then quietly reappear. With persistence the doctor can eliminate them, but there are no shortcuts.

Parents are more upset over their children's warts than their own and insist that I get rid of them. The children don't mind their warts, but the treatment terrifies them. So if there are only a few, I stall by prescribing a bland cream. Since half of all warts disappear within a year, I get credit for many painless cures.

Never imitate the occasional patient (always male) who announces: "I'm tired of these things! I want you to get rid of them. I don't care how much pain and misery it takes!"

If the doctor is foolish enough to launch an all-out assault, this patient will indeed experience pain and misery, not to mention more warts. Warts thrive on hatred. Like pimples or cockroaches or gray hairs, the more you loathe them, the more you see. Life is short. Enjoy it. Try not to think about warts. This is an essential part of a successful treatment.

Freezing Warts

Liquid nitrogen is the best treatment for isolated warts almost anywhere on the body. I use it almost exclusively. When a patient arrives, I collect a few ounces from a large Thermos kept at the nurse's station. Patients look uneasy when I enter carrying a paper cup of boiling liquid emitting clouds of steam, but I assure them that treatment is not agonizing.

Dipping an ordinary cotton swab into the nitrogen, I apply it to the wart for several seconds, then dip it again and reapply. Soon the wart turns white—it is frozen. Although a frozen wart is painless, nearby skin soon stings from the cold. I promise to stop whenever a patient asks; some grumble at the discomfort, but only about 1 in 50 refuses to let me finish.

Not a magical medicine, liquid nitrogen simply kills tissue by freezing. It's the best treatment because it doesn't require novocaine (unlike burning), takes only one session (unlike applying chemicals), and doesn't use a $30,000 instrument (unlike a laser). Watching the second hand on my watch, I keep the wart frozen for an amount of time I've determined by experience. A dry, ½-inch wart on a knee might require a minute. Ten seconds is enough for a small, delicate one on a penis.

If it doesn't remain frozen long enough, the wart persists. If I judge the time perfectly, it quietly falls off a few days later. This ideal outcome is not common because it's so embarrassing when the wart persists that doctors tend to keep the wart frozen slightly longer than necessary. In this case a small blister appears around the wart the next day. The blister may contain blood, and the wart itself may turn black, but this is not an ominous sign. Leave it alone. After about a week, the wart sloughs off, leaving behind a raw area that heals without scarring.

Unlike drugs, which any doctor can use after looking in a book, even the simplest technique takes practice. Mostly doctors practice on patients, but I also learned by practicing on myself. Liquid nitrogen is fun, and in my free moments I froze dozens of blemishes, age spots, and a few seborrheic keratoses on the back of my hands and face. So I consider myself adept.

Other doctors may not use liquid nitrogen enough to become expert, or they may not use it at all. Doctors tend to stick to the first wart technique they learn, growing more skilled as years pass, so their results are good. In any case, if you have a regular doctor, you don't have a choice. Here's what to expect from other treatments.

Burning Warts

Burning uses an instrument called a hyfrecator that buzzes loudly as it generates an electric spark. Children become hysterical and adults look nervous as the doctor approaches—despite local anesthesia. It made me nervous, too, so I was reluctant to practice and never learned. Older doctors often use it routinely because liquid nitrogen wasn't around when they began.

Burning (officially called electrocoagulation or electrosurgery) is less convenient than liquid nitrogen for small warts but quicker for large areas. After scorching the warts with the spark, the doctor scrapes them off with a rakelike instrument called a curette. He or she continues to scorch and scrape until no visible wart tissue remains. If it works, only one treatment is necessary.

Using Corrosives

Acids and other corrosive chemicals work the same as burning. After painting the area, the doctor scrapes off dead tissue, then applies more acid to any remaining wart. Depending on how quickly the corrosive works, this treatment may require several visits, but it enables the doctor to remove 100 percent of the wart with a minimum of normal tissue, so it's good for tricky areas such as the bottom of the foot. I became familiar with this technique in college, where a doctor took half a dozen visits to scrape away a plantar wart. While not excruciating, it was fairly painful.

Surgery and Lasers

Because it produces too many recurrences, surgery without burning is rarely used today.

Laser advocates say that the concentrated light beam destroys the wart more precisely than an electric spark. They're probably right, but lasers are expensive and not widely available. They may be useful for stubborn or very large warts.

Treating Genital Warts

Many patients with genital warts take one look at my sizzling cup of liquid nitrogen and refuse to allow me near. When this happens, I offer podophyllum, an evil-looking black liquid that comes in a small bottle. Since it doesn't bubble or emit clouds of steam, patients are less frightened.

Using a cotton swab, I paint podophyllum onto each wart, carefully avoiding normal skin. If this is the first treatment, I order the patient to wash it off with soap and water after 4 hours. A few can't wait; they feel burning soon after and must wash it off quickly. Most feel nothing and can leave it on longer during later visits. Warts melt away painlessly when podophyllum works, and it works almost as well as liquid nitrogen, but only for soft warts in damp areas like the genitals.

Wrinkles

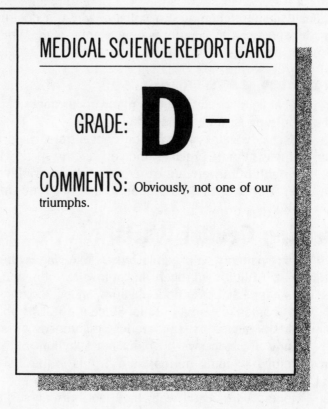

MEDICAL SCIENCE REPORT CARD

GRADE: **D** –

COMMENTS: Obviously, not one of our triumphs.

Dry skin itches, cracks, peels, and flakes, but it doesn't wrinkle. Therefore, keeping skin moist and oiled is a healthful activity that prevents several tiresome skin problems. But it won't prevent wrinkles.

The outermost layer of your skin, the epidermis, is actually dead tissue. It gradually wears away and is replaced by more dead tissue that grows up from the lining base about $\frac{1}{32}$ inch beneath the surface. Just as minor injuries and pimples in the epidermis disappear without a trace, wrinkles would do the same if they were confined to that surface layer.

Wrinkles are permanent because they originate in a deeper layer called the dermis, which is made of tough, flexible material. This material is known as connective tissue because it holds together the blood vessels, nerves, muscles, and glands that run through it. When connective tissue shrinks, wrinkles appear in the epidermis just as shrinkage of a plum produces a prune. However, although a prune's wrinkles are the result of dehydration, your wrinkles are not. The dermis is laced with blood vessels and bathed in body fluids. It never dries out.

What Causes Wrinkles?

After about age 25, cells in the dermis slowly begin to die off. With fewer cells, the dermis must shrink. This appears to be an inevitable part of aging.

Many body cells (nerves, muscles, and bones, for example) gradually die off as we age. Others (fat, unfortunately) increase. Still others (blood, intestinal lining, and epidermis) maintain their numbers.

Stretching to the Limit

The dermis is rubbery and flexible when we are young but grows stiffer as the years pass. The more often it's stretched, the flabbier it becomes—another cause of wrinkles. The face is the most mobile part of the body, so that's where the most wrinkles appear. Compare the face to the relatively smooth small of the back.

So there's some truth after all in the old advice (given to women, never men) that to prevent wrinkles you must avoid frowning or squinting. That constant stretching causes wrinkles also tallies with the finding that smokers develop wrinkles ten years sooner than average. No one is sure why, but they probably squint a great deal when smoke drifts into their eyes.

Radiation Damage

The admonition to avoid too much sun is misleading. Even a tiny amount of sun causes harm, so if you expose yourself to a modest amount of sun, you suffer a modest amount of skin damage. The sun's ultraviolet rays penetrate into the dermis, killing cells. Aging does the same. It's literally true that sunlight causes premature aging. Under the microscope, sun-damaged skin looks exactly like the skin of the elderly.

Sunlight is absolutely unnecessary for your health as long as you get sufficient vitamin D from other sources. If you lived your life in a cave, the only visible effect would be a smoother complexion.

Plastic Surgery and Retin-A

The exciting treatment for wrinkles is not worthy of the term *best medical care*. A plastic surgeon eliminates wrinkles during a face-lift by cutting into flabby connective tissue and pulling it tight. Although breathtakingly expensive and never covered by insurance, face-lifts do what they're supposed to. But they never do what (secretly) patients really want—make them look younger. I see many older women who have had a face-lift. Their wrinkles are gone, but as I watch them converse and move about I would never mistake them for anyone younger. They look like older women with smooth faces.

Retin-A has become wildly popular as a wrinkle treatment. It is almost entirely useless for this purpose. However, I recommend it and use it myself because evidence suggests that it prevents many tiresome precancerous skin conditions.

PEARL

Suntan lotion protects against sunburn but not against premature aging. Tanning is not a sign of health but a protective reaction to radiation—just as tears flow after eye irritation. A tan offers some protection against subsequent ultraviolet radiation, but having a tan is evidence that you're already suffering damage.

My wife insists that my skin is now smoother; I haven't noticed, but I am aware of some annoying side effects.

Retin-A thins the epidermis, and now and then I see an angry red abrasion, probably the result of a minor scrape. It heals in a few days. My face has also become dry despite the religious application of sun cream. Before leaving for work or a hotel call, I must head for a mirror to check for flaky patches that would detract from my professional dignity.

Although worthless for the wrinkles of aging, Retin-A does smooth away the fine wrinkles that result from sun damage, so it has a good cosmetic use, but you're better off staying out of the sun entirely.

PART TWO

How to Get the Best

Getting
the Best Doctor

American doctors rate a "C+." This grade means that we'll cure you occasionally and make you feel better most of the time.

Basically you need two things from your doctor: skill and concern.

I used to tell readers about both because everyone wants a nice doctor, but secretly I didn't rate concern highly. Personally, I told myself, when I get really sick, I want the smartest doctor, regardless of personality. Many patients agree. They're wrong, and so was I.

I realized this when my wife received news that her mammogram was abnormal. Immediately she phoned her gynecologist, who explained that the next step was to see a surgeon. Did she have a surgeon in mind? My wife mentioned one that a friend had used. He was fine, said the gynecologist, who then wished her good luck and ended the conversation. It took about a minute.

The gynecologist earned an "F" for that encounter, but my wife and I could have done better, too. Like many patients, we assumed that the doctor knew how upset we were. We should have told her.

PEARL

It's as foolish to conceal your feelings as to conceal your symptoms.

An outstanding doctor will understand your feelings just as he or she will drag out the symptoms you failed to mention. An average doctor might not.

Improving on an "F" isn't hard, and the surgeon did better, but not dramatically. He took 5 minutes to assure us that he had never seen anyone die of the findings on my wife's mammogram, then sent us to a clerk's office to schedule the biopsy. A week later, after the biopsy results were back, he assured us that my wife could expect a complete cure after a mastectomy. That also took 5 minutes. As soon as we left the office, my wife began peppering me with questions that only the surgeon could have answered—a bad sign.

As a physician, I have a better feeling for other doctors than you do, and my feeling was that he was probably a good surgeon.

An Oppenheim rule: If you find yourself saying, "He's *probably* a good doctor," *something is wrong!*

Ask Around

At this point, I finally did what I tell readers to do. I actively searched for a better doctor by asking the opinion of *more than one* other doctor. When several spoke enthusiastically about one particular surgeon, I chose him. And they were right. He spent half an hour with my wife explaining her tumor and the pros and cons of his recommendation, then another 45 minutes with us together going over every detail and drawing questions from us. Concerned about our fears, he seemed willing to spend whatever time was necessary to relieve them. Later he did little things that (in my experience) doctors don't do well; for example, when he said he'd call back at a certain time when lab results were available, he called. Even his office personnel were nice. He was terrific.

As for his skills, I had to trust the doctors who recommended him. Sheer medical knowledge is hard to determine, even for other doctors. Finding the most brilliant doctor is even harder and only important if you have an obscure disease or require a complicated procedure that's rarely performed. If you have a heart attack, breast cancer, or another serious but common disease, your chance of surviving depends more on the course of the illness than the brains of the physician. You should try to get an excellent doctor, but you must absolutely have a concerned one.

The Case for Concern

The first weeks after my wife's mammogram were awful. I thought she might die—even though (deep down) I knew this was unlikely. Her cancer appeared on a routine mammogram; it was so small doctors couldn't feel it. Yet it wasn't nothing—it was *cancer*. The first surgeon assured me that an operation would cure her. None of this made us feel better. It wouldn't make you feel better, either. Only the right sort of doctor can help.

At some time in your life you'll face the possibility of your death or that of someone you love and expect to have around permanently. If it hasn't happened already, you don't realize how devastating this will be—and you can't mentally prepare for it.

The first event may be a heart attack, but it may be simply an abnormal Pap smear or mammogram or an electrocardiogram showing that one coronary artery is uncomfortably narrow. When the news arrives you will realize that (1) up to now your life, for all its problems, has been pretty good and (2) it will never again be as good. It doesn't matter how much you know about medicine or even if you're a hypochondriac or a veteran patient with a host of medical problems. Your life will never be the same.

Eventually you'll pull yourself together, but you don't want to go through this experience alone—without an expert who understands how bad you feel. You need an outstanding doctor—not one who can work miracles (although that's always nice)—but one who comprehends your pain and is obviously doing his or her best for you. Having such a physician lifts a weight from your shoulders. You know you're in the right hands; you're never forced to say to yourself, He's *probably* a good doctor.

This is where I differ from others who tell you how to get the best medical care. Finding a smart doctor isn't difficult. A solid minority are what I call sharp: intelligent, alert, unlikely to be ignorant of something they should know. They tend to use the best treatments I discuss in these chapters (at least for serious diseases; for others such as bronchitis, all bets are off).

These sharp doctors are fine for your annual physical, rashes, minor injuries, respiratory infections, or bellyaches, even serious bellyaches. But sooner or later something happens that requires more than brains. It could be a life-threatening disease or something as simple as a diagnosis of high blood pressure. You might think that high blood pressure is an easy burden compared to cancer, but sometimes it isn't. Studies of job absenteeism show that workers with high blood pressure have a much worse record than average—even when their pressure is controlled. These people aren't physically sicker; apparently these workers feel unhealthy. Their doctors may have prescribed the best treatment and assured them that their life expectancy is normal, but they haven't lifted the burden of illness. The best doctors lift this burden.

Where Not to Look

When you're looking for a doctor, some of the resources that might seem to be the best are not.

How *not* to find the best doctor (1):   Go to the Mayo Clinic or another famous institution.

The Mayo Clinic is probably the best clinic in Rochester, Minnesota, one of the best in that state, an excellent choice if you live in the Midwest, and a good clinic overall. Its doctors, however, are not superior to those available in any reasonable-size city.

Writers traditionally tell you that the best doctors congregate at medical schools and their clinics, but that's an exaggeration. As a medical student at New York University for four years, I grew familiar with the faculty. A few were genuinely outstanding, and I still worship their memory. Many were very good. But I wouldn't recommend a fair number, mostly because of their personalities. Incompetents were rare, although when the pure researchers came out of the lab to take their turns teaching, interns and residents looked bored and ignored their advice. Overall, doctors in reputable clinics have better-than-average skills, but true humanitarians are no more common in famous clinics than elsewhere. Choose a doctor from a medical center if you must make a quick choice.

How *not* to find the best doctor (2): Examine his or her credentials.

If you need brain surgery, you'll want to use a board-certified neurosurgeon. Finding such a doctor is unlikely to require research, however, because few U.S. hospitals allow noncertified surgeons on staff. For your regular care, a trained internist or family practitioner is probably fine, but don't make too much of that impressive certificate on the wall. I'm board-certified in family practice, and I achieved this by passing a test that wasn't hard. In fact, I must take it every six years, and I recently mailed in $500 for my third certification. Although I'll be taking the same test as trainees fresh out of residency, I'll pass easily—despite missing most questions in areas I don't practice, such as obstetrics. The test is so easy that I question the competence of doctors who score much lower than I but still pass. You can't question them because you won't know their scores; only the doctor and the testing organization know.

Feel free to determine if a doctor is board-certified, but obtaining this kind of information is not as valuable as you might think. Let's say you need plastic surgery. Should you be satisfied if the doctor displays a certification from the National Society of Plastic Surgeons? No. I invented the name. Did you guess that? What about the American Board of Cosmetic Surgery? That's genuine, but it's just an organization of doctors who perform plastic surgery. They don't have to be (and usually aren't) trained plastic surgeons, who are accredited by the American Board of Plastic Surgery. You could go to the library and consult a directory of medical specialists, but if your library resembles mine, its directory is several years old.

How *not* to find the best doctor (3): Ask your friends.

On the other hand, asking your friends is better than picking a name out of the phone book. If half a dozen are enthusiastic about one particular doctor, that's a fairly good recommendation. He or she is certainly a humanitarian. Your friends' enthusiasm doesn't say anything about competence, however.

Never take the word of only one or two friends. People have different tastes, so every doctor has fiercely loyal patients. Neither my brother nor I was happy when my mother's gynecologist advised her to have a hysterectomy. Her problem didn't seem to require one. When we hinted that she get a second opinion, she became upset. She liked her gynecologist and was not about to question his decision. So we shut up, and she had the surgery. Once you find a doctor you love, you won't welcome the idea that he or she could be wrong. Experts who urge you to get second opinions and challenge your doctor's judgment live in an absolutely reasonable universe, but not the one that you and I inhabit (mind you, I approve of second opinions, but many patients find the thought terribly disturbing). If you're going to have absolute faith in a doctor, make sure you choose an outstanding one.

Ask Other Doctors

When it comes right down to it, there is really only one rule for finding the best doctor: Ask other doctors.

Outstanding doctors aren't rare! Probably 10 percent of us practice humanitarianism, problem solving, and healing at the highest level, so you shouldn't have to travel to find one. Furthermore, these doctors are known to their colleagues. Ask.

But don't ask only one. Like your friends, doctors have strange tastes. They like their friends and often refer patients to one particular specialist out of habit. When you ask, notice whether the doctor gives the recommendation with pleasure and without qualification. Finding a spot on her chest x-ray, my mother's doctor referred her to a chest surgeon but cautioned that he lacked charm. The surgeon turned out to be positively rude and often reduced my mother to tears. When she complained, her doctor assured her that he was a wonderful surgeon despite his personality.

The truth is that he was a competent ass. My mother's surgery didn't require great technical skill (most operations don't), but surgery is so frightening that surgeons should be even more humanitarian than the average doctor. Don't accept less.

Both the surgeon and the oncologist now taking care of my wife are terrific. The doctors I asked told me so. They knew because patients they referred reported back, *and* they saw these doctors in action and found them sensible, skilled, and caring. You can't beat that sort of recommendation.

Don't expect every doctor to know someone terrific in every field. I know half a dozen specialists because of either personal experience or reputation. But, for example, I don't know a terrific urologist. The one I use seems good, but I haven't referred enough serious problems to him and I don't know him personally, so I have no evidence that he's outstanding. But "good" isn't bad.

My wife likes her gynecologist, and I'm sure the gynecologist is at least "good," although she flopped badly when handling my wife's mammogram. Because of this, I'm uneasy thinking how she would behave if my wife came down with a serious gynecological problem. If I followed my own advice, I'd make a dozen phone calls and find a terrific gynecologist; however, my wife is not interested in switching, and I often ignore my own advice. But you shouldn't.

The Best Doctors: What They Do

Hurrying to a meeting, an internist reached an elevator as it began to close. Naturally, he put his hand between the doors. Rushing to the same meeting, a surgeon also saw an elevator closing. A surgeon must never endanger his hands, so he thrust his head between the doors."

Internists tell this story to illustrate that surgeons are not so smart. On their part, surgeons believe that internists love the intellectual side of medicine so much that they rarely do anything useful. Surgeons get things done.

Far back during medical school, I recall morning rounds on a medicine ward. One patient with a rare disease required a new and poisonous drug. The professor in charge, together with the residents, interns, and students, remained in the hall for half an hour discussing how the drug worked, how to give it safely, and what happened as it worked. After 10 minutes, one student who later became a surgeon detached himself from the group and paced the hall restlessly. Although this was rude, he was only a medical student, so the others ignored him. Over dinner later, he proclaimed loudly to anyone who would listen that he had just spent the most boring period of time in his life: 30 minutes discussing how to give a drug. How could anyone endure something so dull? In fact, I found it interesting.

Although you're aware of differences in bedside manner, you probably don't realize how doctors vary in other areas. We had various reasons for going to medical school. Once there, we enjoyed different subjects and chose a specialty for different reasons, and in practice we enjoy some medical problems more than others. You should know all this because it affects the quality of your care.

Choosing a Doctor

Whom should you see for an earache? Most likely it will be a family doctor like me because we're the cheapest and most accessible. But if money and convenience were not a problem, you might choose an ear, nose, and throat (ENT) specialist because he or she knows the most about ears. Choosing a specialist would be a mistake. When I see someone with an earache, I sometimes find an infection and give an antibiotic. Equally often, my exam is normal, so I know that it's a less serious problem that will go away with only symptomatic treatment such as a decongestant.

An ENT specialist is a surgeon, which means that he or she prefers action. *Action* never means waiting or prescribing an over-the-counter drug, so when my earache patients go to an ENT specialist they always get an antibiotic. Similarly, I don't x-ray every sprained ankle I see, but an orthopedic surgeon does.

Sheer medical knowledge is only one of three qualities that make a good doctor. The best doctors combine all three, but certain specialties attract doctors who excel in one. These qualities are:

1. Humanitarian
2. Problem solver
3. Healer

Humanitarians sympathize with suffering and want to help. They prefer primary care specialties such as family practice and pediatrics. Problem solvers enjoy gathering information and carefully putting together clues. They enjoy the intellectual specialties such as neurology, pathology, and all the subspecialties of internal medicine: cardiology, endocrinology, gastroenterology, respiratory medicine, and so on. Healers want to make a sick person well—preferably quickly. They choose surgery.

I enjoy questioning patients and performing tests in order to solve a difficult problem, but few of a family doctor's patients require this. All family doctors get a thrill from healing—converting a sick patient into a well patient on the spot. I do this when I remove a sliver, take a foreign body out of an eye, drain a painful boil, or sew up a laceration. But once again, I don't do this often.

Mostly I take people who feel bad and help them feel better. Rarely does this form of care involve making a difficult diagnosis. Although I heal many patients (but still a minority), it usually takes time.

The Doctor Helps, Maybe

There's often a difference between what you *believe* your doctor does and what *actually* occurs.

If your doctor is a skilled humanitarian (number 1 above), the odds are that you give credit for more of numbers 2 and 3 than he or she deserves. But that's fine. You both benefit.

I am a hotel doctor. Vomiters make up my most urgent calls from hotels. They are miserably sick, and reassurance that this agony rarely lasts long brings no comfort. They want to see me.

After 95 percent of my exams, I announce that my diagnosis is the common stomach virus. Guests are always impressed at my acumen because they blame an upset stomach on their previous meal. I follow this diagnosis with advice, medication, and perhaps an antivomiting injection. Leaving, I assure the guest that the worst is over, and I'm usually right.

When I phone later to check, guests express effusive

thanks, and it's clear that they believe my efforts have cured them. The truth is that these illnesses run their course no matter what a doctor does, but my presence comforted the guest, and my medications probably made the symptoms not quite so bad. I enjoy these visits. A pure problem solver or healer would find them unchallenging.

Getting the Best

No matter what other skills you need in a doctor, you want a humanitarian. You certainly want one for a family doctor, but it's no less important for a specialist. I can almost hear what you must be thinking:

"I hear what you're saying. Some people need that—people like my Aunt Minnie. She's a hypochondriac. She goes to the doctor all the time. But not me. I don't go unless I'm really sick. No one has to hold my hand. When I have a stomach problem, I want a good stomach man. When I have a heart problem, a heart man."

I hear this viewpoint all the time, invariably from men who have not yet been terrified by a medical problem. These men *really* need a humanitarian. They'll understand this better after hearing the first bad news about themselves or someone they love. I discuss that in the previous chapter.

The Physical Exam

I give medical science a "D" for physical examinations. This means that they rarely save a life but sometimes make the patient feel better. The "D" rates the exam: what the doctor does with hands and a few instruments like the stethoscope.

I evaluate tests in the next chapter.

Like most doctors of my generation, I left training believing in the value of a regular checkup. A few weeks after beginning practice with a medical group, a veteran general practitioner complimented me on the length and complexity of my physical exam.

"But you're not an intern anymore," he went on, "and the patients aren't sick. You're spending too much time and falling behind. Physical exams are mostly public relations. A patient wants to feel good after one. If there's a real problem, you and I can tell as soon as he walks in the door. Maybe he's fat. Cigarettes in his pocket. The nurse has already put his blood pressure on the chart. What else are we going to find?

"Making patients feel good takes 20 minutes, no more. Ask a few questions. Do a quick exam. You have to put your hands on their body. There's magic in a doctor's hands. Include one embarrassing thing like a rectal exam. That tells them that you're thorough. Then order tests. Patients want lots of tests: bloods and at least one x-ray. You could x-ray their big toe, and they'd be happy. Patients love that machine. . . . If you want to, ask a lot of questions—if their grandmother had diabetes, that sort of thing. If you want to write a long scientific analysis in the chart, go ahead. But nobody cares. Hands and tests: That's what the patient wants."

Old doctors get cynical, and young doctors think they know it all, so I brushed off this advice. But as the months went by, and my schedule of four physicals a day grew into hundreds, it became obvious that I was discovering very little hidden illness. Puzzled, I looked through the medical literature. At the time, experts approved of a regular physical, but when they tried to prove that it saved lives, they couldn't. They're still trying. Even today, there's no proof that periodic checkups (even obvious good things like a breast exam) save lives.

Like apple pie and baseball, the complete physical is an American tradition. It doesn't exist elsewhere in the world. A healthy person who asked a British doctor for a head-to-toe exam would be treated like a hypochondriac or shooed out of the office.

Great (but Unrealistic) Expectations

A physical exam has some uses, but before I tell you what they are, here are illustrations of what it *doesn't* accomplish.

- Mrs. Jones, a 40-year-old school principal, comes in at the end of every spring semester. Except for tension headaches and an appendectomy, she has always been well. When the results are in, and I tell her they are normal, she is pleased.

  "I guess I have a clean bill of health for another year," she said once.

279

Mrs. Jones believes that a complete physical gives her a clean bill of health.

- Mrs. Smith, a 35-year-old housewife, had a different reason for her physical. During routine questioning I asked if she had any problems.

  "Just some pains in my stomach. Otherwise I feel fine."

  I asked several questions about the pain, then moved on to other subjects. Unlike Mrs. Jones, Mrs. Smith was not pleased that her exam was normal.

  "But what about my stomach?" she asked. "It keeps me up at night. I've lost my appetite. My husband thinks it's an ulcer." Hearing this, I reversed gears and spent a long session concentrating on her stomach. My next scheduled patients waited.

  Mrs. Smith looked on a physical exam as a "superappointment." A regular appointment was fine for an ordinary problem, she believed. But if it was serious, one should have a complete physical.

- Mr. Johnson was a 22-year-old student, recently married, with no complaints. That aroused my suspicions. It's rare for someone so young to want a physical. Did he have any aches and pains? No, he felt fine. Had a friend come down with a serious disease or died? No. Had he read about a medical problem that applied to him? No. Any problems at school? Socially? No. What about his sex life?

  Silence. Bull's-eye!

  Mr. Johnson's physical was his admission ticket: an acceptable reason for seeing a doctor. Many people are embarrassed to mention a problem directly. During a physical exam, they hope, the doctor will discover what's wrong and painlessly correct it.

Don't make these mistakes. A regular inspection is less important for a human than for a Boeing 747 or Chevrolet. A heart sounds normal just before a heart attack—and often while it's occurring. No doctor can detect early emphysema by listening to the chest with a stethoscope. By the time your lungs sound sick, you're really sick. On the other hand, a physical can be useful. Follow these guidelines.

Never get a physical if you're sick.   If you belong to a health maintenance organization (HMO), the initial appointment will take months to set up, and the doctor may simply record your complaint on the "problem list," plow through the exam, then give you another appointment to deal with the problem. A complete exam is not a deluxe appointment but a way of gathering routine data about you. In fact, it's more for your doctor's benefit than yours.

Never get a physical from someone you'll never see again.   When the backlog grew too large, an HMO that employed me scheduled physicals on weekends and offered us extra money to churn them out. I declined. That weekend offer struck me as medical hell. When a doctor dies and goes to hell, he's put to work doing complete physicals on an endless line of healthy people. It's dreary labor for the doctor and almost useless for the patient.

Always get a physical from your regular doctor. Get a regular doctor as soon as you're too old for your pediatrician. Young adults mostly ignore this advice for a stupid reason ("I never get sick"). Few would put off getting medical insurance with that excuse. Taking pot luck with emergency room doctors when you're sick and miserable is an experience you want to avoid.

A physical exam "bonds" a doctor to a patient. It enables us to get familiar with you and record routine information without the distraction of your being sick. Doctors have a proprietary interest in their own patients. They are more likely to give advice and prescriptions over the phone and more willing to fit you into a crowded schedule if you're sick. At major clinics, a doctor whose schedule is filled can always send a patient to the walk-in clinic where people like me work and where the patient might wait for hours. But doctors—at least the ones I approve of—see familiar patients when they call even if it means staying late. An important part of your health care is making sure a doctor knows who you are.

Go yearly after age 50.   Reaching 50 is a milestone in everyone's life; one of the lesser stones is that your chance of needing a doctor rises rapidly from now on. Don't go for a complete exam, but go to keep up the relationship and check for a few unpleasant diseases.

Getting to Know You

Beginning in middle life, parts of the exam become essential—but not, unfortunately, the parts you look forward to, such as those involving the stethoscope, ophthalmoscope, and reflex hammer. As my patients grow older, their heart sounds grow more interesting (meaning abnormal), their eyes show colorful changes, especially if they have diabetes or severe atherosclerosis, and ankle reflexes often disappear. Although worth recording in the chart and useful for checking on a problem already present, these changes are less important for finding new diseases.

Above all, you need a finger in your rectum once a year. If you're a man, it will keep track of your relentlessly swelling prostate (and you're better off if it's the same finger). More important, it will feel for the small, hard lump that indicates prostate cancer, something you definitely want diagnosed early. In both sexes it will feel for a rectal cancer, then smear a piece of stool on a slide and test for blood. Colon cancers sometimes ooze a small amount of blood.

The rest of the exam is unlikely to save your life, but I detect plenty of skin cancer, gum disease, cataracts, and enough accumulated earwax to cause profound deafness. Mostly I call attention to paunches, lack of exercise, and inadequate diet and sympathize with constipation, insomnia, and worries about mortality. You want this sort of relationship with a doctor, and you must get it before you need it.

Lab Tests and X-Rays

Lab tests and x-rays are good when properly used, but patients exaggerate their importance. I give them a "B." Tests are best at confirming what a doctor already suspects—a chest x-ray is superb at finding or eliminating the possibility of pneumonia. They are not so good when a doctor isn't sure what's going on. When a patient has had an annoying cough for months but isn't sick, a chest x-ray rarely gives the answer. They're bad when a patient feels fine—if your doctor automatically orders a chest x-ray during your annual physical, he's behind the times; no expert recommends them.

Telltale Tests

Long ago, a whole family came to my office in great distress. A week before, they had participated in a free multiphasic screening series offered by the husband's union. A local laboratory had performed 30 blood tests plus urinalyses, chest x-rays, and electrocardiograms on everyone. A few days later the mail brought the results: several impressive computer printouts—each with a warning to see a doctor.

I understood their concern. The family assumed they were in good health, yet the husband's chest x-ray showed "evidence of emphysema." The wife's blood revealed an overactive thyroid, and the son had an abnormal liver test.

I assured them that none of this was true. The husband did not have emphysema; he was simply thin. A chest film looks abnormally dark in emphysema because destruction of lung tissue leaves less to stop x-rays before they strike the film. A thin, healthy person also has less lung because his chest is smaller. A doctor seeing the film without knowing the patient can't tell the difference.

The wife did not have thyroid disease. She was pregnant. Pregnancy (and birth control pills) produce changes in the blood that make thyroid hormone appear elevated. The gland itself continues to work normally.

The son did not have liver disease. In children and adolescents, several blood tests are normally higher than the adult level.

Tests Aren't Perfect

It's easy to understand why patients value tests so much. For one thing, they involve expensive and complicated machinery. Americans love technology. For another, the working of a doctor's mind is mysterious, so it's hard to speculate on what's going on. But a test seems easy to understand. Doesn't a blood sugar tell if you have diabetes? Doesn't an electrocardiogram show how healthy your heart is? The answer to both is: sometimes. Tests have limitations. Here are four.

No test measures everything. A stomach x-ray does not tell everything there is to know about the stomach. A urinalysis reveals something about kidney function, but you can have kidney disease and normal urine.

No lab is perfect. In the average laboratory, an error rate of 2 percent is considered excellent.

A normal test doesn't mean healthy—and an abnormal one doesn't mean disease. In statistics, normal results include exactly 95 percent of the population—but not 100 percent. Everybody outside that range is abnormal. A woman 4 feet, 10 inches tall is certainly outside the 95 percent range, so she is abnormally short. But is she diseased? Maybe, but we need more information. That's why doctors are useful.

Many factors can distort a test result. Among them are age, youth, pregnancy, medications, minor illness, even stress.

Tests at Patient Request

During the 1970s, hypoglycemia was purported to be the leading cause of headaches, fatigue, and general unhappiness with life in young patients who were otherwise in good health. I still hear of hypoglycemia, but it's been superseded (as I write) by Epstein-Barr and chronic yeast infections. Another disease may have appeared by the time you read this. Young Americans expect to feel perfect. Doctors (who are neither young nor as healthy) tend to be unsympathetic, so such patients look elsewhere for an answer—just as overweight patients do. Fad diseases come and go as often as fad diets.

Doctors check for hypoglycemia with a 5-hour glucose tolerance test (GTT)—giving a drink of sugar, then measuring blood sugar at intervals for the rest of the morning. During its heyday, many patients announced (defensively; they had consulted non-M.D. practitioners who claimed expertise in their problem) that they had hypoglycemia and then handed me a printout of their 5-hour GTT. Sure enough, one or two readings were below normal. Remembering the guidelines earlier, I always asked, "How did you feel during the test?" Almost everyone answered that they felt no different from normal.

Early on, I would announce triumphantly that this proved that they *didn't* have hypoglycemia! To make the diagnosis, one must have symptoms of hypoglycemia (hunger, headaches, sweating, palpitations) at the same time that the blood sugar is low; normal people often have low results during the test. No one believed me. Their blood sugar was low, they repeated firmly. That meant that they had hypoglycemia. Today, I look respectfully at the lab slip and nod sympathetically.

Despite these limitations, tests earn a "B." Thousands exist, so many that they require an entire book.

In the meantime, don't exaggerate their importance. Despite the wonders of technology, doctors make almost all diagnoses by listening to what you tell them. To break it down, a doctor gets information from:

- History (i.e., your description of what's going on plus answers to his or her questions)—90 percent
- Physical exam—5 percent
- Tests—5 percent

Why Test?

"I was okay until I got to work, then I began to shiver and my head hurt. So I took my temperature and . . ."

"You have influenza."

Young doctors enjoy showing off by announcing the diagnosis before a patient finishes explaining. Although other doctors are impressed, patients aren't. They *want* a chance to describe their miseries. Young doctors soon learn to keep their mouths shut.

After greeting a patient, I ask the reason for the visit, then wait until he or she runs out of gas. Sometimes I prod with "What else?" or "Then what?" At the end, I'm almost always certain of what's going on. I'm rarely surprised by the results of the exam or tests. Your history is so important that you should make an effort to do a good job on it. Tell a coherent story. Give the facts. Never say:

- "I can't describe the pain." (Your cat can't describe pain; humans have this ability.)
- "I've had this since I got home from vacation." (When, exactly, was that? Some doctors can read your mind, but don't count on it.)
- "It really doesn't bother me, but my wife insisted." (Never apologize for the visit; I hardly ever order patients to leave on the grounds that they're not sick enough.)

- "I think I've got strep throat." (That's *my* line! I give the diagnosis; your job is to complain.)

Despite the low yield in usable information, lab tests are an important part of practice. I order them for several reasons:

- To gather more information
- To reassure a patient
- To satisfy my curiosity
- To cover myself in case of a malpractice suit

Gathering information. This is the most important function of the tests. Although you probably believe that knowing what test to order is the mark of a good doctor, knowing what *not* to order is a better mark. Doctors order far too many tests, and inexperienced doctors order even more.

I'm always entertained observing younger colleagues during the flu season. Unlike most patients, flu victims look miserable. They shake with fever and ache all over. They can barely hold themselves erect for an exam. Diagnosing flu isn't difficult, and treatment is simple.

Confronted with someone who looks so sick, some doctors feel they must do more. Infections elevate the white count, so many doctors order a blood count. Sure enough, the white count is high. A urinalysis may show protein. Protein isn't normally present in the urine, but a high fever can change this. Sure enough, there it is. Flu victims often cough. Since a cough can also be a sign of pneumonia, some doctors order a chest x-ray. Flu victims may have a sore throat; this can lead to a throat culture. In the end, we all reach the same conclusion: The patient has flu.

On the other hand, tests can be essential in some cases. You can suspect pneumonia or strep throat on the basis of a history or exam, but only a test can confirm it. I don't order these tests for every cough or sore throat because, after the history and physical, I may not suspect pneumonia or strep. However, I may order one anyway for another reason.

Reassuring patients. This is an essential part of a doctor's job, and a test is often the safest way.

Unlike some doctors, I detest giving antibiotics for viral upper respiratory infections, but many patients are visibly unhappy if a doctor doesn't "do" something. So I sometimes take a throat culture even when I'm confident that it's not strep. Two days later when I call with the results, the patient usually feels better and is pleased to hear that it was "nothing." Two days earlier this would not have been good news.

Satisfying curiosity. Although this sounds like a strange reason to order tests, you're better off if your doctor does a bit of sleuthing now and then. It means that he or she enjoys practicing medicine.

As an example, if I see a hotel guest with an upset stomach and yellow eyeballs, the diagnosis is almost always hepatitis. With a simple urine test I carry in my box, I can confirm it. That's all I do, unless the patient is very ill (at the patient's leisure, he should get a test to refine the diagnosis to hepatitis A, B, or C).

Seeing the same patient in the office, a doctor will order a battery of liver function tests, a blood count, and perhaps a collection of other tests. Then he'll see the patient at intervals and repeat the liver functions. I also see hepatitis patients regularly because it's important to make sure that the test results return to normal (occasionally hepatitis becomes chronic), but I do this with a single test. Very few doctors order a single liver test.

The truth is that we enjoy looking at abnormal results, provided the patient isn't seriously ill. In garden-variety hepatitis, a patient who feels mildly under the weather may have a blood alanine aminotransferase (a measure of liver damage) of over 5,000. Since a normal level might be 40, this spectacular number sends shivers down a doctor's spine no different from what a baseball fan feels reading that his favorite pitcher has struck out 17 batters. He may show the lab slip to colleagues and listen to their oohs and aahs.

Covering myself in case of a malpractice suit. When questioned, doctors agree that testing for this reason is an almost universal practice . . . but that they personally never do it.

I do it now and then. A typical situation might be a mother who brings in her infant who has fallen out of the crib. Except for a huge lump on the head, the baby is fine, and my physical exam is normal. A baby is resilient; if it didn't lose consciousness and has nothing wrong on an exam, the chance of brain injury is almost zero, and no test can detect the rare child with an injury. Skull x-rays won't.

"So you don't think he needs skull x-rays?" the mother asks after hearing my explanation. Most patients are too polite to demand a test, but when I hear this hesitant question, it puts me on the spot. Furthermore, I need only look around to feel the pressure. The family is staring at me hopefully. The nurse is also awaiting my answer—probably holding an x-ray slip already filled out. If I am working for another doctor or a clinic, I must wonder what my boss would do; looking at the nurse gives a hint. I also know that doctors are sued for failing to order a test—never for ordering something useless.

Finally I know that if I change my mind *everyone will be happy!* The family will smile. The nurses will relax. I'll feel the pressure disappear. That's a powerful temptation, and I sometimes give in.

Prevention

Medical science gets a "B" for overall prevention. As befits such a high grade, proper prevention often saves lives and almost always makes you healthier. However, depending on the disease, medical science earns different grades:

- Prevention of polio: A
- Prevention of bowel cancer: B
- Prevention of osteoporosis: C
- Prevention of the common cold: D
- Prevention of Alzheimer's disease: F

When I say prevention I don't mean turning the clock back. If you already have high blood pressure or diabetes, or you've just had your first heart attack, you need treatment, not prevention. Advice in this chapter may keep things from getting worse, but it's unlikely to eliminate damage already present.

Nothing spurs my patients' interest in prevention more than their first serious illness, which usually happens as they near middle age. I wish younger patients shared their enthusiasm.

Because it would take an entire volume to discuss prevention of all common diseases, this chapter focuses only on our leading public health problems.

Preventing Heart Disease

Prevention of coronary artery disease really must be graded according to when preventive measures begin:

- From childhood: A
- From age 35: B
- From age 55: C

Coronary artery disease, the number one cause of death, is entirely preventable, although it requires a diet that most Americans won't tolerate (see the chapter on angina). Children, of course, tolerate whatever they're given (don't nit-pick about spinach). "A" prevention begins in childhood with a diet very low in cholesterol and saturated fats. Vegetarianism isn't required, but meat is less important than Americans tend to think it is.

Don't feed infants this low-fat diet, however. They need whole milk and plenty of fat for normal growth. Begin the heart protecting after age five. If a child reaches adulthood with a cholesterol under 150 and maintains this throughout life, the risk of coronary artery disease, hardening of the arteries, and heart attacks is essentially zero.

Preventing Cancer

Cancer prevention earns a "B."

Although cancer is not entirely preventable, you can lower your risk a great deal. Like osteoporosis and the gradual decline of many organs such as kidney and lungs, many cancers are an inevitable part of aging. Here's a summary of the best preventives.

291

- Never smoking gets an "A" for lung, mouth, tongue, throat, esophageal, and larynx cancer and a "B" for bladder and pancreatic cancer and leukemia. A heavy smoker who stops does one grade better, so quitting is still worthwhile.
- Staying thin earns a "B" for breast and uterine cancer.
- Never being pregnant or having only one sexual partner earns a "B" for cervical cancer.
- Remaining a virgin is an "A" preventive for both cervical and penile cancer and a "B" for prostate cancer.
- Having many pregnancies earns a "C" for preventing breast and ovarian cancer.
- Taking birth control pills reduces the risk of uterine and ovarian cancer enough to earn a "B."
- Keeping out of the sun reduces skin cancer to almost zero, an "A."
- Avoiding alcohol gets an "A −" in preventing esophageal cancer (and a "B" for accidents, murder, and suicide).
- A very high fiber diet gets a "B" for colon cancer, provided you follow it from childhood on.

Keeping Blood Pressure Down

The grade for high blood pressure prevention depends on the age at which the measures are started:

- From childhood: A
- From age 35: B
- From age 55: C

Completely avoiding salt is all that's necessary, but (as in the diet to eliminate coronary artery disease) this takes more "avoiding" than most Americans would tolerate. Among primitive tribes, where salt intake is extremely low, high blood pressure doesn't exist, and pressure doesn't rise with advancing age as it does in all advanced countries.

I still hear experts insisting that excessive salt intake

doesn't cause high blood pressure. Being experts, they point to studies in which people were interviewed to learn how much salt they consumed. It turns out that the high salt intake group has no more hypertension than those classified as low salt.

This example shows how a single flaw in a good study ends up producing nonsense. In this case, researchers weren't comparing a high salt intake with a low salt intake. Their "high" group had a titanic intake; the "low" group's intake was merely huge.

The typical American diet includes an immense excess of salt—10 to 20 times what the body requires. When experts found that those eating 10 times the body's requirement (their "low-salt" group) had just as much hypertension, they came to the wrong conclusion because they'd picked the wrong group.

In fact, it's hard to find anyone in the United States who consumes as little as twice the daily requirement. Avoiding salt to this degree involves avoiding almost all commercially canned, frozen, baked, precooked, and processed food and restaurant food. But that's a diet that prevents high blood pressure.

Stopping Strokes

Preventing strokes earns an "A−."

Almost all strokes result from high blood pressure or atherosclerosis, so anyone with the fortitude to prevent those conditions receives a stroke-free report card as a bonus.

Preventing Diabetes

Preventing diabetes earns an "F" for type 1 and a "B" for Type 2. (See the chapter on diabetes for an explanation of the types.)

No one is certain what destroys insulin-producing beta cells in Type 1 diabetes, so we don't know how to prevent it. A good deal of research is in progress, so this state of affairs may change in the next decade.

Staying thin helps prevent the insulin resistance that leads to Type 2 diabetes. The fewer calories you take in, the less beta cells must work to provide the necessary insulin. Becoming thin is almost as good as staying thin, so it's never too late.

Preventing Other Disorders

Our prevention report card wouldn't be complete without a few more biggies:

Preventing accidents: grade C.   Driving safely and avoiding alcohol are the major accident preventives. Wearing seat belts and using safety seats for children earns an "A−" for preventing death and injury.

Preventing chronic bronchitis and emphysema: grade A.   These conditions are rare in nonsmokers.

Preventing pneumonia and influenza: grade C. Immunizations for both these conditions work fairly well. Everyone past 65 or with a chronic disease such as diabetes or emphysema should get immunized.

Preventing suicide: grade B−.   Being married and avoiding alcohol both lower the risk of suicide. Doctors make a major contribution when they treat depression.

Preventing cirrhosis: grade A−.   Chronic hepatitis occasionally results in cirrhosis, but alcohol causes well over 90 percent.

Drugs

Drugs get a grade of "B − ." Humans have an uncontrollable urge to take a drug when they feel ill, and physicians have always obliged. Depending on the culture, a healer may or may not cast spells, dance, thrust needles, or enter a trance, but *all* prescribe potions. Until recently only a few drugs had a useful action (opium relieved pain and diarrhea; quinine suppressed malaria). Many made sick people sicker. Doctors and patients once believed that a very unpleasant action meant that the drug was powerful; both looked with approval on those that produced vomiting, diarrhea, sweating, and hallucinations. But most drugs were useless.

Until 50 years ago, doctors discovered most useful drugs by accident. This was literally the case for one major advance in cancer treatment. According to a story, the discovery followed a ship explosion in an Italian harbor during World War II. The ship carried nitrogen mustard, the basis of mustard gas, a popular weapon of World War I (no one has explained why this poison was aboard). During the weeks that followed, dozens of sailors died of bleeding and infections as a result of bone marrow suppression. Tissue in your marrow makes blood cells: red cells that carry oxygen, white cells that fight infection, and platelets that produce clots.

Observing this effect, doctors remembered that bone marrow cells are wildly overactive in leukemia; later they tried nitrogen mustard in a few patients—and it worked. Nitrogen mustard was the first effective leukemia treatment.

Designer Medications

Although accidents are still useful, today scientists know so much about human physiology and disease action that they can decide what a drug must do, then design one. Thus, during the 1950s doctors noticed that penicillin no longer cured staph infections. Researchers found that resistant bacteria had begun producing an enzyme that broke the penicillin molecule at one spot, rendering it useless. So scientists attached a bulky molecule to that vulnerable spot on the penicillin molecule, shielding it from the enzyme. That particular form of penicillin continues to kill staph.

This talent for designing drugs has produced a flood so great no doctor can keep track of them. It has also diminished one class that dominated previous centuries: useless drugs that were fairly harmless. Today drugs are more likely to do what they're supposed to but also more likely to cause problems. A drug that slows the heart may slow it too much. An antibiotic that kills an amazingly large variety of germs will miss only obscure, nasty ones that nothing can kill, so these multiply and become important.

Nevertheless, this is progress. I expect it to continue, but I hope human nature will catch up. So far patients still come to the doctor yearning for a drug. They rarely yearn for surgery, sigmoidoscopy, or cardiac catheterization—useful procedures with unpleasant features. Yet drugs can be equally unpleasant.

Everything Has Side Effects

A good rule to remember: The more essential the organ, the more difficult it is to make the drug work right—efficiently and with tolerable side effects.

PEARL

When you're sick, go to the doctor for help, but let us decide what form that help should take. If you even hint that you want a drug (". . . so you don't think I need an antibiotic?"), you're more likely to get one.

You can't do without a heart, so cardiac drugs are powerful and tricky. Family doctors overprescribe them. In a patient whose heart has many extra beats, for example, it's not always necessary to treat these extra beats. Yet the sight of an irregular electrocardiograph tracing makes some doctors nervous, and they feel they must do something. Fortunately, they usually give an inadequate dose of the drug that treats this condition and their elderly patients frequently forget to take it, so I rarely encounter side effects—which, when they happen, are often a consequence of the intended effects. Drugs that stimulate the heart tend to make it more irritable and susceptible to irregular rhythms. Drugs that suppress irregular beats tend to suppress normal ones, too, so the heart pumps more weakly.

Unlike most health writers, I don't spend much time warning about the side effects of drugs. It does more harm than good. When a patient announces that he's just read that a drug I prescribe causes impotence, bleeding, cancer, or a rash, my heart sinks. The patient is probably right—many perfectly good drugs do cause side effects. But my heart sinks because I know that I can never trust that patient to take that drug, even if I seem to convince him that it's essential.

No drug is completely safe, but a good doctor prescribes it when the benefits outweigh the risks. *Never make a decision on a drug on the basis of what you read here or anywhere else.* You'll almost certainly make the wrong one. If you're worried, discuss the drug with your doctor. If you're not satisfied with the explanation, don't stop the drug. Find another doctor.

Antibiotics Cure Bacterial Infections

Antibiotics are a triumph of twentieth-century science. In combination with two triumphs of nineteenth-century science—sanitation and immunization—they have reduced bacterial infections to a minor health risk. Throughout most of history such infections were the leading cause of disease and premature death; this is still true in poor countries (where, in most cases, antibiotics are sold over the counter like aspirin).

No antibiotic cures everything. Each infection has a treatment of choice—the best antibiotic, given in the proper dose, for a certain amount of time. Other antibiotics don't work as well for that infection. Some are entirely useless, so having a doctor decide what you need is still helpful. In fact, when my patients arrive and announce their diagnosis, they're right most of the time. When patients go on to announce the antibiotic they need, they're usually wrong. One reason patients have such poor judgment is that many doctors give them antibiotics for unpleasant minor ailments for which they don't work. One delight of practicing medicine is that patients give us credit when their illness goes away, so doctors who misprescribe antibiotics produce grateful patients who become mystified and upset when they encounter the rare doctor who doesn't. Remember what follows on viruses.

Fighting Viruses

Drugs for viral infections earn only a "D."

This is an improvement over the "F" of a generation ago. Acyclovir (Zovirax), a herpes treatment, was the first relatively nonpoisonous antiviral drug. Others, such as AZT and interferon, were developed during the 1980s, and many more are in the works. So far not one earns an "A."

Older antiviral drugs produced the same side effects as cancer chemotherapy—vomiting, destruction of the immune system, anemia, abnormal bleeding. In fact, many *were* anticancer drugs.

Viruses are hard to kill. Antibiotics, as I repeat, have no effect, but doctors routinely give them anyway. Review the chapters on bronchitis, colds and flu, sinus infections, and throat infections to see what you're up against.

Helping the Heart

I would give drugs for heart disease a "C+."

Reviewing current research for this chapter, I thanked my lucky stars that I gave up salt, fat, and cholesterol in the 1960s before it became fashionable. Although cardiac drugs do important things, they can't wipe out a disease and restore you to perfect health. Unlike insulin or thyroid, they are not a natural replacement for something you've lost. Unlike antiulcer drugs, they can't suppress a normal activity that isn't essential (you don't need stomach acid).

The heart is a pump. When diseased, it responds to drugs to make it pump more strongly, slower, faster, or less irregularly, but these drugs can't turn the clock back. Mostly, they make an unhealthy heart behave better, and they do it fairly well.

Here's a quick review of what heart drugs do.

Digitalis (digoxin, Lanoxin). By increasing the force of the heart's contraction, digitalis reverses heart failure. Another digitalis action slows the heart, helping disorders in which it beats too fast. These arrhythmias have names like atrial fibrillation, atrial flutter, and paroxysmal atrial tachycardia.

Nitrates. These drugs relax blood vessels outside the heart (so that the heart doesn't have to work so hard) and inside (so that the heart itself gets more blood). They help relieve angina, and you can read more about them in the chapter on angina.

Calcium channel blockers (Isoptin, Calan, Cardizem, Procardia). These also relax blood vessels and relieve angina. In addition, they lower blood pressure (nitrates do the same, but the effect wears off too quickly to be practical).

Beta-blockers (Inderal, Lopressor, Tenormin, Blocadren, Corgard). Beta-blockers block the action of adrenaline. Since adrenaline stimulates the heart, beta-blockers do the opposite, so they relieve angina, lower blood pressure, and control rapid arrhythmias.

Adrenaline is not all bad; a heart needs stimulation—during exercise, for example. A healthy heart can tolerate a great deal of adrenaline, but the hormone makes a diseased heart more irritable and prone to dangerous arrhythmias. Doctors suspected that many people who drop dead had suffered such a rhythm disturbance, and they wondered if a beta-blocker would prevent it. Sure enough, in a large study of subjects who had already had a heart attack, those taking beta-blockers had a 40 percent lower death rate over the next three years. Whether a beta-blocker prevents deaths in those who *haven't* yet had a heart attack isn't certain, but it might.

An important class of arrhythmia drug resembles novocaine (lidocaine, Procan, Pronestyl) and provides a similar local anesthetic effect on the heart, dulling nerve conduction to suppress wildly dangerous rhythms. Doctors often give these drugs during a heart attack when the muscle is especially susceptible.

Aiding Digestion

Drugs for diseases of the digestive tract earn a "B."

Here my rule on essential organs works nicely. Stomach function isn't essential, so drugs that affect it earn a high "B + ."

H_2 blockers are a class of drugs that turn off stomach acid production. Currently four are available: cimetidine (Tagamet), ranitidine (Zantac), famotidine (Pepcid), and nizatidine (Axid). More will soon appear, because every drug company is eager to share in the bounty. H_2 blockers are the most lucrative drugs on sale today, partly because no generics will be available to lower the price until Tagamet's patent expires in 1994. But the most important reason is that H_2 blockers work brilliantly.

Remember, when a drug works brilliantly for one problem, doctors vastly overprescribe it for problems that it doesn't help. Stomach disorders are extremely common, so most patients taking an H_2 blocker don't need it.

Naturally, the "B + " applies only when H_2 blockers are

given correctly—for ulcers. Sucralfate (Carafate), a drug that coats the stomach, works equally well. It's my treatment of choice; you can read more about it in the chapter on ulcers.

Digestive Enzymes

The small intestine digests food. Since this is essential to life, my rule states that drugs for this organ aren't so effective. Sure enough, digestive enzymes (Viokase, Pancrease, Arco-Lase, Cotazym, Zymase) earn a "C−." Why shouldn't digestive enzymes work better for disorders where there's a deficiency of these enzymes? Experts are puzzled. Fortunately, disorders of digestion are rare.

The most common occurs in chronic alcoholics who destroy their pancreas as well as their liver. The pancreas produces most of your digestive enzymes, so people with chronic pancreatitis digest poorly.

If you're not alcoholic but you're certain you suffer indigestion, you're probably wrong. Most pains, reactions to food, gas, cramps, and diarrhea are not the result of poor food digestion—even if your doctor says so and prescribes enzymes. True small intestinal diseases that interfere with digestion have names like sprue, blind loop syndrome, regional enteritis, and Whipple's disease. All are uncommon and serious. I see a case every few years.

Digesting Milk

There is one common form of indigestion—the inability to digest milk and most dairy products. That disorder is known as lactose intolerance, and good treatment exists: the enzyme lactase (which breaks down lactose, the sugar in milk).

Milk is baby food, so infants' small intestines have plenty of their own lactase. Adults gradually lose the enzyme as they age, but enough remains so that most don't notice. But 10 to 20 percent of Caucasians and up to 75 percent of blacks and orientals lose so much that a glass of milk or a dish of ice cream is followed by an explosion of flatulence and diarrhea. Although they can't digest milk sugar, the germs in their colon eagerly ferment it, producing a great deal of gas. Many people who have lactase deficiency learn to avoid dairy products, but they can buy lactase in any drugstore. Added to ordinary milk, it breaks down enough lactose to make it tolerable. Lactose-free milk is also available, but it's expensive.

Gas Remedies

Gas remedies earn a "D," but I'd break this down by giving activated charcoal a "C" and an "F" to the rest.

Activated charcoal bears no resemblance to plain charcoal or burned toast, a folk remedy. It is purified carbon, heated and exposed to steam so that the surface is extremely absorbent. Doctors use it to treat poisoning; fish lovers add it to aquarium filters to keep the water clean. You can swallow it and hope it absorbs gas. Experiments show that volunteers fed beans produced less gas if given activated charcoal, and some of my patients think it helps. You don't need a prescription, and it's safe. Other gas remedies such as simethicone don't work. Lactase works only if you're lactase deficient, so it's worth a try.

Help from Hormones

Hormones earn an "A" as hormones and a "B" as drugs. They work brilliantly when doctors give them to replace a deficiency and fairly well when given to treat other diseases.

Available since the beginning of the century, thyroid is one of the first miracles of modern science. Most of this hormone, however, is prescribed to people with a normal thyroid who complain of fatigue or have difficulty losing weight. It doesn't work for these conditions.

When replacing a deficiency, a single daily dose of thyroid, cortisone, estrogen, growth hormone, and a host of other hormones works fine. A single dose doesn't work as well with insulin, which accounts for its "B" in the diabetes chapter. Eventually insulin's performance will improve. Medical science must develop the ability to vary the insulin dose as quickly as the human body does to keep blood sugar within narrow limits. Assured of a normal blood sugar, diabetics will stop following a special diet and not suffer premature atherosclerosis and other complications. They will be as normal as thyroid patients taking thyroid.

Hormones as Drugs

Cortisone deficiencies exist, but they're rare. Far more often we prescribe cortisone for its pharmacological action. In huge doses, cortisone suppresses inflammation, so it eliminates the pain of arthritis, the diarrhea of ulcerative colitis, the itch of eczema, and the wheezing of asthma. It does these things so quickly that doctors were thrilled when cortisone appeared in the late 1940s. So were patients when their crippling joint pains or maddening rashes vanished.

So was the Nobel committee, which gave the developers its prize the following year. Normally the committee waits about 20 years, so many scientists who yearn for the world's greatest honor lose their eligibility by dying of old age. This delay helps preserve the Nobel's enormous prestige, because many brilliant discoveries turn out to be not so brilliant or complete flops as the years pass, and several speedy Nobel prizes became an embarrassment. (The surgeon who developed the lobotomy got one.)

Cortisone deserved its prize, but doctors soon learned that suppressing inflammation has drawbacks. It slows healing, reduces resistance to infection, and weakens tissues. Children on high doses stop growing. Adults discover that their bones and skin become frail, and they have a higher risk of cataracts, diabetes, ulcers, and high blood pressure. Despite all this, cortisone is a lifesaver and the only source of relief for many victims of serious diseases. Take it if you need it, but be sure to obey my rule on taking dangerous drugs: Always know when your next doctor's appointment will be. Something is wrong if you don't. The only exception is if your doctor is easy to reach.

Short courses of cortisone are a different matter. I use them all the time—most commonly for poison ivy. A large dose silences the burning eruption, but I only give a two-week supply. By that time the poison has worn off. Similarly, injecting cortisone into an inflamed joint for arthritis or near a joint for bursitis gives dramatic relief. You should welcome it, but repeat injections are a bad idea.

Sometimes You Don't Need a Drug

I doubt if drugs are more popular today than in past ages, but they are certainly more useful and more dangerous. Despite these changes, the old bad attitudes remain. Patients go to a doctor hoping for medication, and doctors comply with useless drugs or good drugs for conditions they don't help. Being the responsible party, doctors are more to blame, but patients shouldn't encourage them.

The Rest
of the Best Treatments

I'd love to write another book on the best treatment of an additional 60 or so disorders. That will probably happen, but not for several years. Until then, where can you find the best treatment for systemic lupus, malaria, glaucoma, or some other disease not covered in this book?

Where Doctors Look

Current Therapy, edited by Robert Rakel, M.D., is published by W. B. Saunders every year.

A reference popular with family doctors like me, it contains over 1,000 pages and several hundred chapters on innumerable diseases. To encourage us to buy it often (and because even experts have different ideas), each year's edition is entirely rewritten, with every chapter by a new author. Because of this, I don't discard old editions, and my shelves contain *Current Therapy* for every odd year since 1975.

Naturally it goes into more detail than I can here and, like a good medical book, discusses the bad along with the good effects of each treatment in enough detail to make you very nervous. I don't encourage you to read medical books—but not because much of the writing is too technical. You'll understand plenty, but you'll find more information than you want, plus plenty that you *don't* want to know.

I still remember the occasion in 1980 after a doctor found a skin cancer near my nose. Returning home, I opened a dermatology text to the appropriate section. Staring up from the first page was a gruesome photograph of a patient with a gaping hole in his face. "To hell with research!" I exclaimed, slamming the book shut. I did not pursue the subject.

If you buy *Current Therapy,* make sure there's a doctor available to answer questions. You'll have plenty. If you're a glutton for punishment and have children, you can buy *Current Pediatric Therapy* from the same publisher.

Problems with Health Books

Most health books written for the general public are awful. Avoid any that promise dramatic new treatments; it usually takes two years from the time a writer begins writing until the book is in the stores, and despite popular belief, important medical advances do spread quickly. Furthermore, don't worry about missing a good new treatment. As I stress in this book, you should worry more about not getting a good treatment that's been around for 20 years.

Don't assume a book is good just because it's written by a doctor. Were it not for libel laws, I could list many prolific doctors who turn out the most amazing nonsense. On the other hand, you can trust anything by Jane Brody, a *New York Times* columnist who also writes health books. As for doctors who write health books, I have a high opinion of Kenneth Cooper and Art Ulene.

I also approve of anything published by Consumers Union, which also publishes the magazine *Consumer Reports,* but you must understand its philosophy. Consumers Union treats the medical profession no differently from the way it treats General Motors, General Mills, or Procter & Gamble—as a large institution with too much political influence that could make an excellent, inexpensive product (and sometimes does) but that more often turns out something overpriced, fragile, ineffective, unhealthy, or unsafe. Although I consider this a bit harsh, it's not wildly off base.

A Consumers Union book teems with facts and common sense but frowns on new technology. When Consumers Union recommends a treatment, you can bet that it's a good treatment. You can also bet that it's not the most expensive and not the newest, so occasionally it's not the best.

You can trust a book written under the auspices of the American Medical Association, American Pharmaceutical Association, or other professional medical associations, but you must also take into account *their* philosophy—which is different from the Consumers Union philosophy. Books endorsed by professional organizations tell about good treatments, but they assume that that's what you'll get. Because they take for granted that doctors practice the best medicine, they're no help in detecting when you're getting less than the best.

Beware of Magazine Articles

Magazine articles are the most unreliable of all, and I speak as an expert who has written for most of the women's and health magazines.

Editors of these magazines are mostly intelligent and feminist, yet they treat readers as creampuffs: hypersensitive, hypochondriac, and easily offended—typical Victorian ladies except for an interest in sex. This analysis holds true whether the magazine is a swinger like *Cosmopolitan* or more conservative like *Family Circle*.

In this book, I write as I please. My editor never suggests that I change an opinion except when it might get me sued. You might assume that no magazine editor would tell a doctor what to say. Beginning medical writers assume this, too. Until they change their minds, they remain beginning writers.

Here's a conversation I once had with a magazine editor:

"Doctor Oppenhéim, you say on page 2 that the average American doesn't need vitamin supplements. Is this scientifically proved?"

"Yes."

"Don't some doctors prescribe them?"

"Doctors do plenty of dumb things. But Americans don't need extra vitamins."

"At this magazine we don't like to give one side of an argument. Since some doctors disagree, shouldn't your statement be more balanced?"

"No. Nutrition experts agree with me."

"But there's a real difference of opinion here, and our readers expect us to be fair . . ."

Don't be misled by this concern with "balance" and "fairness." This particular editor refused to allow me to tell readers that they don't need vitamins, and she was trying to get the message across to me without giving a direct order. Unfortunately, this experience occurred early in my writing career, so I worked hard to convince her that my statement was the simple truth. Eventually she gave up. I assumed that I had won the argument and looked forward to the appearance of the article, which I submitted in 1981. I am still waiting.

Health and women's magazines publish good educational articles, but only in certain areas. They are fairly dependable on the topics of aging, well-known diseases, preventive medicine, and birth control. They are not too bad on sex, although they approach it with the solemn worshipfulness I once associated with music appreciation. On anything concerning obesity they are dreadful. In fact, you can't trust them on any subject readers have strong opinions about—such as nutrition, psychology, and stress.

You should also realize that magazines have a firm rule that articles must be optimistic, positive, and exciting. Moreover, nothing appears in a women's magazine that might irritate a large segment of readers. Nor will they permit an attack on any popular health belief unless it's accompanied by a disclaimer. Thus, the blunt statement that Americans don't need extra vitamins killed my article. A sophisticated writer would soften it to "Experts claim that the average American doesn't need vitamin supplements, but many doctors feel that patients benefit." This might pass. Reading the average health article, you'll notice plenty of similar mushy statements.

Turn to Your Doctor

Asking your doctor for information can be tricky. Doctors know the best treatment of ailments they treat, but they may be surprisingly ignorant of the latest miracle antiaging drug or a new, deadly disease that is sweeping the country but hasn't arrived in your city.

For example, Lyme disease hasn't yet appeared in Southern California, so we haven't seen a case. Although we've all read about the symptoms, we also immediately forgot them. Doctors have a hard time remembering diseases they've never seen. Despite the absence of Lyme disease in our area, patients regularly come in wondering if they have it. This always produces a minor crisis. The doctor wanders the halls, consulting colleagues who have also never seen a case. He or she pores over medical texts, which are not helpful, because books describe all the possible symptoms, and the patient always has a few that fit. After a series of phone calls, an expert advises a blood test for Lyme disease and another appointment in a few weeks. The blood test isn't helpful early in the disease, but after a few weeks the patient stops worrying and doesn't return, so the problem is solved.

The best doctor to consult is someone you know socially who never sees you professionally. You'll get an honest (although not necessarily correct) opinion. Don't be surprised to hear laughter as he reads the magazine article that provoked your question. I'm amazed at what gets into print.

Don't always expect a satisfactory answer. Some disorders have more than one best treatment; others have a best that's not too good. Be patient. From the beginning to the end of the twentieth century, medical science improved its grade from barely passing to better than average. We should continue to improve.

Index

A

Abrasions, 150
Accidents, prevention of, 294
Accutane. *See* Isotretinoin
Acetaminophen, menstrual cramps and, 180
Acetylcholine, depression and, 75
Acid, ulcers and, 246–48
Acne, 3–8
  comedones, 4–7
  cystic, 5–8
  hormones and, 3–5
  malnutrition and, 5
  myths about, 5–6
  papulopustular, 4–7
  treatment for, 5–8
Acquired immune deficiency syndrome (AIDS)
  condoms and, 34
  media disease, 17, 127, 168, 221–22, 245
  warts and, 255

Acupressure, muscle aches and, 194
Acupuncture, muscle aches and, 194
Acute sinusitis, 228
Acute urinary retention, prostate enlargement and, 214
Acyclovir (Zovirax), herpes and, 129–30
Adrenaline
  anaphylaxis and, 14
  panic and, 206
Age spots, 9–11
  familial tendency of, 10
  treatment for, 10–11
  warts vs., 255
Aging, cancer and, 56
Agoraphobia, panic attacks and, 205
AIDS. *See* Acquired immune deficiency syndrome
Air pollution. *See* Smog

trichomonas, 251–52
yeast infections, 34, 251, 285
Varicose veins, hemorrhoids and, 123
Venereal disease, condoms and, 34
Viral illnesses
antiviral drugs, 298
bacterial vs., 50–52, 226–27
bronchitis, 51, 52
herpes, 126–30
measles, mumps, and chicken pox, 66–67, 128
upper respiratory infections, 65–68
Viruses, Alzheimer's disease and, 17–18
Vitamin E, breast pain and, 48

W

Warts, 254–59
acquired immune deficiency syndrome (AIDS) and, 255
cause of, 255

genital, 259
seborrheic keratosis vs., 255
treatment for, 255–59
Weight loss, rules for, 197
Weight Watchers, obesity and, 198
Wrinkles, 260–63
cause of, 261–62
treatment for, 6, 262–63

X

Xanax. *See* Alprazolam
X-ray studies
low back pain and, 164–65
pneumonia and, 208–9, 211
pros and cons of, 279, 283–89

Y

Yeast infections, 34, 251, 285

Z

Zovirax. *See* Acyclovir